Oneota Flow

AMERICAN LAND *&* LIFE SERIES

Wayne Franklin, series editor

Oneota Flow

The Upper Iowa River & Its People

BY DAVID S. FALDET

foreword by WAYNE FRANKLIN

University of Iowa Press, Iowa City

University of Iowa Press, Iowa City 52242

Copyright © 2009 by the University of Iowa Press

www.uiowapress.org

Printed in the United States of America

Design by Richard Hendel

The University of Iowa Press is a member of Green Press
Initiative and is committed to preserving natural resources.

Printed on acid-free paper

Library of Congress Cataloging-in-Publication Data
Faldet, David S., 1956–
    Oneota flow: the Upper Iowa River and its people / by David S.
Faldet; foreword by Wayne Franklin.
        p.   cm.—(American land and life series)
    Includes bibliographical references and index.
    ISBN-13: 978-1-58729-780-9 (pbk.)
    ISBN-10: 1-58729-780-9 (pbk.)
    1. Upper Iowa River (Minn. and Iowa)—History.   2. Upper Iowa
River Region (Minn. and Iowa)—History.   3. River life—Upper Iowa
River (Minn. and Iowa)—History.   4. Upper Iowa River Region (Minn.
and Iowa)—Social life and customs.   5. Upper Iowa River Region
(Minn. and Iowa)—Biography.   6. Upper Iowa River Region (Minn.
and Iowa)—Environmental conditions.   7. Natural resources—Upper
Iowa River (Minn. and Iowa).   8. Human ecology—Upper Iowa River
(Minn. and Iowa).   I. Title.
    F612.U77F35 2009
    977.7'6—dc22   2008031470

09 10 11 12 13 C 5 4 3 2 1

To RACHEL,

who walks along

the river

with me

Contents

Foreword

WAYNE FRANKLIN

Nature writers who take to the water express a profound human impulse to move on. They respond to the way that, even as flowing water washes our feet, it slips around the next bend on its way someplace else. If it abides, it stagnates and dies. So, we think, will we. Naturally enough, little in the everyday world so satisfies our wanderlust, our desire to be free of entangling commitments and settled habits, as a mighty river aiming past our boundaries and out of sight. We follow it in our imaginations even if we cannot follow it in fact. Huckleberry Finn faked his own murder in order to gain the center of the Mississippi, and we know why. We read his story as an allegory of our own.

Yet, if we are honest with ourselves, we have to acknowledge that part of us always remains back on that abandoned shore. We wish to abide as much as we wish to move on. Resist the river's call long enough, sit watching its ceaseless disappearances, and we will come to view the water as always in retreat—as going down, down, to nothing but the vast sink of the restless sea. Being human often means staying put.

There are, it follows, two ways to write about rivers. The first, and most natural, is to launch yourself onto the water and let it take you where it will. Flowing water glitters and shimmers, but most of all it has its own way as it heads downstream. Once you push out from the shore and let it take over, it will deliver you to perpetually new scenes. It may overset you, even drown you, but if you exercise due care and if it is a true river, with a reasonable gradient and sufficient volume, it will take you on and on for what seems like forever. The sea awaits, but you do not think of that. And very few decisions dog you as you drift or steer. So if you are a writer, your prose will display this same drifting aesthetic. You may write of the shore, as Mark Twain did, as a series of ephemeral appearances always melting rearward into the great gray forgetfulness of the past. Nothing is real but the river. Even in Mark Twain's memoir, *Life on the Mississippi*, which is concerned with the navigational realities of the river (for he was a pilot before he was a writer), the river snakes alluringly away from any fixed social or geographical or intellectual positions. It is a system unto itself.

Mark Twain placed his most foolish characters on shore—from the puffed-up adults of St. Petersburg to the idiotic Grangerfords with their duels and their dull poetry—but allowed enough of their foolery out onto the river that poor Jim, free by virtue of his human dignity, is chased by owners and bounty hunters alike. Jim's life afloat is hellishly determined by the fixed ideas of the society at the water's edge. That Jim runs away to escape those ideas and their legal and institutional shadows, much as Huck runs away to escape the alcohol-fueled violence of Pap Finn, is what makes the novel so seductive. The shore may follow you out onto the water— even Huck's mind keeps putting Jim in his place long after Jim has literally left that place. But finally Mark Twain would have you think that the worst trash from the shore gets washed away by the big-hearted river. Even Pap Finn is called to account by the Mississippi, his body left in a house that has been pushed off its footings and set adrift. The river is freedom.

The other way to write about rivers involves the opposite perspective. It starts with a stubborn abidance on the shore. Not that you take the ways of the shore people as right or inevitable or even tolerable. Just that you know something deeper about the human condition—the biocultural fact that, having emerged eons ago from the ocean and come up on land, humans really can't go back to the watery world. One consequence is that you begin to view a river quite differently once you fix yourself and, as it were, let it go its separate way. The river ceases to be a vehicle for your fantasies and becomes a margin for your actual life. Its passing provides boundaries and frames. It also gives structure.

I have always lived within close haul of flowing water. As I write these words I look out my back window down through a patch of woods to the glint of a brook that arises within a mile or so and, another thousand feet from my house, takes one last turn and empties into a marsh-fringed stream. That stream soon dumps into a small trout-fishing river that gathers up other such tributaries in its short run and then merges with the Connecticut River twenty-some miles above the latter's disappearance into Long Island Sound. The brook behind my house is no big thing—it is so intermittent that I have christened it, only half-jokingly, "Sometimes Running Brook." But, especially at the start and end of the year, when the oak and hickory and maple have not leafed out, or when their leaves glow and then fall and dry, I gain access into the brook's little gully, nestled under a low crown of fragrant spicebush. Then that thread of water becomes a twisting line of light. I cannot boat the brook, and though I sometimes fantasize about putting my canoe in the marsh and proceeding down to the Salmon River and the Connecticut and the Sound, for the most part I am happiest simply regarding that silver crease in the otherwise dark woods.

Water there gives me a second sky. That is the sort of gift for which a shore-dweller ought to be munificently grateful.

≋ David Faldet's river winds through a decidedly inhabited human landscape. He goes out on the Upper Iowa, to be sure, and as we follow him in his literal explorations we come to know that stream, the only one in Iowa cold enough to harbor a self-sustaining trout population, as a rare and valued thing in a state that bears a heavier load of human purpose than any other. I have seen that river, and drifted on it, and wet my feet in it, and I agree that knowing it this way is good. But David Faldet wants us to know it in far more profound ways than a drifting boat trip allows. For those who inhabit a river's basin, they and it come to sustain a deep ecological and emotional symbiosis. For one thing, although the river ceaselessly passes through such landscapes, its insistent passage provides a perpetual reminder of all the human and natural life that has arisen and arrived there, and of how it has fared on its own passage through time to eternity. History becomes an adjunct of nature. Contrary to Mark Twain's insight, the more the water runs, the more the life on its shores endures. And rivers therefore make you want to know the past.

They also make you appreciate how permeable are the boundaries we customarily draw between past and present, shore and stream, figure and ground. Not only does new water pass into a river all along its journey, from brooks and springs and storm drains and a thousand other sources, but it also wicks out into the soil, evaporates into the air, and spills over our premises in flood times. And those are only the more obvious kinds of interpenetration between river and land. More subtly, as David Faldet's exquisite anatomy of his river and its place shows, a river's people are biologically, and spiritually as well, its best, its deepest tributaries. Our bodies are continuous with the bodies of water we drink from, discharge into, eat from, swim in, look at, speak of, write about—and love.

Oneota Flow provides some of the most profound insights into the place of rivers in our experience that I know of. It plumbs the Upper Iowa—no mean task—but it moreover shows us how to understand any river. It offers a philosophy of water and life. And it does so in a prose of remarkable clarity and buoyancy. The words here belong together like the molecules in a stream. They mirror a landscape where things cohere, for well or ill, as they never can when we skip through space in the vain hope that something newer or better lies around the next bend. Rivers, David Faldet reminds us, always bring us home.

Acknowledgments

Without generous gifts of time, money, and assistance from Luther College, I could not have written this book. I received sabbatical supplement awards from the Paideia Endowment. The Doris and Ragnvald Ylvisaker Endowment for Faculty Growth helped pay for my work on chapters 6 and 7. I did the final editing through the Dennis M. Jones Distinguished Professorship in the Humanities. Much of the research for the book was done during summers, aided by a string of able and patient assistants—Seth Ansorge Jaavag, Joy Wotherspoon, Gwen Rudy, and Katie Blobaum—who spent long hours in archives and at microfilm readers to provide me with great material and who accompanied me on small adventures to make sure I didn't get lost or killed. Sarah Warner, Ryan Gjerde, Sarah Clark, Amanda Valo, and Denise Warner also helped.

The Luther College English Department and my Environmental Studies colleagues provided editorial advice, helpful conversations, moral support, and good cheer. Loyal Rue first introduced me to bioregionalism. Robert Wolf got me started on regional writing. Lora Friest helped me get my bearings on environmental issues in the river basin. Richard Bernatz, Lori Stanley, Richard Kellogg, the late Jean Young, John Staeck, David Stanley (of Bear Creek Archeology), Cindy and Merl Steines, Phyllis and the late Dervin Faldet, Ted Wilson, Kevin Lee, David Lee Smith, Reed Fitton, Midge Kjome, Hubie and Avis Bolson, Ransome Bolson, Gaige Wunder, Cathy Henry, Patrick Henry, Merrill Chesebrough, Jack Anundsen, Rick Fromm, Darrell Henning, the late Cliff Chase, the late Lloyd Vine, Stan Jeffers, David Halverson, Dave Pahlas, Jerry Freund, and Bruce Adair provided information and wisdom. Jon Jensen and his Environmental Forays class, Beth Lynch, Colin Betts, Gene Tesdahl, Samantha Greendeer, Linda Kinkel, Laura Beard, Susan Jacobson, John Moeller, Harv Klevar, Bill Craft, Sarah Andersen, and Tim Olsen generously gave me advice and editorial response.

The Luther College Library, the National Archives, the Decorah Genealogical Society, the State Historical Society of Iowa, and the Winneshiek County Historical Society provided crucial resources and help.

Though their names do not all appear in the Bibliography, I owe much to the writings of William Cronin, Wes Jackson, John McPhee, Ian Frazier, and William Least Heat Moon.

My wife Rachel's skillful editorial collaboration from start to finish, as always, made my writing what I meant it to be. She and my daughters, Elizabeth and Pearl, were patient and encouraging and gave me the peace I needed for writing.

Oneota Flow

The Smell of Rain

Where It Starts

Scrutiny of even the most familiar and simple elements of experience can lead to surprise. Several years ago, a soil scientist informed me that the most common smell identifiable as "rain" is made up of bacterial spores, bursting into reproductive frenzy with the impact of raindrops on dust. The *actinomycetes* bacteria that produce these fragrant spores are also the source of drugs that save people from infections that would otherwise kill us: tuberculosis, leprosy, and cholera. The smell of rain, for which I long on a hot, dry day, is the birth cry of friendly bacteria. This knowledge has not changed my imprecise habit of calling that certain delicious smell "rain." The excuse for my inaccuracy is this: what is obvious to my nose remains invisible to my eye.

This book of essays is my attempt to depict precisely the story of a river that begins as rain. The chapters bring to light elements of the river's life and history invisible to casual observation. I have spent forty years in the basin of the Upper Iowa, a stream that winds from the flat farm fields of southern Minnesota through the wooded valleys of northeastern Iowa to the Mississippi. As a child I fished and swam in the river. As an adult I cross the river every day. My office overlooks the river, winding out of sight in two directions; with my windows open on warm days, I hear the raspy crowing of pheasant cocks in tall grasses along the river's bank. On the map, the Upper Iowa is a blue line that, together with the crossing of two state highways, explains the position of the town I call home.

The blue line masks the complexity of the river's course and makes it easier to think of the river and the people who live along the river as having separate lives. But people and the river are like the smell of rain, a mix where one element runs temporarily out of sight in the other. We are mostly water: water that runs through us in a circular stream. We tap into that stream drinking a glass of water or a cup of coffee. With an additional load of nutrition and oxygen, that water eddies through the farthest-flung capillaries of our fingertips. Having done that in any number of round trips lasting less than a minute, it passes from us, continuing its necessary errands, fanning out salts, acids, and unused additives like caffeine into the watery world of which we are a mobile part.

The sense of being an intermittent but integral part of a river system was innate in the people who gave their name to the Upper Iowa. The Ioway called the water world *nyí*, and their sophisticated vocabulary for water distinguished between the ripples made by a river rock or a moving animal, or between a flood caused by rain versus a flood caused by snowmelt.[1] In an 1837 treaty signing, the U.S. government asked No Heart and Moving Rain, representatives of the Ioway, to draw a map of their tribe's ancestral territory. They drew a diagram of Iowa rivers, branching, like the veins in a human hand, from the intersection of the Missouri and the Mississippi. After nearly a thousand years of familial residence in the place, the basic orientation of these two Ioway men to the land they called home came to knowing where its rivers ran.

Unfortunately, our sense of being physically connected to a river system is no longer innate. Though forgotten, the connection is gradually being reaffirmed for us by science. Forensic tests of hair can now plot the geography of a person's life. The change in the hydrogen and oxygen isotopes of rain clouds passing over land gets registered in drinking water. The place-specific weight of isotopes gets passed on to the hair, teeth, and bones that water builds. Conversely, the cocaine level in a river is a fair measure of the drug problem in cities upstream. The levels of caffeine and antibiotics in the Upper Iowa, measurable by sensitive tests, are a modern revelation that residents are really, like No Heart and Moving Rain, walking tributaries of the nearest stream. If I am home and healthy, I am a brim-full extension of the Upper Iowa. My water and sewer bills ensure that the valves stay open between the rest of the river system and me.

The relationship between people and rivers is reciprocal. While we depend upon rivers like the Upper Iowa, they also depend on us. Since piss and dishwater are part of our contribution to river systems, it is easy to think of them as waste disposal mechanisms, something we would rather forget. But this lack of mindfulness takes a harmful environmental toll. Witness my home, Iowa, the most ecologically altered state in the Union. In a frenzy of development, the settlers of Iowa replaced its horizon-to-horizon prairies and wetlands with furrowed fields, efficiently drained by a network of tile. Their descendants have resisted the river-cleansing rules of the 1972 federal Clean Water Act for a quarter of a century. The state's waters typically run brown. In February 2006, as legislators considered passing rules that would bring Iowa's municipal water treatment up to the 1972 federal clean water standard, a lawyer for interested environmental groups complained, "There is no state that is out of compliance like Iowa."[2]

Though the Upper Iowa is the Iowa river most intensely used for recreation, the Iowa Department of Natural Resources (DNR) classifies it as "impaired." Its load of soil, chemicals, and human and animal waste has lethal consequences up and down the river system and up and down the food chain, from an increase in bacteria to the disappearance of mussels, which are canaries in the mineshaft of my liquid element.[3] The river, like a keen memory, carries a record of the past to which we too easily deny our contributing part.

What goes for people goes also for the land on which they live. Little of a river's course looks watery. The river starts in small explosions of rain, splashing off dust, leaves, and the fur of animals. In the beginning, water that will make up the river drips from trees and roof edges. It flows over fields, barnyards, lawns, and parking lots, seeking out low points. It seeps into soil, making its slow and unseen way down. From these channels, water runs into creeks and springs that look, at least, like a recognizable part of the river system. But a river flows across every particle of its basin.

To see rivers in the context of their entire course, including their human one, makes ecological sense. Though such perspective seems inexact, it has an accuracy we need to regain in scrutinizing our environment. Aldo Leopold called the processes of ecology a "round river." What comes down as rain eventually goes back up as mist and fog, as the respiration of trees, in the evaporating bursts that include the bacterial smell of rain, and in the steamy breath of the farmer in his field. In the course of that circle everything imaginable gets mixed up in the channel of water. Ecologically conceived, all processes in nature work in this tangled way. When Leopold devised a general label for the stuff of the ecological world, he called it "the land." Leopold's "land" includes not only soil but also plants, animals, air, and water, all of them caught up in a single stream.[4] So, too, the actual river, gathering force as it passes through the land, is marked by each of its channels, mingling with the soil, the people, and the bacteria through which it passes, carrying away remnants as it goes. Because it is so much more than it seems, the measures of the river's health are written in the entire landscape through which it flows.

The essays that follow hold true to Leopold's conception of land as a community in which water, people, and soil play interactive parts. The book tells the story of the Upper Iowa River as it flows through land and people. It begins with the prehistoric beginnings of the river, and it surveys the river basin's resources. The chapters move through the history of peoples' lives along the Upper Iowa, always focusing on the way they depend on the river, the environment, and the resources of the region. The story includes ways people have relied on the watershed that have proved mutually sustaining over hundreds or thousands of years. It also chronicles mistakes from which we will do well to learn. I've kept the survey familiar by putting the present up against the past in each chapter, including stories of people living along the river today as a reminder of how the past braids through the present in this place with a river at its center.

My research involved conversations with people and readings from the historical record but also required conversation with the river itself. To talk about the river I learned to talk *with* it. One hot August afternoon, draped like a damp dish towel over a black inner tube, I floated down the Decorah stretch of the Upper Iowa. Splashing to correct my course, I lost my wedding ring. After twenty minutes on my knees, groping my slow way through sand and gravel an arm's length down in the cloudy water, I uttered a kind of prayer to the river. My thumb and index finger closed on the ring. Instead of groping *through* it, I had to ask the current directly to give back what it had taken. The work of this book has been no different. It is the record of a series of conversations I've learned to have with a river that responds to questions not in words, but in little revelations. To write this I've learned not only to recognize the surprising meanders and permutations of the river, but to recognize a voice that speaks through a bed of sand and rock, ripples and depths, colors and smells of water, and the life cycles of pocketbook mussels or of beaver.

This history of the Upper Iowa and its people is a reminder that none of us can afford to divorce ourselves, in our own thinking, from the fluid world of which we are a dynamic part. We are walking tributaries. The smell we sense in rain, in an ocean, or on the banks of a midwestern river attracts us because its familiarity runs deep.

The Two Names of the River
Geological Beginnings

As we swing around the bend, the water suddenly swarms with a shoal of redhorse suckers that arch and dive in a shadowy tumble. Suddenly, though, the fish are gone and the canoe crunches to a stop against a sheet of ice. Jabbing hard, I do nothing except chip a large notch out of my wooden paddle. The ice remains uncracked, stretching out before us for hundreds of feet. This, then, is the end of our trip: trapped by the current against an immobile sheet of ice too thick for us to break but too thin to support our walking weight. What made us think we could canoe a partially frozen river?

It started with me, thinking that canoeing with Karl Knudson would shed a little more light on an enigma. The river we are canoeing has two names. Its usual name, the Upper Iowa, was drawn from the Ioway people whom French explorers encountered when they first came to this hilly countryside. The river's local name, however, and the name printed on maps for a brief period a hundred years ago, is Oneota. W. J. McGee christened the river with this second name in the nineteenth century, claiming that Indians called the last rock outcrop to the north of the river's mouth "Oneota," also calling the river by this name. "Oneota" means "people who sprung from a rock." The river Knudson and I are canoeing goes by one name in public record and by a familiar alias among close acquaintances. But the names are distinguished by a certain logic. Locals use Oneota for the rock valley through which the river flows. The springs feeding the river flow from this rock. "Upper Iowa" is reserved for the waters of the river itself. The Upper Iowa's waters flow from the Oneota's rock.

I thought Knudson, a lawyer who daily consults the Upper Iowa like some people do the weather, could help me understand this conundrum that entwines itself deeply in legal questions.[1] The waters of the Upper Iowa, like the air above them, are a public resource, recognized by law, though they flow through a bed that is mostly private property. As if in a

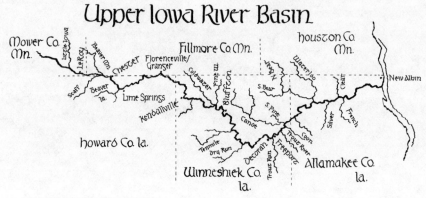

Upper Iowa River Basin

UPPER IOWA RIVER BASIN

hot air balloon, canoeists making a leisurely float trip below the limestone bluffs that tower over the waters of the Upper Iowa typically pass over the private property of dozens of Oneota Valley landowners, often without setting foot on any of this private land.

The river is politically complex as well, paying no more attention to civic boundaries than to property lines. In its 135 miles the Upper Iowa runs through two states, six counties, and several small towns. Squiggling its way through a grid of townships, it does not define the border of any of them. It is not contained by any one of these places, so its use is governed by them all.

I ask Knudson to do some late-season canoeing because it has been a drought year. For anyone planning to canoe, low water means getting out of the boat and walking now and then—pushing us out of our legal use of a public resource and onto the contested rocky bed of the river. Knudson can tell me plenty about that. While he was in public school his father, George Knudson, was embroiled in a political debate about the future of the river. His father favored increased public ownership. When Karl and his dad once landed their boat on private property to do some fishing, the angry landowner, who happened to be a leader in the fight against the public initiative, charged Karl's father with criminal trespass and confiscated their canoe. In law school Knudson became a member of the board for the Iowa Sierra Club and carried on his father's battles. Through the Sierra Club, Knudson published a book in 1979 appealing for the people of Iowa to protect their scenic waterways. He used the Upper Iowa as his case in point. In addition to being a lawyer, he ran a canoe rental business from the early sixties until 1992. Since childhood, he has stayed close to legal battles between those who see the river's future in its continued redevelopment, mostly through private ownership, and those who see the river's future in its preservation as a public resource. Knudson, as a lawyer, has sometimes represented the latter group.

Knudson's schedule in the late summer and fall of 2003 is filled with legal cases involving development, but one bone-chilling Sunday in mid-November he has a free afternoon. A little after noon, in Knudson's dusty old Pontiac, we pull up to the public boat landing next door to his old canoe business. We roll out in scruffy cold weather gear that makes us look like a couple of refugees from a tundra hike that went wrong. As I stand at the river's edge, nervously eyeing the thin ice that stretches like a sheet of antique glass from the bottom step of the landing, Knudson solo lifts the canoe to the bank and noisily throws in our gear. As he slides the canoe into the ice, little geysers of water bubble up through the weak spots. The frozen sheet below our boat crackles, groans, and breaks away as we step in and push off. Knudson tells me that in high school he canoed the river in winter for the adventure of trying to impale fish in the open water with a spear fashioned from a sapling. It's clear that a trip down the river propels him backward to what feels like a more primitive time.

Somewhat perversely, the route I have chosen, starting on the west edge of Decorah, will be through the least primitive section of the river. We will skirt the north edge of the town center and pass the village of Freeport before getting into the countryside and ending up at a bridge east of town. The eastward course of our journey is the direction in which Decorah, the biggest town in the river basin, is developing.

Aldo Leopold argued that soil, water, and animals are an interdependent community, where each needs to be granted the same rights. The Decorah stretch of the river we are floating is a test of that. It shows how the Upper Iowa's waters spring from Oneota rock, and how people depend on both rock and water. We argue, however, about how to define that relation legally.

Below the canoe landing we float past the mouth of Twin Springs, a favorite local trout stream. Scattered leafless trees border an opening of water that looks pure enough to drink. Knudson's father, George, a chemistry professor, wrote the handbook for river canoeists like us: *A Guide to the Upper Iowa River* (1970). In it he warned, "Do not drink spring water." The reason for this caution was geological: "the water . . . may not have been purified by filtration through soil or sand."[2] Instead of soaking its way downward, water in the river basin pours through the heavily cracked bedrock of limestone, a geological feature called "karst topography." In the valley where the town sits, the groundwater's swift fall is halted by a layer of water-impervious Decorah shales. Water flows horizontally until it finds a way past these shales, often seeping or pouring out at the hillside edge of the Decorah layer as Twin Springs does.[3] The contaminants Knudson's father warned about mostly come from septic systems and farming on the land surface, for which the springs and the river serve as a drain. Springs are often called "sources," but in the Upper Iowa landscape, the waters of the river's so-called sources already carry a history that the basin's geology doesn't have time to erase.

The waters that feed Upper Iowa springs often enter the ground through a rock feature called a sinkhole. A sinkhole is created when water nibbles out a widening funnel as it descends into the rock below the surface. These funnel vents collapse under the weight of the rock and soil above them, creating pockmarks, the most visible intake pores of the underground circulatory system of the river basin. The Upper Iowa may be fed by as many as six thousand of these. My childhood along the river taught me that sinkholes were repositories. Into the sinkhole on my family's acreage I dumped branches, leaves, lawn rakings, and grain sacks full of clinkers and ash. Over the biggest depression on our land, a previous landowner had parked an outmoded horse-drawn hayloading machine. It towered, rusting, over our pasture sinkhole like the skeleton of some prehistoric reptile. Having made deposits, I expected returns; some of the best cure-all bottles, animal skulls, and antique curiosities I found in my childhood ramblings came from sinkhole depressions. Because of the predictable effect on groundwater of dead pigs, chemical containers, and junked refrigerators, it is now illegal to use sinkholes as dumps, which means a diminishment of life for young explorers but an enhancement for everyone else.

George Knudson's guide is a trusty companion for canoeists. I am also glad to have Karl Knudson, the former canoe businessman, in the stern. He has mastered the elusive j-stroke and knows the river well. Karl called his rental operation Knudson Canoes, a lyrical name since Knudson sounds like the two-word question, "Canoed son?" Owning Knudson Canoes was, in season, exhausting work. Knudson went out after high water to cut up snags that posed threats to boats. He watched whole flotillas of drunken students sail off in his boats and dislodged the canoes of first-time paddlers from beneath submerged logs. On his wedding day, Knudson rented out his livery of fifty canoes to a dozen parties in the morning, sent them upstream, got married, and then rushed back to collect his boats. Most of his business involved people putting in somewhere between Kendallville and Decorah and taking out somewhere above town. People avoided the stretch we are floating, choosing instead the rural and dramatic scenery that starts thirty river miles upstream. Their itineraries confirm that Knudson is not alone in preferring the primitive when he ventures onto the river in a canoe.

Below Twin Springs I see ice that looks more serious than the brittle shelf into which we launched. Our canoe grinds onto a sheet that stretches from bank to bank. There is nothing to do except use our paddles as ice-breakers. I hack into the sheet in front of the canoe with my paddle. Knudson wedges his into the opened corners of ice and pushes us forward. We leave a small channel of open water in our wake, finally breaking clear. The smooth water doesn't last long. On the next riffle, the canoe groans to a stop. I throw down my paddle, lumber out, and help Knudson pull the canoe forward into deeper water. To do that, Knudson and I are stepping on rocks that are partly our own; the floodplain through Decorah belongs to the citizens of the city.

Because the Upper Iowa crosses town, county, and state boundaries, the U.S. government has the most important public interest in the river. Iowa was created from federal land governed by the Northwest Ordinance of 1787, which states, "The navigable waters leading into the Mississippi . . . and the carrying places between the same shall be common highways and forever free."[4] As Knudson settles in again to his j-stroke, he tells me, "There's argument based in federal law that navigable rivers are public highways, no matter what the state law says." Steven Long, a former school administrator from New Hampshire, did one of the federal government's first very informal surveys of the Upper Iowa in 1817. Long stayed on his boat on the Mississippi but wrote in his log, "the Little Ioway River . . . is navigable in time of high water about fifty miles."[5] In our low water trip, we are twenty-one river miles farther inland than Long predicted.

Iowa landowners were furious when the craze for lightweight canoes that began in the 1950s opened the river to more boating. Canoeists in the 1960s began cutting the pasture fences that crossed the river to allow free passage downstream. In 1965 the state attorney general passed down an opinion that property owners had the right to fence the river, though the ones who continued the practice eventually used techniques that allowed boaters to get over or under the wires. Today, fences across the water have almost disappeared. Still, the attorney general's opinion stands. For Knudson, this legal territory is as familiar as the Decorah stretch of the river. As he summarizes it, "The land underneath that portion of the Upper Iowa near the Mississippi is public land. Most everything else on the Upper Iowa is private property that just happens to have public water flowing over it."

The Decorah section of the river valley belonging to the city has been developed as parkland. In the long and shallow curve above the town, the river has cut through over one hundred feet of rock, exposing on our right a long wall of stone. The exposed, unglaciated rock of the area gives the region its geological name: the Paleozoic Plateau. Red cedars and white pines grow from the bluff edge that glows dull white far above us in the cold, cloudless sunlight.

As the West Decorah Bridge comes into sight, Knudson and I pass the river-gauging station, a small, concrete block building topped with a satellite antenna. Constructed by the Army Corps of Engineers, the little sentry house contains equipment that measures the flow rate of the river and beams this information to the U.S. Geological Survey. A few yards downriver from this measuring station, a white plastic tube runs to the center of the river to measure the Upper Iowa's nitrate levels. These two monitors on the upstream edge of the town demonstrate the federal government's active interest in the river.

Settlers sited Decorah on the river in 1849 to make use of its waterpower. But after nearly annual inundations, federal, state, and local governments teamed up to create a levee system that rerouted the river away from the central business district, then separated the town from the river with a series of dikes visible on both sides above the West Decorah Bridge. Because of its role in constructing the levees, the Army Corps of Engineers shares concern about flood levels with the Iowa DNR and the town. The rate of flow on the day of our canoe trip, seventy-nine cubic feet per second, is a mere vapor compared to the roughly thirty thousand cubic feet per second anticipated by the builders of the dikes, but a flood in 1941 reached that rate, and waters have been near that level several times since.[6]

The second monitor pipe, just below the river-gauging station, is the perimeter of a wall of defense against pollution. Iowa's streams have the highest level of nitrate pollution in the nation. Nitrates, an oxidized form of nitrogen found in animal waste and chemical fertilizers, are linked to the health problem called blue baby syndrome, where a child's blood becomes oxygen depleted. According to the Environmental Protection Agency (EPA), ten parts per million of nitrates in drinking water constitute a health hazard. In spring flood, the Decorah monitoring unit has registered a nitrate level as high as twenty-two parts per million. In those conditions, the city water has registered a level as high as eight, uncomfortably close to the EPA's maximum permissible level. The river and the water supply have different readings, but there is a shadow effect: the nitrate level of the city wells rises as river floods carry more nitrate. The small buildings that house the pumps for Decorah's six wells string out like a necklace along the river's southeast edge. Unpumped, these wells, sunk in the greenbelt that accommodates the river levee and the floodplain, would fill with water to a depth of twenty feet. This means that there is a relatively thin layer of very porous ground between the water that feeds my household taps each day and a river that sometimes carries over twice the government's permissible levels of nitrates.

The federal government's interest in river pollution goes beyond nitrates. The Upper Iowa also carries a fertile load of topsoil and phosphorus to the Gulf of Mexico. The rich mix creates an explosion of algae growth and decay that ultimately sucks the oxygen out of a portion of the Gulf that, in a bad year, grows as large as Lake Ontario. Over 20 percent of the fertilizer in the Gulf comes from Iowa. In slow response to the Clean Water Act of 1972, the EPA will eventually begin fining watershed governments for the excess nitrogen and phosphorus they send into the Mississippi. In addition to reading the threat to city water, Decorah's monitor will tell state and federal officials how much nitrogen originates upstream. The nitrate the river carries southeastward with our canoe unites the interests of the city, Gulf shrimp fishermen, and Washington, D.C. When it comes to water pollution, we all live downstream.

≋ Just above the West Decorah Bridge, the river shrinks to its narrowest width in forty miles, catapulting forward at double speed in a rapids where waves usually rise higher than the bow of the canoe. Today, however, instead of having a fast ride, Knudson and I are splashing through shallow water. As pickups and pedestrians cross the bridge above us, we hike in winter coats, carrying one hundred pounds of portaged canoe over more City of Decorah gravel. Back in the water downstream, the boat nears a sandbar where the surface churns with the fins of white suckers swarming to escape our dark shadow.

Fish in the Decorah stretch of the river have also drawn the attention of higher levels of government. In 2002 the Iowa DNR and the federal EPA took sample fillets from carp and smallmouth bass in the stretch of the river that passes Decorah. They found traces of mercury, PCB, and chlordane, with mercury levels in the bass exceeding the level recommended by the

EPA. The federal government banned the manufacture of PCB, an industrial chemical, in 1977 and banned the use of chlordane, a pesticide, in 1988. These chemicals in living fish are a legacy of collective carelessness, for which Upper Iowa anglers now pay the price. Mercury also may be an issue only the federal government can manage. The main source of mercury in streams like the Upper Iowa is coal particulate from electrical plants. Though federal standards have scrubbed much of the poison from smokestacks, the mercury in fish swimming beneath our boat is a mark of the current failure of the national government to protect us from ourselves.[7]

Not far below the bridge, Dunning's Spring enters the river. In Victorian times the power of this spring was used to cut and polish a limestone marketed as Decorah marble. Decorah marble came from a quarry just below Dunning's Spring. The reciprocal relationship of water and the river basin's stone is written in the origins of layers of bedrock such as Decorah marble. The stone in the hillside below Dunning's Spring was all sprung from water, but it happened over four hundred million years ago, the equivalent of seven million successive human lifetimes past, in a time when what is now the river basin was the sloshy edge of a large inland sea. For tens of millions of years, the slow currents of warm seawater swirled above this spot, strumming the bottom with a steady pulse of waves. It was a time before people, before mammals, before fish, before anything with a backbone: a world of water-dwelling invertebrates. These soft creatures took in water, and from it they extracted minerals they recast into their hard outer skeleton: shells of calcium carbonate. After the animals died, their skeletons continued through the rivery change that, in rock, is termed *diagenesis*. In seafloor sediment the nonskeletal organic matter decayed, pressure squeezed out the oxygen, and calcite bonded together the pieces. Weathered particles of other rock, bone, and fossil packed themselves into the interstices. One of the layers of limestone chocked with these fossils became Decorah marble.

Decorah marble shows how folks in the little municipality, past which we are gliding, rely on rock. In an economic crisis that peaked around 1880, the town looked to its abundant building stone as an exportable commodity that could replace wheat, and to the decorative "fossilized granite" industry as a replacement for the manufacturing of agricultural equipment. The public relations engines of the frontier town began to whir. A Boston geologist said of the Decorah marble quarry in the 1880s, "Nowhere in the United States is there to be found a stone that equals these fossil ledges in revelations given of the past." Town leaders used a piece in the counter of the town's new post office, where everyone would be sure to see it just about every day.[8] They tried to send another block of Decorah marble to be included in the Washington Monument.[9] In 1884 the power of water stripped clean the quarried rock and ran thirty stone saws in the mill above the quarry.[10] After a few years, however, the fossilized granite industry went belly up. Despite the names given it by spinmasters, the rock wasn't granite or marble. Sedimentary limestone proved a poor replacement for igneous or metamorphic stone.

≈ In the back of the canoe, Knudson surveys the river. Downstream from Dunning's Spring, the whisper of the current spreading out over gravel rises to a threatening sizzle. Knudson's eyes narrow to a squint, and he stands, hoping with a little altitude to read the water for the still, inverted "V" of deeper channel that promises safe passage. Dropping down, he leans hard into his stroke to give us momentum as the water thins out with a wind-tunnel roar. We stop anyway. Knudson jumps out onto the rocks to give us a push. We scare some fish as we finally float clear. "Have you ever had bass jump into your canoe?" he asks as twitchy fins disappear ahead of us. "It used to be when you'd go canoeing you'd see lots of bass jumping into the canoe, or alongside the canoe," he says. "You never see that anymore." Nostalgia runs strong in his thinking.

≈ Just downstream from Dunning's Spring, Ice Cave was formed when a long wall of limestone slid toward the river. The top of the wall tipped back against the bluff, creating a cold, pyramidal cave at its base. Rock all along the river moves and changes. The highs and lows created by the major joints are exaggerated by water cutting downward through the low places. Within the rocks are pockets and veins of calcite crystal, where the calcium carbonate molecules of the rock rearrange themselves in regular hexagons. Broken open, these creations of darkness glint in the sun like the clear center of so many eyes.

Secondary deposits introduced by water soaking down through stone sometimes attract more interest than the base material in which they have located themselves. Beginning in 1856, in the last phase of the Iowa "lead rush," entrepreneurs set up mining operations along the lower stretches of the Upper Iowa to extract galena ore from the sandstone and limestone in an area that was given the name New Galena. J. D. Whitney reported in the 1857 *Geological Survey* that "along the face of the bluff . . . a number of shafts have been extended into the rock." From these, he reported, "between fifty and one hundred thousand pounds of lead had been obtained"[11] by a company employing up to a hundred men. But the deposit was not well defined and the mining proved difficult. The New Galena Lead Mining and Real Estate Company, within one short year of operation, exhausted the resources of its chief financial backer, a New York speculator named Jasper Moulton, and drove him to drink.[12]

Lead deposits provided their flash-in-the-pan interest, and Decorah marble was a short-lived draw. Construction-grade limestone, however, has proved a steady treasure to the area. One of the many Norwegians to settle around Decorah in the nineteenth century was my great-grandfather, Ole Faldet. He emigrated from a small, cold farming valley in Norway to a creek along the Upper Iowa where he could work as a stonemason. In Norway, his great-great-grandfather had discovered and started a copper mine, but Ole's family had fallen on such hard times that his father died a miserable death working away from home in another copper mine, three hundred miles north of the Arctic Circle. In the whole of his American life, Ole never owned a horse, a wagon, or, later, a car. He walked from home to his building projects with his tools, often carrying his mortar tub on his head. Ole and men like him broke limestone from local quarries before the age of dynamite and straightened the necessary edges with hammers and chisels. In Decorah and the countryside around it, they laid stone after stone into the foundations of houses, barns, and business buildings; stacked stone into retaining walls along streets, bridges, and creeks; bent rings of shaped stone around cisterns and wells; and arched long lines of it to be buried as storm sewers.

≋ After Knudson and I pass the mouths of Sampson Spring on the left and Dry Run on the right, we are beyond the residential core of Decorah, as well as its wide grassy band of levee and floodway. We are entering the commercial and industrial fringe. On the right, at the same point in the river where huge power lines sweep into Decorah from the east, are metal garages; the butt ends of parked cement mixers; and the towers and smokestacks of a concrete, gravel, and asphalt company. The firm specializes in gravel from beds deep in the river plain. Several of the other largest area employers crush rock from local quarries, four of which form a spotty ring around Decorah. Many people in the area find work in the stone business, not just because of the ready availability of rock, but also because of its quality. The rock business is steady because, as the director of one local company once told me:

If you look, just about everybody every day uses limestone. You walk on it. You drive on it. Your house is partially made out of it—if you're using concrete—and a lot of times the filter rock in septic systems and drain tiles is all limestone. Everybody uses it every day. Some people, some firms, even get into industrial limestone, and that's used for toothpaste, antacids . . . those do the same as what we do when we apply lime to a farmer's field: take the acid out of it. Antacid is calcium—just really an expensive limestone that you're eating.[13]

This description of people's relationship with limestone is a fine short primer in human ecology. We add limestone to our environment to make it more hospitable. With bodies that are an extension of the mineral environment in which we live, we ingest calcium when our system is thrown off balance by a greasy lunch or too much stress.

The heavily developed stretch of the Upper Iowa east of Decorah has caused Karl Knudson plenty of stress. As we pass the equipment parked on the bank, he pushes back his stocking cap and shakes his head in frustration. Twenty-five years ago, he summarized in his book the values that made him follow his dad in urging public protection of rivers like the Upper Iowa. "Scenic rivers are eminently worth preserving in their natural condition,"[14] he wrote. A second, more practical reason he cited in his book for leaving floodplains open is that taxpayers often end up paying for the mistake of unwise private development along rivers where flooding destroys property. For this reason, if for no other, he argued, "The flood plain is best preserved in its open state."[15] The stretch of the Upper Iowa we are now entering is developed in all the ways he argued against a quarter century ago.

It is here that we meet our nemesis: the long, solid sheet of ice that chips my paddle. In reality, the worst we probably face is inconvenience. If we can get to shore we are a two-minute walk from the busiest stretch of highway in town. But Knudson, who has canoed the river in ice before, is not ready to give up. He suggests we try to hit the ice hard, in unison, and he begins calling out "stroke!" like the coxswain on a crew team. It works. Our combined strokes lift the boat and drop it as our paddles push us forward. Slowly and boisterously we break a path downstream. A flock of mallards lifts from a riffle ahead when we finally reach clear water. I feel a surge of pioneer accomplishment, along with relief that Knudson is in the stern.

We are now at the midpoint of the Upper Iowa, the mouth of Trout Run Creek, where a shift in the bedrock bends the river from its southeasterly course to a northeasterly one. On the east bank beyond Trout Run are clustered a hodgepodge of business buildings. A long wall of bank stabilization rock gleams below the concrete walls of Decorah's Wal-Mart Supercenter. Knudson has been part of a three-year litigation against the city and the largest retailer in the world to prevent the fill and development of the floodplain for this 187,000-square-foot building. His clients are the landowner on the other side of the river and several riverside homeowners upstream. Though the lawsuit has kept the doors of the completed building closed for a year, Knudson's clients have, just weeks before our canoe trip, settled out of court. The Iowa Supreme Court found the building illegal under the current laws, but after the ruling, the city council had begun to write new laws to allow the store to open.

This is the first time Knudson has been down this stretch of the river since the start of the case three years earlier. His concept of multiple-use preservation is to keep the maintenance of a pristine river corridor a high priority, with fifty feet of stream bank and steep forested hillsides left wild, the floodplain restricted to agriculture. The concrete box of merchandise that looms ahead of us is the antithesis of that idea. Knudson remains bitter that local and regional governments are fainthearted in protecting the river's need to flood from land developers hungry to eat up floodplains.

The stream bank below the supercenter building—a highly engineered channel of stone resembling an open-topped culvert—is part of what annoys him. To protect itself from the waters that come directly at this key bend in the river during a flood, the corporation added eight feet of fill to its site to raise the ground level well above the state-mandated standard and then lined the entire bank with rock riprap. This high wall of rock continues far downstream. I stick my paddle into the water along the bank and cannot touch bottom. A stream contained by hardened walls often deepens and speeds up, channeling the water away faster. Looking at the banks of broken stone through which we float, Knudson scoffs, "To take care of the flooding problems here they're going to simply treat this river like a ditch: a ditch lined with riprap." Considering the river a ditch is, for him, like mistaking the cosmos for a sanitary landfill.

The fact is, city engineering extended to this stretch of river close to twenty years ago. In the last stretch of rock riprap below the new town-center-in-a-box, we pass the outflow pipe of the municipal sewage system, built in 1985. A million gallons of water that entered the system from riverside wells dutifully carries its load of effluvia to this facility every day. This outflow pipe is the tributary my neighbors and I have built to connect ourselves to the Upper Iowa. Here is what we do to the water we send toward the river. The first stage of processing screens out the plastic ducks, pocket combs, and perfume bottles. Smaller heavy solids are then settled out, all to be trucked to the landfill. At the heart of this water-cleansing process, organic matter still in the water is consumed by bacteria in aeration ponds and anaerobic tanks. The mineral sediment that remains is hauled out, spring and fall, to be plowed into farm fields. The methane given off by frantic bacterial activity heats the plant and anaerobic tanks and lights an eternal flame that burns from a pipe at the plant entrance. The cleaned water is exposed to ultraviolet light in the hot months to kill any lingering bacteria and then piped into the river. Gravity, microbial feeding, and light are the three simple means by which the town's sewage becomes acceptable river water. Though the plant manager, David Halverson, uses lab analysis to test the purity of the outflow, his favorite test is in the river itself. "We see plenty of trout around the downstream side of that outflow," he is happy to say. "They seem to like it there."

It's important that Decorah puts clean water back into the river, in part for the sake of the groundwater of the region. Decorah contributes one-third of the river's wastewater, and before 1985 it contributed over half of the river's municipal water pollution.[16] At the next bend downstream, the river cuts into a steep hillside of sandstone. The layer of rock exposed in this hillside is called the St. Peter: the first major layer of rock to lie below the shale level that sheds polluted surface water off through hillside springs. The two best underground channels for water below northeastern Iowa are the porous St. Peter and Jordan sandstones. The river is among the sources of water that gets drawn into this sandstone. Thousands of people draw their drinking water from these aquifers. Decorah's wells, for example, are in the St. Peter. Much of the surface water that makes its way into these levels of stone will next see daylight from the drinking water tap in someone's home.

These sandstone layers below the river are part of a record of the very long prehistory of the area. The St. Peter, for example, was built up during an ancient period of low water that exposed old formations of sandstone to erosion and deposition over the large areas of remaining sea. One strange twist of water and rock on the Upper Iowa River is that the rock bed gets older as you float forward. The prairie streams that feed the beginning of the river flow from the Iowan Surface underlain by Devonian rock, 350 million to 400 million years old. The Galena layer of stone through which the river cuts above Decorah is Ordovician, between 425 and 475 million years old. The final stretch of the river is a passage through Cambrian rock, containing the oldest remains of life, well over 500 million years old.

Just below the outcrop of St. Peter sandstone, Knudson stands up in the back of the canoe and surveys the water ahead. It is so shallow we paddle to a river island to carry the canoe to deeper water. This time our foot journey is on county land, the site of the farm originally purchased to maintain the county home for the infirm and the insane. Here we stop to stretch. My calf muscles feel like set cement and my shoulders ache. Standing in the sunshine and shaking our khaki legs, we are as warm as we are likely to get on this nippy November day. As I munch a candy bar, I feel juiced up and contented. This stretch is pretty. The oak leaves on the hillsides glow a rusty orange against the gray of the bare forest trees. The pools below the riffle on both sides of the island are turquoise green.

River islands are notorious for shifting position or vanishing altogether. That and the animated water flowing past call to my vagrant mind Heraclitus, the dark, mistrusted seer of ancient Greece. He said, "You cannot step twice into the same river, for other waters and yet others go ever flowing on." You stay the same. The bank stays the same. But the water is always being pushed downstream by newer waters behind it. Heraclitus was drawn to running water as he was also drawn to fire because he believed change is the single element you can count on in a universe where everything—water, trees, the land itself—will pass away. Town centers get caught in that relentless flow. River islands disappear. Even the riverbed is caught up in a process of flow. The rock that forms the base of the river valley, and the hard foundation over which the water slips its way, is moving. The coral fossils in Upper Iowa stone prove that the rock below the water of the river is on a long, slow odyssey. Corals are tropical, growing in warm equatorial seas. The rock bed of the river, now forty-two degrees north, spent a long past south of the equator. The sea of which it was once the floor covered a portion of the single landmass, Pangaea, that two hundred million years ago split apart to begin drifting into today's continents. The whole landmass of what is now North America tilted to its present orientation; what is east today was once south.

To picture this long migration from the warm equator to the cold north, I think of the earth beneath my feet as being like a mollusk. The pearl of heavy elements at the earth's core is surrounded by doughy material, the spongy upper edge of which is called the mantle, the same name as the layer that makes the shell of a clam. From this mantle, the thin plates that make up the earth's crust are generated. The mantle circulates in currents sufficient to propel the plates of the outer crust in the migration that takes eons. Oceanic ridges lift up. New sea floor spreads out. Plate edges buckle under. Old sea floor lifts into mountain ridges. Though the hard crust of the earth below the Upper Iowa is sixty miles thick, it floats on the mushy core of the planet like a leaf on water, spinning to its current orientation and migrating north to where it is today at a rate of centimeters per year. The lesson of river islands in elemental history is this: even rock floats.

≋ Pushing the boat off the island, Knudson and I start floating again, too. Because of the dry spell, the water is clear enough for me to watch the riverbed pass. Occasionally, the inner side of an empty shell flashes up from the bottom. Twice I see the white flesh of a freshwater mussel, gleaming like a sliver of moon between the dark shells that house it. I ask Knudson about who owns the fish and who owns the mussels. He tells me they are public property, their acquisition limited by government rules. Knudson has a legalist's love of this kind of question. Knitting his brow and raising the pitch of his voice, he goes on, "But if you trespassed on private property to collect clams or to fish, it makes the act of your entering onto that property more culpable than if you just wandered onto it." Although mollusk species far outnumber vertebrates, freshwater mussels are, it turns out, some of the more endangered creatures on the Upper Iowa. Their census is one of the single best measures of the river's basic health, and their decline in number is one reason the river's water quality is listed as impaired. When the Iowa DNR prepared its management plan for the newly designated Protected Water Area of the river in 1990, it listed five local species as threatened.[17] Though a state survey found six species in the Decorah stretch of the river in 1985–1986, a follow-up thirteen years later found none.[18] Today I am surprised to see any mussels at all.

A clear stream bottom and a clean river are less important to humans than to their twin-shelled neighbors. Yet if property rights were strictly a matter of getting there first, mussels would have humans beat hands down. Shells, in fossil form, pack the rock over which we float, among them the marine ancestors of today's river mussels. Even the names of the mussels that make their life in the upper stretches of the river today sound older than bedrock: elktoe, pocketbook, heelsplitter, and squawfoot. If you want to go looking for these, you have to avoid the mud and silt that washes into the river, creating surfaces where mussels can find no grip to anchor or pull themselves along. The best place to find mussels is in a section of river with a mixed sandy and rocky bottom and strong current, just below an area of deep water. Wedging its foot securely between the rocks in such a place, a clam is happy, with the river water carrying food down into its mouth and hauling its waste downstream.[19] A mussel in that kind of water settles down for an enjoyable stay.

Though people walk around on land and keep their heads above the water, they depend on water as absolutely as a clam does. Water needs to move through us just as relentlessly as it moves through a clam. Heraclitus, the champion of the running stream, proved the wisdom of his own observation by passing away from dropsy: too much water retention. Too much body fluid and a sinking sense of disappointment in his fellow humanity caused him to die at sixty. The threatened future of mussels in the river suggests that the deepest problems with the stream start, not in the corridor of riverbank and trees, but in the land surface that is washing away on the uplands to bury the kind of river bottom that best suits these once-upon-a-time sea creatures with an ancient adaptation to fresh water, but no protection against rivers of mud and pesticide. Knudson's idea of river corridor preservation is more than aesthetic. A strip of forest, grass, and shrubs at the edge of the river and bordering the streams and watercourses that feed it stops silt and other pollution before it leaves the land surface. Wild-looking stream borders improve the environment for river-bottom mussels.

Knudson and I don't run into any more ice or run aground on any more rocks. In one unexpected way, then, our afternoon expedition becomes the Upper Iowa canoe trip of Knudson's dreams: all our foot travel, even in this season of low water, ends up being on public land. We pass the Freeport bridge, the golf course, a very visible subdivision, the near buildings of two farms, and two more bridges. We catch sight of a new water tower. But beyond Freeport, the river regains more wildness. We see a big-antlered buck, eagles, two beaver houses, and a lot of beautiful, flowing water. "We seem to be out in the sticks again," Knudson happily remarks.

We end our journey at a canoe landing adjoined by a white pine stand where Knudson had a part in helping stop a large residential development. When a developer started bulldozing roads into the eighty-eight-acre site, area landowners formed a coalition and filed suit, challenging the legality of the subdivision under the county zoning ordinance. The Iowa Natural Heritage Foundation (INHF) stepped in and bought the entire property. To make the purchase worthwhile, eleven parties granted the INHF over eight hundred acres of permanent conservation easements on lands in the river watershed, pledging to keep land undeveloped in perpetuity. Knudson and his wife, Clara, were among the landowners who deeded away an easement so this small bend in the river could remain a good home for bald eagles. Knudson helped do for one bend what he would like to see done for the whole Upper Iowa River.

Our trip down the one marginally urban and suburban stretch of the Upper Iowa reinforces my sense that although the water and the rocky bed are two separate elements, only the two together make a river. The two can be separated for legal purposes, but the separation is a distortion of what constitutes a stream. Knudson loves the whole thing: the stream and its bed. He continues to advocate collective action to preserve the river valley because a river defies the boundaries of one element, one person's land, one town's jurisdiction, and one state's power to legislate water protection. I admire that passion. His politics express his love and respect for a piece of his home environment. My expedition with him has opened for me a small window on the way rock and water are caught together in the Oneota flow.

Big River in the Driftless
The Ice Age

Using all the stealth I can muster, I sneak to the upstream edge of the pond behind a beaver dam. In the boggy ground around me, the grass and weeds have grown as high as my chest. The glassy center of the pond sharply reflects blue sky and clouds, making the water beneath invisible. I switch my lure to something lightweight that looks like a bug. Stepping onto a tiny island of turf, I flick my pole forward, the lure arcing to the far side and landing with a plop that shivers outward in small rings. The sound is nearly as quiet as a kiss, but in the shadows at my feet I see the dark shapes of trout rippling past into the weeds, alarmed by the shock. The disappointment I feel at having failed to outwit these quick fish is, however, tempered with an answering thrill of knowledge. The stream is alive with a remarkable population of game fish, even though I had once written its waters off as dead.

The stream I am trying to fish, labeled South Pine on the map in the *Iowa Trout Fishing Guide*, is an icy brook where my father and I used to seine minnows. My father and his childhood neighbors called it Spring Creek. Walking against the current, we would push the lower ends of the seining net forward in the dark water, feeling for the bottom like blind men with their canes. The meshes would come up writhing with minnows, shiners, and crayfish. Tossing the smaller specimens of this haul into a pail to use as bait, we would throw the rest back into the stream. But one day in the early summer of 1972, an eerie spectacle: the meshes of the net came up lifeless. We guessed that a farm chemical had made the environment suddenly toxic. The water was frigid and clear, but it had gone as sterile as rubbing alcohol. So it is a surprise when, in the summer of 2004, I find myself fishing the stream.

≋ An environment is not simply a place; it also has a temporal dimension, ceaselessly in flow. A shift in temperature, for example, causes, in time, an environmental shift. Heraclitus, the very first minister of flux, said, "Cool things become warm, the warm grows cold." This plain observation applies to the most drastic environmental change in human history: the great warming, from the Pleistocene cold during which people evolved, to the balmy Holocene present in which we now flourish and in which our carbon emissions further ratchet up the heat. People came to North America because of an Ice Age. Our first environment here was a cool one. That we have remained, even as the climate has warmed, is a testimony to our adeptness at refashioning ourselves and transforming our immediate environment. But like other species, any person who stays in the Upper Iowa basin has chosen an environment that is partly cold.

The fish I am setting out to catch in Spring Creek on an early summer morning in 2004 are brook trout. I recently found that they were living in the upper reaches of the stream even when the creek, near its mouth, had gone dead. The Spring Creek brook trout are testimony not only to resiliency, but also to the cold history of the region. Spring Creek is the only stream in the Upper Iowa basin, the only stream in the state of Iowa, with a naturally reproducing, unstocked population of brookies. Trout fail fast in water where the temperature climbs above sixty degrees and stays there for long periods. Room temperature you and I find comfortable would slowly stew a brook trout. During the Ice Age, the ancestors of South Pine trout could have lived in any clear stream in central North America as far south as Georgia. Those fish thrived in streams at the edge of the glaciers, and from that haven they moved north to populate newly exposed water as the ice melted. As the air temperature climbed, however, so did the temperature of the temperate-belt watercourses, leaving the major rivers insufferably warm. The fish became isolated in the headwaters of streams across the eastern half of the continent. Settlers along the Upper Iowa found what they called speckled trout in shaded creeks cooled by springs. Neither Canoe Creek, into which South Pine feeds, nor the Upper Iowa, today, stay cool enough, year-round, to support brook trout. The Mississippi, into which the Upper Iowa feeds, is famous for being warm and muddy, two conditions that promise death for speckled trout. At some point in the heating that followed the Ice Age, the brook trout of South Pine were trapped in their short, cool ribbon of comfortable water. Later, the fish near the mouth of the stream may have either moved upstream or died from chemical poisoning. But a portion of the South Pine fish survived and reproduced, happy in the stream's cool waters and better disposed genetically than any other trout on the planet to survive there.

≈ It is odd that I should be pursuing this endangered little population with a fishing pole, in part because I haven't fished for trout since I was twelve. When I go to buy my gear I am immobilized by the profusion of lures and tackle in the sporting goods section. A wall chocked with nymphs, jigs, spinners, and spoons dazzles me with color. An artificial minnow glints metallically. Flies fan their audacious hairy tails. Before a lure catches a fish, it has to mesmerize a shopping fisher. What do I know? I know the size I need: small. Beyond that, I can only try to imagine what a hungry trout in Pleasant Township might find tempting for a morning snack. I go for the smorgasbord, tossing assorted lures into my shopping basket along with some lightweight line for my dusty rod and reel. I buy a license and a trout stamp. Notwithstanding my ignorance about trout fishing, I am now legal and equipped to try my hand at catching the rarest fish in the state.

≈ South Pine, Canoe Creek, and the Upper Iowa River are fingers of the Mississippi, spreading northward to what once was the edge of an ice sheet extending across water and land from the North Pole to the middle of the continent. The lower half of the river valley, including South Pine, is part of what in the nineteenth century came to be called the Driftless. The Driftless name is a sign of how totally the descendents of Ice Age Europe had forgotten their cold origins. By the time Thomas Jefferson purchased the Mississippi basin from France, careful students of geology knew that the earth had not always been as it was in their own time. They used a biblical theory to explain the signs of inundation they read in the landscape around them: earthquakes, floods, fire from the heavens. They called the large granite boulders they found stranded far from granite bedrock *drift*, the improbable flotsam of Noah's flood. The landscape, free of boulders, dissected by the fingers of the Upper Mississippi, was being opened for settlement when Louis Agassiz, the leading European geologist of his day, was appointed to a professorship at Harvard in 1847. Agassiz advanced the theory that the northern parts of the United States had once been inundated not by a tremendous flood, but by ice. From the pews of Methodist churches to the chairs of natural history at American universities, his glacial theory was coldly received.

For the next half century, scientists doggedly continued to disbelieve Agassiz's theory that glaciers had covered America. The man who carried out the first geological study of the Driftless, Josiah D. Whitney, rejected glacial theories even as he described the region in official reports to the state of Iowa in 1858 and to Wisconsin in 1862.[1] In the 1870s, W. J. McGee tramped northeastern Iowa, testing the likelihood of Agassiz's glacial theory. McGee's nose for adventure and intellectual mysteries eventually led him to collaborate with John Wesley Powell in geological and ethnological studies, to serve as chair of the National Geographic Society, and to help found the American Anthropological Association. But before his professional career was established, McGee studied the entire length of the Upper Iowa, from the river's mouth to the granite boulders and boggy potholes near its source. Publishing his findings in 1891 as *The Pleistocene History of Northeastern Iowa,* McGee concluded that Agassiz was right. Describing the patterns of erosion and deposit he observed in the landscape through which the Upper Iowa flows, McGee triumphantly reported that "the trail of the ice monster has been traced, his magnitude measured, his form and even his features figured forth, and all from the slime of his body alone."[2] The "slime" was drift, carried by ice to the borders of the Driftless.

Once the glacial theory was generally accepted, scientists refined their picture of the ice event responsible for the creation of the Upper Iowa River valley. At its maximum, the "ice monster" was so massive that its weight lowered the earth's crust beneath it. At its edges, the ice flowed out from under itself across the land surface like an ebbing tide. The glacier leveled whatever stood in its path, carrying before it the rubble of an erased landscape. As the cold deepened, the ice expanded, adding its own momentum to the shift in climate. In heat, the ice sheet threw up a veil of mist to shield it from the sun. When the sun cut through the mist, it reflected quickly off the sparkling surface, providing little warmth. The ice hoarded the snow that fell on it: two inches, twenty feet, two hundred yards, enough snow, ultimately, to compact into ice two miles deep. This tremendous reservoir of ice lowered the oceans. Land bridges impeded the mixing of the cold seas with the warm. The cold dug in and deepened.[3] Even the Ice Age, however, had its seasons and its retreats. The potential for flooding in the warmer periods was far beyond what can be imagined by today's standards. Today's river started much bigger.

The Upper Iowa begins in country leveled by the ice sheets. Granite boulders, carried down from the Canadian border, heavily litter its western stretches. Near its middle the river reaches the Driftless. Over half a million years ago, the entire land base of the river was covered at least twice by a glacier. All subsequent expansions of the ice left the river valley at least partly uncovered: "driftless." In the last half million years, powerful floods poured down when ice dams broke, gouging out the canyon through which the modern river flows. Though the modern Upper Iowa erodes the valley, its force and channel are minor in comparison with the rivers of churning water, rock, and ice that ran from hilltop to hilltop through the entire valley, dissecting the earth before them. By ten thousand years ago the climate had warmed, but the Pleistocene inundations had left a new riverbed carved into the landscape.

≋ The August morning that ends at the pool above the beaver dam is cool, in the fifties as I drive through the mist to an overgrown public parking area on Spring Creek Road. My destination on Upper South Pine Creek is a good mile of hiking through state land, mainly old meadows and prairie, yellow with blooming goldenrod. I tramp through wet grass, fishing pole in hand, half a dozen untried lures in the tiny new tackle box that rattles in my pocket.

≋ Though brook trout have survived from glacial times, many of that period's other creatures vanished with the ice. The signature species were mammoths and mastodons. Many of the deep beds of loose gravel over which the Upper Iowa River flows were deposited as glacial outwash. Occasionally a mastodon tooth, a bone fragment, or a section of tusk is found in this gravel, a sign that the bodies of these creatures also got caught in Pleistocene floods. Other species from that colder time were similarly large: towering ground sloths and giant beavers, bears, and bison. Unlike South Pine's brook trout, these Pleistocene megafauna failed to survive in the warm Holocene. One reason for their disappearance may be the arrival of a new species. The first people arrived in the region near the end of the last ice advance ten thousand to twelve thousand years ago. During this episode the landscape of the river was, at its coldest, a mix of tundra and parkland. As the climate warmed and the ice moved north, the land produced evergreen forest. The earliest people entered this environment in small bands, armed with stone weapons, to hunt large prey.

Visitors today pour in steadily to catch trout. Rainbow trout and brown trout are stocked in Upper Iowa tributaries, but they belong to a different genus of fish than the brook trout that once lived in these streams. The rainbow is native to streams west of the Rockies. The brown trout is a European fish. Rainbows can stand warm temperatures, tolerating waters up to seventy-two degrees; they readily migrate out of the streams into which they are stocked to live in the river. Of the 110,000 fish stocked yearly in local streams by the Decorah trout-rearing station, roughly 85 percent are rainbows. Most of those are caught quickly in what is called the put-and-take fishery.

Put-and-take fishing is a big business in northeastern Iowa. Along the creek bottom at Highlandville, northeast of Decorah, the campfires of trout fishers burn all summer. Grandparents bring restless children visiting Decorah to feed the fish at the Decorah Fish Hatchery, run by the Iowa DNR between Siewers Springs and the waters of Trout Run. Sometimes retired truckers or beaming fourteen-year-old boys also show up at the trout-rearing station with a ten-pound rainbow, reporting on where they hooked the fish and asking how long a fish of that size might have lived in a stream. The questioner expects an answer in years. Yet it has probably been minutes, hours, days, or for a smart fish, weeks. Monster-size trout in the put-and-take streams that feed the Upper Iowa spend their lives in the trout-rearing ponds of the Manchester Fish Hatchery, eating commercial fish pellets and producing eggs. Iowa farmers understand this concept well; brood stock, big animals kept in confinement mainly for producing young, are culled for consumption once past their reproductive prime. The culled, oversized rainbow are planted in the same Iowa streams into which thousands of their offspring have preceded them on their way to the frying pan.

The DNR stocks other trout, at a very small size, to grow in the stream. In the right streams, some will not only grow, but also reproduce. The fish most stocked as fingerlings to grow and reproduce in northeastern Iowa streams are brown trout. This species, imported to America in the 1880s, is moderately tolerant of the varying stream conditions caused by humans, including temperatures up to seventy-five degrees. Browns grow to a large size, even in small streams. One famous brown, for example, tantalized fishermen in Highlandville through several summers of the late 1930s. Then, on a Sunday evening in May 1939, Decorah lawyer Ed Acres tied a large streamer fly on an invisible, light leader. To keep his line from breaking once he set the hook, he set the reel tension low. Once the six-pound-two-ounce fish hit, he played it for forty-five minutes before pulling it from the pool in Bear Creek, where it had evaded the best efforts of local fishers throughout a long life.

≋ It is hard to emphasize sufficiently the rarity of South Pine brook trout. To protect them, the DNR has designated South Pine as a catch-and-release stream. Each fish caught must be returned to the stream. Bill Kalishek is the fish biologist for the Iowa DNR whose job it is to develop good trout habitat in streams that feed into the Upper Iowa. He says that of the three species of trout, brook trout are "the most sensitive to high temperatures, the most sensitive to pollution, the most sensitive to habitat degradation."[4] That's why, though the Upper Iowa and most of the streams that once fed it were home to native brook trout 150 years ago, South Pine's brook trout are, according to Kalishek, "the last population that's spawning successfully on their own and still maintaining a population through that spawning."

Kalishek uses fingerlings raised from the fertilized eggs of South Pine fish to reintroduce a native strain to half a dozen of the healthiest creeks in northeastern Iowa. So far, he's had success in five. The keys to the survival of reintroduced trout are genetics and habitat. South Pine brook trout are better disposed to survive in Iowa streams than hatchery-raised brook trout. For habitat, they need cold water that runs clear, over a bed that has plenty of clean stretches of gravel. Most important for habitat, Kalishek says, is the consistent cold temperature. Kalishek kept a monitor on South Pine for the summer of 2003, when the air temperature frequently went over ninety degrees. The stream temperature, in contrast, registered more than sixty degrees only on four days in the course of over four months. Otherwise, the water consistently remained between fifty and fifty-seven, night and day. Though the state owns a one-mile stretch of the stream, and one county road crosses South Pine, more than two-thirds of it remain in private hands. So far, landowners have worked with Kalishek, putting land stewardship practices in place that will help keep the little creek running clear and cold.

≈ The grassy track I hike to South Pine is not worn with use. I fish for three hours. The only noise I hear that sounds like a motor is the low-frequency buzz of a hummingbird attending to jewelweed flowers. The only signs of fishing are the muddy prints of raccoons and blue herons—predators not subject to the catch-and-release restrictions to which I need to attend. Mud, flattened grass, and a line of flotsam show the water has been up about two feet within the previous week. This was not the first or the worst flood of the summer. Signs of the torrent make me worry, once again, whether there will be fish, because a gully-washer completely scours out a creek. A fish strikes, however, at one of my first casts. Though the maximum size of a South Pine brook trout is about twelve inches, I feel the same electric thrill in my arm that Ed Acres must have experienced when he snagged his record brown.

≈≈ South Pine stream is a cool island of refuge, but there are other relics of Ice Age cold along the valleys of the Upper Iowa: cool microclimates in the relative warmth of the larger basin. The U.S. Fish and Wildlife Service designated this archipelago of small islands of perpetual coolness the Driftless Area National Wildlife Refuge.[5] The Ice Age plants and animals that inhabit these cool spots are not able to move beyond them. The northeastern Iowa landscape, through which the Upper Iowa flows, is a refuge for fifty endangered species of plants.[6] Some of these plants, as well as several types of snails and insects, depend on stable cold to live.

The most fragile and tiny of these environmental islands are called *algific talus* slopes. Talus is the debris that forms at the base of rock cliffs. Cold air, heavier than warmer air, sinks and enters the ground through cracks and vents in the upland terrain. In the cold winter months, ice forms near the ground water level where seepage occurs in these air passageways among the rocks. This ice preserves a temperature between thirty-seven and forty-five degrees in the air spaces between the talus through the summer months, when heavier air from above settles over it. Air displaced from talus crevices passes out at the base of the slope.

Cold-loving mosses and ferns cover these cool, damp rock piles with a mat of soil and roots. In the coldest part of winter, ground air warms the talus environment, keeping it less arctic. In these cool pockets the roots of plants such as northern monkshood and golden saxifrage find a comfortable climate. In the case of the Iowan saxifrage, its only near relatives grow near the melting edges of glaciers.[7] In the 1950s several snail species, used in fossil form for decades to help archeologists date Ice Age soils, were discovered alive and contentedly reproducing on these algific talus slopes. Some of the tiny islands of cold that support these species are no more than a few square yards in size. A disruption of the moss or the weight of a single heavy footfall is enough to break up the fragile blanket of mosses that makes the place hospitable for these remnant communities of Pleistocene snails. The Nature Conservancy, the Iowa DNR, the U.S. Fish and Wildlife Service, and right-minded landowners have worked to map and protect this patchwork scrap of the Ice Age past.

Cold climate remnants also extend beyond algific talus areas to the sides of many north-facing slopes. The most famous is a balsam fir stand, protected as a state preserve, along the river below Bluffton, Iowa. Along the steep bluff from which that small town takes its name are thin, needle-pointed evergreens you would need to drive north almost to Duluth, Minnesota, to see again. Balsams along this short stretch of bluff have remained protected from logging, too much sunlight, and the killing effects of heat since the days when the whole region was a boreal forest. Beneath these balsams, and on the floor of other north-facing river slopes, grows the Canada yew, a ground cover that more commonly thrives in northern evergreen forests. On northern and eastern crests of hills throughout the river valley, white pines tower above neighboring trees. At the southern edge of their range, they were a welcome sight to early settlers. Yankees were familiar with them from the Northeast, and early builders found plenty of uses for their massive logs. In one of the more colorful accounts of the settlement of Winneshiek County, the story is told of how two men, John McKay and Mr. White, harvested two white pines from along Trout River to make a flagpole eighty feet high, erected it on a ridge on July 4, 1851, and ran up a flag assembled from red, white, and blue fabric and tin stars. The men honored the day by calling their new home in the Driftless by the name Washington Prairie.[8]

Though the strike on the first bend seems promising, my luck through the rest of the morning shows me why the speckled trout in Spring Creek survive. In a deep, slow section of the stream where a black willow leans from one bank to the other, I see fish dart from under the shadow of the tree trunk. For the next hour I toss a shiny spinner, pulling it through the center of the little school of twenty, dispersing their ranks briefly before they scoot upstream to the nearest shady hole. Tossing the line again, I watch them rocket back to their previous hiding spot. As the quiet morning passes, I realize that even if they had not seen me, the sound of the lure plopping in this church-like silence is enough to set these wild fish on edge.

≋ Like brook trout and Pleistocene snails, people also draw on the area's cold resources to survive the hotter seasons of life along the Upper Iowa. In the Great Depression, one successful summer tourist attraction in Decorah was Ice Cave. Just east along Quarry Road from Dunning's Springs, Ice Cave is a large and accessible example of the same ice sink effect that creates algific talus slopes. Beginning in 1930, tourists could pay a dime to escape the heat and see a wonder of nature by visiting the cave and its environs. The cave is free of ice during the fall and the frozen months of winter. When the ground thaws in the spring and water runs down through the bedrock, cold air sinks down with it, freezing a large formation of ice in the lowest part of Ice Cave. This formation cools the temperature of the cave, keeping the ice intact far into the summer. The cave reverses the ice formation pattern of the outside world.

Ice Cave received its greatest moment of national renown in 1911, when Stephen Muller reported to the local newspaper that after visiting the cave regularly during several days of peak hay fever season, his symptoms of that illness disappeared. The Associated Press picked up the story, with its St. Paul agent adding the following off-the-cuff speculation: "It is said that local capitalists will erect upon the site of the cave a mammoth sanitarium for the cure of hay fever." The wire posting inspired the following story in the Lafayette, Indiana, *Daily Courier*: "Decorah, Iowa, comes forward and offers a cave as a substitute for the storage department of a brewery as a cure for hay fever. It makes one curious to know what is in that cave."[9] A visit to the state preserve site today shows that there is not much in Ice Cave except aging graffiti and a few cigarette butts, but in late summer, the air inside still provides cool respite from the August sun.

Until electric refrigeration became widespread in the 1950s, people used river ice to preserve little islands of winter coolness through midwestern summers. Decorah's ice business was owned by the Dirks family. During January a team of twenty men harvested ice from an impoundment of water above the Tavener milldam in West Decorah to fill the Dirks's icehouse with 1,200 tons of Upper Iowa River ice. In addition, the crew filled the icehouse along the rails at the east end of town to supply the creamery, the egg and produce companies, and the railroad.

Through warmer months of the year, ice was distributed to the town of Decorah. The first load each morning went to the businesses along Water Street. The biggest customer was the Sugar Bowl ice cream factory, which needed a lot of cold to make, store, and ship their ice cream. At Shimel's tavern on Washington Street, 1,500 pounds of ice had to be carried across the floor, down the back stairway to the basement, and stacked around the beer kegs. Additional ice was chipped into the reservoirs around the coils that fed the taps to cool the stream of lager. By midmorning the teams began residential rounds.[10] Today, in the western stretches of the Upper Iowa, river ice cools the milk Amish families sell to the local dairy in July and August. In these ways, people have cultivated their own little pockets of perpetually iced air along the river.

≋ On several occasions the brook trout on South Pine have almost *not* endured. Genetic analysis shows that those fish are distinct from the strains of native brook trout in Minnesota and Wisconsin. It also shows that at several points in history, the population became severely reduced. One of those occasions may have been the last time my father and I seined minnows on the stream. According to Bill Kalishek, "You don't have much genetic diversity, much genetic variation," in South Pine fish. "But that's fairly common for small, isolated populations of trout." When I ask about how much a stream's fish census could decline, Kalishek tells me about a population of naturally reproducing brown trout in another Iowa stream. "We went in to sample one fall. We hadn't been in there for several years, and we found we were down to fourteen fish: thirteen males and one female. That was twelve years ago. Today we're back to normal numbers, and they're all descended from that one female." As I speak with Kalishek, in an office where the shelves hold books like J. David Allen's *Stream Ecology* and specimen jars with labels like "silver lamprey *Ichthyomyzon Unicusons* 9-30-99 Upper Iowa R Iverson Bridge," I realize with creeping horror that my own childhood seining expeditions must have occasionally netted fingerlings from the most endangered fish population in Iowa. That activity, today, could have landed me in jail. I was an unwitting part of the environmental pressure that has reduced this fragile community almost to extinction.

I don't want to take any fish away today. I want to hold one in my hands and see its colors shine in the morning sun before I release it. I move to the beaver pond only after thoroughly jangling the nerves of the fish beneath the willow. Among the alarmed fish I see swimming out from the shadows in the pond is a specimen that, I swear, is at least a foot in length. Though I don't get to look that fish in the eye, I have confirmed that the speckled trout of South Pine are alive, well, and favorably disposed to evade the onslaughts of a designing though unpracticed fisher. That being enough, I crank in my line for the last time and stroll back to my car.

≋ When J. D. Whitney used the word *drift* in the first geological study of the Upper Iowa basin, he understood it as alluvium, deposited by flowing water. It was part of his denial that glacial action helped create the landscape of the river. The ancient world of ice was not mentioned by the middle eastern authors of the Bible or accessible to the imaginations of staid Victorians. When I ask Bill Kalishek about South Pine's fish, he explains another use of the word *drift* that exposes a prejudice, as dangerous to my understanding as Whitney's flood theory was to his geology. *Drift* is the term used to describe random changes in genetics that cause populations to evolve over time. My prejudice is to want to believe that the fish I see gliding through the shadows of South Pine are the product of the Ice Age. But evolution fights that in several ways. First, natural selection means that as the larger South Pine environment has changed in the last ten thousand years, the fish that survived there are the ones most suited to those changes. As Kalishek explained, "Even though South Pine is a good watershed, you know there are a lot more row crops there now than there were in the 1840s or the 1700s. The genetic strain of fish would not be the same there now as it was in those times." For this reason, Kalishek is indifferent to whether South Pine brook trout have lived there since the Ice Age or whether they were introduced seventy years ago. Their beauty, to him, is their perfect disposition for survival in that stream due to natural selection and conditioning.

In addition, however, a population will "drift" in its genetics in ways that are often independent of natural selection. This is especially true of tiny populations, like those in South Pine, where accidents might randomly eliminate a huge percentage of an entire generation. On the basis of his conversations with fish geneticists, Kalishek believes that within twenty years, drift alone will make an isolated population of fish genetically distinct from the parents that produced it. The fish I see moving between the shadows in a morning of fishing are genetically distinct from the fingerlings I scooped from the water over thirty years earlier. The fish I disrupt share the same love of cold that may have brought their ancestors to South Pine. But the fish I see are not Ice Age trout. They are the product of the Ice Age, but also of chemical spills, floods, my own past excursions to these cold waters, and the partially random workings of genetic sequencing. Though it is appealing to think of those nervous fish as a remnant of the prehistoric past, part of the truth is that they are also uniquely new. Their cool streaks of life and color fit not only just this place, but also only just this August morning moment in the long flow of time in the basin of the Upper Iowa.

Roots and Fire

8,000 – 500 B.C.E.

Measured by volume, the greatest pollutant of the Upper Iowa River is, and has always been, soil. Tons of soil get flushed into the river with every spring rain. In the water, the thick brown cloud chokes the insects, mussels, fish, and plants that make the river their home. A cloudy burden of silt fills in the channel and the sloughs of the Mississippi River south to New Orleans, a city that sits on a delta of silt that spreads into the Gulf like the root fan of a brutally upended tree. In the Upper Iowa basin, the single most important way to slow soil runoff is to put down permanent roots: either grass, a mixture of grass and trees, or forests. The challenge is that the basin's main industry is agriculture based on the annual plowing and tilling of much of the land surface, and with the industrialization of agriculture, fewer and fewer farms depend heavily on perennial grass or forests.

The most serious problem of soil loss in the basin is on the plowed hillsides where the prairies originally met the forest in a watershed called Trout Run. Out of the 640,000 acres that make up the Upper Iowa watershed, there are 2,000 acres where soil loss on each acre each year would fill a string of dump trucks. Half of those acres are in Trout Run. Although the Natural Resource Conservation Service would like to see soil erosion limited to between five and ten tons a year on cropland, on some of the steeper fields along Trout Run, farmers lose forty tons of soil per acre per year. This ongoing ecological catastrophe is in part the symptom of another one: deforestation. Those steep fields on Trout Run were once forested. In the thirty-three-thousand acre Trout Run watershed, 87 percent of the timber, twenty thousand acres, is now gone. In the whole Upper Iowa watershed, with twenty-eight major tributaries, 10 percent of the lost timber acreage is in Trout Run. Ironically, Trout Run is home to Iowa's second-largest coldwater spring and the area's largest trout-rearing station. It is a watershed that needs to keep its soil in place.

With that in mind, I make an appointment to meet Richard Kittelson at a coffee shop a few blocks from my house. Kittelson directs the Trout Run Reforestation Project for Northeast Iowa Resource Conservation and Development. His work promoting reforestation on Trout Run is, in the spring of 2004, the current best hope for slowing runoff in the watershed to an acceptable level. I find Kittleson, an amiable man in plaid shirt and jeans, at a window table. After introductions and ordering coffee, he pulls out a folder of maps. The first map looks like a hand with a very bad rash. In fact, it is the fan-shaped Trout Run watershed with the highly erodable acres marked in red. "If we could take the worst seven hundred of those acres out of row crop production and put it into timber it would stop 28,000 tons of soil loss every year," Kittelson says as he spreads the map out on the table. That is a lot of mud to keep out of a small stream. It sounds easy enough, until he pulls out the next set of maps, each of them the aerial photo of a section of land with the acres eligible for the program marked in yellow highlighter. Succeeding in that simple goal of seven hundred acres might mean convincing something like eighty different farmers to put eight to ten acres of their land into forest and promise to keep it in forest for the next ten to fifteen years.[1]

≈ The cover of *Soil Survey: Winneshiek County, Iowa* (1968) features an aerial photo of a country church with flat upland fields in the foreground, crazy bands of contour in the middle distance, and here and there copses of trees and more fields fading into the far horizon. The scene is part of the Trout Run watershed, chosen not because of erosion problems but because it embodies the poster-perfect dream of rural America. The *Survey* was compiled in careful detail by the soil scientists of the U.S. Department of Agriculture (USDA) in 1968.[2] To give you an idea of its purpose, one of the 120 maps in this thick book tells me that the soil on my house lot, the place where I am sitting to write, is deep and moderately eroded Sattre loam with a 5 to 9 percent slope. The *Survey* also tells whether deep and moderately eroded Sattre loam is suitable for farming, for use as fill, or as the base for a road or a reservoir. It tells me what I would need to make it produce crops, and what yield I am likely to get from it each year in corn, soybeans, oats, or hay. It tells me the color, properties, and thickness of each horizon (A, B, and C) down to a depth of five feet. And in some cases, it tells me if soil is forest-formed (podzolic) or prairie-formed (brunisolic). For all that complexity, if you own agricultural land in Winneshiek County, your property tax is determined by a simple formula based on acreage and only one soil factor: its suitability for corn. That narrow interest in the production of row crops is at the heart of the soil-loss problem from one end of the river to the other.

≈ Kittelson and I leave the coffee shop for a road trip through the countryside of Trout Run. His first stop is an acreage planted thickly in ash and walnut seven or eight years ago by a landowner who is also a conservationist. The trees stretch fifteen feet tall in the bottomland along the creek. As we walk up to the stream through this young forest, a pair of wood ducks lifts from water running clear enough for trout. But the bank across from us is eight feet of eroded black earth: the silt from a century and a half of farming.

As we pull away in the car, Kittelson shows me, field by field, the acres that qualify for his program. Almost every farm we pass has slopes with a gradient over 14 percent that would qualify for his program. Some are in pasture or crop set-aside acres of rough meadow. As with many of the government's current conservation programs, these grassy acres do not qualify for Kittelson's richer incentives because they are already protected from soil loss. Many of the steep slopes, however, are plowed for corn and soybeans. "I have to admire the tenacity of these guys," Kittelson admits. "It can't be easy to maneuver machinery on these kinds of grades." The very steepest land is still forested. Many times a rock outcrop twenty or thirty feet in height looms up from the hill, surrounded by trees. The variety of the landscape, these little copses, and strips of trees make it pretty country: a likely choice for the cover of the *Soil Survey*. But as soon as the land begins to taper into a gentler slope, the trees end and plowed land begins.

Kittelson has discussed the land, field by field, with landowners, but the sign-up period for the federal crop set-aside has not even been announced. So far he has few hard commitments. "This one," he says, pulling up at the base of a steep hill with a band of woodland that cuts diagonally across its middle, "would fit perfectly. Just extend that wood down to the road. The landowner even wanted to do it, but he's got the farm leased on a two-year contract, and look what the renter did." At the very edge of the road ditch the land is scarred, and the broken remains of timber stick up from the ground. A wooded fence line has recently been scraped clean by a bulldozer. "That guy bulldozed down a row of trees in the old fence line, and for what? For an extra row, maybe two rows of corn." As we drive I notice two-story piles of bulldozed timber at the edges of fields and woods on many of the farms. The deforestation is going forward at a steady pace.

This picture-perfect section of northeastern Iowa is undergoing the same kind of environmental catastrophe most people associate with the Amazon basin. Kittelson's reforestation project is going to have to reverse a steady tide of tree loss that so far has not been turned.

To a person who neither gardens nor farms, soil is simply dirt. But people who work in soil eventually learn that it comes to you with a personality. Roots help create that soil, and they keep soil anchored in place, even in the heaviest rain. Only the upper layer of soil, the "A horizon," or topsoil, is alive. There, at the junction of earth and air, the literal base of the food chain, dead material is rekindled into a living frenzy. Whatever dies—plant or animal—and falls to the earth surface becomes food for invertebrates, bacteria, and fungi. Plants, setting their roots in the soil, convert carbon dioxide, water, light, and minerals into leaf, stem, flower, and seed. This alchemical magic starts in the roots, in the dark, in the stuff most people call "dirt." And dirt's personality has been determined by its origins.

In Trout Run basin, reintroducing a mix of forest canopy and roots would be the best way to slow down the eroding power of rain and runoff on the steep crowns and sides of hills. The vegetation in a forest arches in an umbrella designed to catch rain as well as sunlight. That visible growth is roughly matched in volume by the root system spreading into the darkness underneath the ground. As they stretch beyond the A horizon—the living upper layer of soil—roots introduce a living presence into the layer of pure mineral below. Sliding, creeping, and burrowing along that highway of roots come the fungi, the bacteria, and a host of animals, from single-celled protozoa to worms, insects, and voles. The amount of organic material in a forest that falls to the soil as leaf litter when it dies is roughly equivalent to the amount of material that dies only after it has penetrated the soil (mainly in the form of roots) to live. Beneath the leaf litter, which serves as a kind of skin, the soil of a forest tends to be acidic and loose, a crumbling black humus that gives off a rich and musty bouquet. The mixture of canopy, undergrowth, leaf litter, and roots is one of nature's better ways of holding steep hillside soil in place.

The Upper Iowa watershed sits on a biological divide. To its east stretches a region called the Eastern Woodland, and to its west is the Tallgrass Prairie. Such junctures of two distinct types of environment are called ecotones. Before Euro-Americans settled here, the river basin was a mixture of both: prairie in the west, where it began, and forest in the east, at its mouth. But along its whole length were patches of both prairie and woodland, and perhaps as plentiful as either was savanna that was a mixture of the two, oaks growing alone or in clumps but surrounded by expanses of prairie grassland.[3] Wherever the water sat still, marshes developed, with their deep peaty soil base. These environments made up the biome of the Upper Iowa. Trout Run sits at the midpoint of the river, where the line of the ecotone was most distinct: a forested area at the edge of a vast prairie. Over the millennia during which people have lived here, the vegetation has moved back and forth with changes in climate and the occurrences of fire. Grasses had the advantage in the drier and hotter climate when fires swept through easily. Trees succeeded in cooler and wetter times, and wherever the fire line broke. In the steeper reaches that make up much of Trout Run, forest almost always won out.

A few of the fields we pass in Richard Kittelson's car have freshly turned soil. I remember the maps he has showed me. Each contour of land was labeled with its soil type. Many of the contours Kittelson had marked for inclusion in the Trout Run Reforestation Project were Fayette soils, described in my *Soil Survey* as "gently sloping to very steep . . . on convex ridgetops and side slopes. The native vegetation was trees."[4] Every layer of Fayette described in the *Survey* includes the words *brown*, which fits most every plowed field we look at, and *friable*, which means that this soil will break apart and erode easily. The *Survey* suggests that such land be used for hay and for meadows, plowed for corn no more than one year in four, preferably one year in six. The tawny earth of most fields we pass is mixed with last fall's corn stubble. The sequence is corn followed by corn or an even less soil-holding crop: soybeans.

Though several of the farms we pass still have dairy cows that need pasture and hay, many have gone out of livestock production or are raising hogs, animals that do not need hayfields. Dairy families lived in this neighborhood thirty years ago, but the pattern of land use has changed. The steady money, from the markets and subsidies of the Farm Security Agency, is no longer in small dairy operations. The money has gone to row crops and the hogs that consume a steady diet of subsidized grain from infancy to slaughter. As farmers try to make the land along Trout Run follow that money, the steeper fields are being shifted to corn and beans. A northeastern Iowa farmer using contemporary farming techniques on hilly soil would sleep easy harvesting 4.5 tons of corn off an acre of tilled soil in a year.[5] On the Trout Run, however, the trade-off is sometimes ten times that amount of topsoil washing off an acre in a single season. The formula does not allow for a long future of farming.

On a steep bend, our car meets a logging truck that pulls over to pick up walnut tree trunks stacked by a farm drive. Just having seen piles of bulldozed wood, I am about to complain when Richard Kittelson puts in his perspective: "It's good to see that logging. We've got to keep that out in front of farmers, that one day they can log forests, and make a good profit on their land." In addition to this financial incentive, there is the promise of a long future for farming forested land: "Selective cutting is an excellent way to use this land, and to keep it in use for generations," Kittelson says. The packet Kittelson hands out to landowners includes a graph that illustrates the rate of return for land that produces logs. The return, over time, is as good as for raising row crops. The figures are based on the price of walnut boards. The challenge is that those trees need to stay in place for forty years, a person's working life. The way Kittelson sees it, reforestation is a good way for farmers to bank for retirement or to pass on an inheritance to their children. In an era of high overhead, shifting farm policies, and high government support for corn and bean production, that type of long-term investment is not proving an easy sell.[6]

≋ The story of the soil on Trout Run has a far deeper history of human interaction than the last 160 years of crop farming. As the damp and cold of the Ice Age climate passed, grasslands spread. The last glacial era ended in this region nearly ten thousand years ago, and by seven thousand years ago, the climate here reached its warmest temperatures in a period called the Altithermal. As the climate leaned out toward that peak and then edged back over a period of four thousand years, the dominance of prairie also ebbed and receded. The human remains of the Altithermal and the millennium and a half that followed are called Archaic. Early Archaic people, like the Ice Age people before them, relied mainly on hunting, including the hunting of large grazing animals. One broken hunting point roughly ten thousand years old was picked up in an upland field area that overlooks the confluence of Trout River and the Upper Iowa. Made of Moline chert, this fluted Folsom point would have been used near the end of the Ice Age to hunt a large, now-extinct species of bison. Near this Paleoindian point were other points, including a local chert fragment of unfluted, lance-shape pattern from the beginning of the Archaic. These fragments of hunting tools mark between them the shift from the Pleistocene to the warming of the Holocene. Disturbed and eroded upland sites like the one near the mouth of Trout River are the only type where Paleoindian and Early Archaic remains have been found in the region. Undisturbed Early Archaic sites have not been found on the Upper Iowa. One reason may be that they were located in areas that were dry during the hot millennia of the Altithermal but have since become deeply buried by new soil, eroded upland soil, or carried away by flood.[7] The fate of these sites is a clue to the history of people and the soil; the living soil along the Upper Iowa mostly formed and deepened during the period in which people lived here. People were part of the ecological equation in the soil's formation, just as they are now in its elimination.

In the human prehistory of this ecotone region, culture followed the pendulum swings between a dominance of forest or a dominance of prairie. As the climate became wetter and cooler, people entered the Middle Archaic period. They depended more heavily on gathering forest foods. Middle Archaic sites are the first to produce *manos*, the grinding stones that turn acorns, hazelnuts, walnuts, hickory, and other seeds into gritty flour.[8] Sites from this period have been found on the bottomlands near the mouths of rivers in the Upper Mississippi, and bone remains show that people exploited the new abundance of wetland foods such as clams, turtles, waterfowl, and fish. Further south, on the Iowa side of the Mississippi in what is now Dubuque, a local archeological firm uncovered the remains of three houses on what had been the tributary fan of the Maquoketa River in Middle Archaic times. These house sites included pits that seem to have been footings for upright logs that formed the architectural skeleton for round houses.[9] Axes appear in sites of this period. People had, by six thousand years ago, begun to more fully exploit the timber of expanding woodlands for houses and to settle for longer periods in their homes at the woodland edges of local streams.

≈ Along the high, plowed edges of woodlands like those of Trout Run, farmers occasionally find arrow, spear, and knife points, some of them Archaic. One casual collector of such points was my uncle Julian. Dressed in blue denim overalls and smoking a Lucky Strike as he walked along a woodland edge near Falcon Springs to check his fence, he noticed something glinting in the dirt. A point made out of quartzite, six inches in length, this notched triangle of stone, the color of pale brown sugar, rested on the coffee table in my uncle's living room throughout my childhood. In my young imagination, it connected with the horse-riding Indians I daily saw firing arrows at cavalry and cowboys on my home television. However, the stone is an Etley point, from 2,500 to 4,000 years old. The person who left it on that hillside had no horse, no cowboys or cavalry about whom to get upset, and no clue about the technology of the bow and arrow. Like my uncle Julian, however, he may have been smoking at the time. Carved pipes appeared in the region 3,500 years ago.[10] That same period in the history of the climate marks an era that struck a balance between the earlier extremes of the forest climate and the prairie maximum. Some 3,500 years ago, oaks began to spread outward into the prairie. The era of savanna had arrived along the ecotone.[11]

The stone for my uncle's Etley point was harvested from a site in Wisconsin. Although nostalgia makes it easy to imagine prehistoric people rooted to one place, the trade routes of the Late Archaic extended from one end of the Mississippi and the Missouri to the other. Obsidian from the Far West, pipestone from the plains of Minnesota, copper from the Great Lakes, and shells from the Gulf of Mexico all moved up and down the rivers that emptied the middle of the continent. The person who dropped that point for my uncle to find made his home near water. His mental map of the known world would have been etched with the flow lines of the Mississippi basin. Part of his map would have included Falcon Springs. The mental map of some of his contemporaries, and maybe his own, would also have included Trout Run.

≋ On Trout Run, the reforestation is being funded by a coalition of government, business, and foundations. On top of that, 10 percent of the reforestation cost is paid by the landowner. Soil protection projects in the prairie stretches of the river rely on similar partnerships. One project, stopping extreme stream bank erosion out in prairie country, pulled together government support, the work and resources of a landowner named Dean Thompson, and help from the Lime Springs Fish and Game Club. On my next excursion to study the battle against soil erosion, I meet Thompson to see how stream bank erosion is being stopped in the flatter, western reaches of the Upper Iowa.[12]

Dean Thompson lives within sight of Chester, which sits in open field country just below the point where the river first flows out of Minnesota into Iowa. When I turn off Highway 63 to Thompson's gravel, road signs give an immediate hint of his problems: "Flood Area Ahead," followed by "Not Passable When Flooded," and if the point of the first two signs is lost on me, there is a third: "Do Not Enter When Flooded." Thompson is a former bar and restaurant owner and former trucker, whose wild driving on a Harley Davidson left him with a steel rod and twenty-six lag bolts in his back and the challenge of retraining for a new line of work at the age of fifty. He also owns one hundred acres of farmland with an erosion problem.

Thompson meets me wearing a Minnesota Vikings sweatshirt and accompanied by two large dogs. Standing on the river bridge below his red, hip-roofed barn, he explains that he put in his first crop of beans on his relatively new acreage in 1993, the year Chester, Iowa, received over ten inches of rain in one night and the river widened into a lake that spread from his barn to the highway a half mile away. "I had forty acres of beans under water three times that season; that was it for my beans," he laments. Another year the spring flood dug so forcefully into the bend on Thompson's farm that it excavated an island of earth six feet deep and twenty-five feet square, floated it upwards, and deposited it on top of the road fifty yards away. The river in flood keeps rearranging Thompson's acreage.

As Thompson's two dogs splash in the water of the river below the bridge, the bank behind them rises dark and black: a rich, thick deposit of prairie earth. "I got everybody else's best farming dirt," Thompson shrugs. His land, however, wasn't always an open floodplain. "You see those oaks over there, and over here?" he says, pointing from the road bridge, "The whole bottom used to have trees like that, and the river ran straighter through it, but the guy who owned the place before me took them out, plowed in straight lines, and planted corn right up to the bank of the river. He hated trees." The deeply eroded grassland below Thompson's barn was, twenty years before, a wood. "This used to be all oak trees with squirrel hunting and horseback riding all the way up and down. We'd come out here and fish off the bridge and catch bass." The earth in Thompson's bottomland is prairie soil, but for generations it had been held in place by a forest. Thompson likes to imagine the whole bottom covered once again in trees, but getting them established is a challenge. He received grants from the EPA and the state to help pay for rock to stabilize the bank. In return, he is supposed to introduce trees. "I put in trees, and if the deer or the rabbits don't get them, then in the winter big ice cakes come floating down, and they cut them off."

The county, which tries to maintain the bridge and road in this floodplain, has paid Thompson money to put in a seven-acre pond to divert runoff and in so doing create a wetland. "When that two-hundred-acre area above it floods, that basin holds some of the water back so it doesn't go down the river. We're on the northern migratory path. The first spring, I don't know how many kinds of ducks were out there: geese, trumpeter swans, pelicans. I was trucking, and a buddy called me up and said, 'Your pond's a little flooded and the ducks have to take a number to land!'" Thompson knows the dam holds back more than water. "That pond also holds back the silt and farm chemicals." Thompson shakes his head at the reason for his county-subsidized wetland. "That's the government. Twenty years ago they paid people to tile, to drain their fields, and now they're paying them to cut the tile and have this. I think all that tiling is the problem. They used to have sloughs, and those sloughs would hold the water back. Now they tile it out and, BOOM, down the river she goes!"

We climb into Thompson's white Pontiac and tool along a grass drive that cuts through his bottomlands; "safari-ing," he calls it. The grass around us is as high as the roof of the car. "Everybody says, 'Why don't you just sell it and move up to Rochester?'" he shouts over the loud whoosh of grass parted by the Pontiac before it lifts back to fill the edges of the drive behind us. "Back when I was a kid with no neighbor kids I'd wander around by myself. Now I'm doing it again. I've lived in California. I've seen the world, but I've come full circle."

In open country in damp ground, where the water wants to move fast, trees seem nature's way to hold back the earth and slow the water down. The farmer who cut the trees in Thompson's bottomland was erasing part of the landscape described by the surveyors who first laid eyes on it in the 1850s. One of them wrote, "The timber is, in general, found skirting the streams, while the prairie occupies the whole higher portion of the country, with the exception of here and there an isolated group of trees, standing like an island in the midst of the ocean."[13] Having talked to Kittelson and Thompson, two men who deal with soil loss on the river at its worst, I decide to observe the management of a place with little erosion: Hayden Prairie, less than three miles southwest of the acreage where Dean Thompson is learning to come full circle.

≋ Hayden Prairie is managed by the Iowa DNR. I plan my visit for a day when they are burning a forty-acre piece of it. Driving west from Highway 63 to Hayden Prairie, I see the small town of Chester to the north, a gathering of trees and houses and a grain elevator surrounded by open farmland where clusters of trees mark the farmsteads. Newly harvested fields of corn and beans dominate the countryside along Beaver Creek, the stream into which Hayden Prairie drains.

It would be very easy to overlook Hayden Prairie, an expanse of weedy-looking grass on a country road with no defined parking areas. Where I pull onto the shoulder, the bluestem grass stands as high as field corn. Europeans who first saw the prairie hung back from it, a trackless barrier that would swallow them up and offer no respite or shelter. A visitor from

Dubuque reported taking a walk through a hilltop prairie above Decorah in February 1859: "We sought an Indian trail, and pass[ed] westward through prairie grasses higher than our heads."[14] What tempted Iowa settlers into the sea of grass where they sank from sight was the soil that fueled that growth. Unlike forests, in the tallgrass prairies the mass of roots, nodules, and tubers beneath the surface might be twice as dense and twice as long as the plant growth aboveground. In a well-established prairie, the living soil is measured not in inches, but in feet. It coheres to itself tenaciously. For the children of farmers used to struggling with rocks in the thin former forest soils of New England, or for young men who had struggled to raise hay on the damp slopes of Norway, prairie soil offered the wealth of kings.

Iowa's prairie was swallowed in an ecological holocaust. Only 0.1 percent of the state's over twenty-nine million acres of presettlement prairie now remains. At 240 acres, Hayden Prairie is a big piece of land, but it was once part of something over one hundred thousand times bigger. Equally important, Hayden Prairie, though it does not stand out from the cropland around it like trees would, hides a bounty lost to all the ground that surrounds it. In woodlands, trees make up the canopy, whereas in prairie the canopy is grass. The big bluestem, or turkeyfoot, that stretches up as high as seven feet, overshadows the Maximilian sunflowers, milkweed, rattlesnake master, water hemlock, coneflowers, wild rose, thistles, and switchgrass that vie with it for sunlight. In the undergrowth beneath these taller plants are wild strawberries, ox eye, indigo bush, yarrow, and clover. The fields around the property grow only beans or corn, a diminishment of the diversity of dozens of species that make up a prairie acre.

In prairie, the action stays on and under the ground. Grass grows not from the tips of the stem like a tree, but from its base. Bison can bite it, fire can burn it, and ice can break it, but as soon as there is enough water and sun to tempt it back, it surges upward in a green arc. Above ground, only the wind and grass sigh. Underneath the surface, the gophers, the worms, and the springtails sift through the soil for food. Bacteria ensconce themselves so snugly around the root masses of legumes like prairie indigo that it would be impossible for a technician with a high-powered microscope to distinguish plant from microbe in the nitrogen-fixing machinery that they form together. Fungi thread through the soil, breaking down carbons, stabilizing proteins vital to other organisms, delivering nutrients to plants, and binding disparate particles in their web. Rich dark prairie humus builds up at nearly twice the rate of forest soil.[15]

≋ People yearn to leave a permanent mark on the soil. Another innovation in human artistry introduced around the time that my uncle's Etley point was chipped from the unshaped stone was a burial practice called "red ochre." People were buried in a pit that was first lined with red pigment. Over some of these burials, small mounds were constructed. Just south of the mouth of the Upper Iowa, Red Ochre people used a stain of red and a hill of earth to leave their mark both in and on top of the soil. The first construction of burial mounds, however, was minor compared to reconfiguring the landscape through the power of fire.

The earliest European visitors to this region were amazed at the ferocity, the extent, and the frequency of its fires. An Italian adventurer, Beltrami, passed the "mouth of the river Yahowa" by steamboat in May 1823 and witnessed a fire he attributed to "Indians, who . . . set fire once a year to the brushwood, so that the surface of all the vast regions they traverse is successively consumed by the flames." Beltrami described the scene: "The venerable trees of these eternal forests were on fire, which had communicated to the grass and brushwood, and these had been borne by a violent north-west wind to the adjacent plains and valleys. The flames towering above the tops of the hills and mountains, where the wind raged with most violence, gave them the appearance of volcanoes, at the moment of their most terrific eruptions." It was, he wrote, an American Vesuvius or Aetna that stretched on for fifteen miles. "[T]he devil himself was jealous" of the inferno Beltrami witnessed.[16] Natural forest and prairie fires are started by lightning, but as Beltrami pointed out, they could also be started by people promoting the kind of environment that would best suit their needs. When the French Jesuit, Jacques Marquette, navigated his pirogue onto the Upper Mississippi in June 1673, he recorded seeing prairie banks on either side, with trees only on the protected river islands.[17] Claude La Potherie, a French native of Guadalupe who visited the Upper Mississippi not long after Marquette, linked the prairies he saw to Indian fire. West of the Mississippi, he reported, "are plains of vast extent, entirely treeless."[18] La Potherie blamed the open prairie on Indian hunters who lighted fires as signals.[19] He also said that Indian hunters used "a ring of fires, which burn the trees," to trap and kill buffalo.[20] The Dakota, the Ioway, and the Winnebago were all reported to use this latter technique.[21] Jonathan Fletcher, the Indian agent managing government dealings with the Winnebago, who lived on the Upper Iowa in the last decade before white settlement, summed up the role of fire in Indian land management: "It is believed that the practice of burning the prairies has a beneficial effect on the health of the country, by preventing the decomposition of vegetable matter; but it injures the surface of the soil, kills the young timber, and thus circumscribes the native forests."[22] From Marquette's arrival until whites settled the eastern half of the river basin, this practice of burning increased markedly, leaving a majority of that region open savanna and diminishing forest exactly as Fletcher describes.[23] Heraclitus observed, "There is exchange of all things for fire and of fire for all things." The ecotone was open country largely because for thousands of years the people who lived there cultivated fire.

Archaic residents of the river valley depended more fully on hunting than later people. They made increasingly sophisticated use of their environment and used fire in their daily lives. It is very likely, therefore, that they used fire in hunting. Though not farmers, those early promoters of fire *were* cultivating soil. By extending prairie into woodlands, they produced topsoil in thick, deep layers, with a root system never touched by the fires that kept the shady growth of trees and shrubs at bay. When Rudolf Kurz rowed down the Missouri in 1852 and saw a number of prairie fires set by Plains tribes to remove the old growth and promote the new spring growth, he observed, "Therein consists the Indians' total cultivation of the land their bands are accustomed to wander over."[24] A fall burn of the prairie helped congregate animals for winter hunting, and a spring burn created a dark, solar-collecting scar, charged with potash, where the spring growth would come first and most lush, attracting herds for the spring hunt. These burns left behind prairies or savannas, beneath which the organic "A" horizon spread downward, rich and tenacious.

≋ Because set fires have promoted roots and soil on Hayden Prairie since Archaic times, I am glad to arrive as four DNR employees and a botanist fire their fuel canister. A drizzle of rain is forecast. The wind being from the south, they begin along the north edge of the prairie, dripping gobs of fire into the dry grass. As the wind shifts and the sky darkens, they move their line of fire around the east and south edges to speed up the burn.

The thin orange line of flame moves across the square of prairie, ahead of it a large expanse of brown and green, behind a growing field of black. The man in charge of the burning, the state wildlife biologist for northeastern Iowa, has a pale, weathered face. He wears a hunter's orange cap and a brown coverall. Like a good cultivator of the soil, he carries a garden rake. Behind the line of the burn, he rakes away the black and gray ash, exposing a thin green layer of mosses and collars of grass. The loudest noise up close is the crackle and pop of the burning and the breathy roar of the flame in the wind. Behind that is the droning of a tractor in a nearby field. It pulls a harrow plow loaded with a tank of anhydrous ammonia to fertilize the picked cornfield. The burn is the holdover of ancient land management techniques. The plow and chemical tank are modern agriculture at work.

At a little copse of trees in the corner of the prairie, the flames burn up to the edge of the undergrowth and then fizzle out. This morning's burn is meant to stop the natural succession from prairie to woodland on this patch of ground where little growths of plum and aspen now stand smoking in the black expanse. "That wood used to be a lot bigger, between five and ten acres, and so thick you couldn't see through it," the biologist tells me. "Now we've got it down and opened up. We're making progress." Workers had girdled the trees in late July, but the shade still had been enough to allow only a thin undergrowth. The rich supply of stored-up solar power in the grass of the prairie petered out at wood's edge. "We've got to try to get rid of those trees. They're a seed source for this whole prairie," the man explains. But he is happy with the morning's work: "You come back here next spring," he advises me with a gardener's pride. "We're going to have a real rich growth here then."

≈ Whether it is plowed or unplowed, burned or watered, soil continually changes. In the case of Hayden Prairie, the soil washes downward in a process called leaching. Almost none of it horizontally erodes. The organic surface, with its distinctive chemistry and minerals, gets washed down with time into the subsurface. As the new soil builds, it buries the soil that preceded it.

Disturbing the soil, as the farmer is doing in the field next to Hayden Prairie during the burn, leaves it vulnerable to erosion. Unlike the beans and corn of the adjoining fields, the prairie plants, like most of those in a forest, are perennials. Not all farmers continue to till the soil. In the 1980s some began to practice no-till farming, leaving the stalks and leaves of the previous year's crop on the surface of the soil to protect it from rainfall, hold back runoff, and retain organic content instead of releasing it into the atmosphere. No-till is a highly mechanized return to low-impact early horticulture. Rather than turning the soil, it hoes or cuts a slot into which the seeds are dropped. The main drawbacks are the high level of herbicide it takes to keep back undisturbed weeds and the diseases that flourish in the undisturbed remains of the previous year's crop. Any modern corn or bean field, however, is based on the planting of annuals that die every year, leaving a barren land surface. In contrast, the bluestem plants lying dormant beneath the field of ash have been putting up shoots for more years than I have been alive. The harvested corn and bean plants will need to be replaced with new seed next year. Between now, in November, and late June of next year, the ground that produced those plants will remain partly exposed to wind and rain. Plant breeder Wes Jackson calls these contrasting practices perennial polyculture and annual monoculture. In the perennial polyculture of forest and prairie, the soil builds faster than it erodes. Annual monoculture, the backbone of agriculture here as elsewhere, allows high returns of grain in exchange for a high loss of soil, even with modern no-tillage or low-tillage farming.[25]

On most of the farmed slopes of the Upper Iowa drainage, strips of perennial grass stop soil runoff. Since the 1930s, when *soil conservation* became a common phrase in the conversational vocabulary of farmers, grass, often in the form of hay, has been used in contour strips that stay in place once the row crops between them are plowed. Grass is also seeded onto the field terraces that level out the slopes of cropped hillsides. Ravines or low spots where the water washes are also left in sod. A web of grassed waterways winds its way through even the most heavily cropped sections of the Upper Iowa, including the fields around Hayden Prairie. Grass is the main seeding required on land placed in the Conservation Reserve Program and in strips planted along streams to stop the soil from reaching them. Even though it subsidizes crop production, the government also subsidizes the seeding of grass for conservation. In this it is promoting the regrowing of soil, using one of the two main systems natural to the Upper Iowa for holding and building the earth.

≈ People are not going to return to a pre-agricultural past, but history has provided a guide for soil conservation along the ecotone. Putting down more permanent roots is nature's way of turning an environment of soil loss into one of soil building. For thousands of years people helped build soil in the Upper Iowa basin with practices that also helped keep them alive. It is important to see from more recent mistakes that the land is not a blank slate. It is written with its history. The soil's erasure on Trout Run, on Dean Thompson's river bottom, and in cropland all along the river is a message from the land about what cannot be sustained.

The Old Ones

500 B.C.E—1633 C.E.

The only remaining passenger pigeon on earth died, age twenty-nine, at the Cincinnati Zoo in 1914. Ellison Orr was the person who last recorded sighting a passenger pigeon in northeastern Iowa. He saw the bird on Williams Run around 1890 and added its solitary white egg to his specimen collection.[1] The passenger pigeon was not a yearlong resident of the Upper Iowa basin. It nested on the Upper Iowa after wintering in states along the southern reaches of the Mississippi River, returning north in February or early March.

As a migratory bird, the passenger pigeon shared a faculty more celebrated in one of its domestic cousins, the homing pigeon. The homing pigeon is bred for its ability to return to its home roost after its release from a distant point in any direction. If necessary, it does this with little prior knowledge of the landscape over which it flies. Races between birds sometimes cover a course thousands of miles long. The homing pigeon does by instinct what has taken people generations of careful study and invention; the bird takes its bearing from the time of day, the season, the earth's magnetic field, the angle of the sun relative to the earth's horizon, and what landmarks it can recognize. Putting those together tells the bird where it is and where it needs to go. In its native ability to perform this complex act of computation, the homing pigeon is a marvel of nature.

The passenger pigeon, *Ectopistes migratorius*, was a marvel in its sheer abundance. Orr recalled that as a boy in the 1860s, he observed a nesting colony of pigeons that covered forty square miles.[2] The dozens of nests in a single tree often broke down limbs. These nesting colonies of *Ectopistes migratorius* varied in location from year to year, depending on the previous year's crop of acorns and nuts. The pigeons were among the first migratory birds to reappear. A Winnebago Indian, whose tribe lived in the territory directly east of the Mississippi from the Upper Iowa, once told an anthropologist that often the weather did their hunting for them; they simply picked up plentiful numbers of pigeons that died from exposure.[3] The weather that presented the greatest threat was snow and ice, falling after the pigeons' return to the north and covering the ground from which they needed to harvest their food. The migration north increased as spring progressed. At its peak, one hundred million birds might fly overhead in an hour, in wave after wave that darkened the sky and made a steady noise that one eastern Iowa observer called a "shrill roar."[4] This same observer also claimed that among the small game in the region, nesting passenger pigeons were second in plenty only to gray squirrels throughout the warmest months of the year.[5] By June, Indians along the Upper Iowa could take the large and flightless squabs from nests or knock them from their platforms with sticks and hurled stones. Winnebago chieftains ordered pigeon hunts to fill the tables abundantly at "chief feasts."[6] Now, on the islands of the Mississippi, the Wisconsin, and the Upper Iowa, where the flight of passenger pigeons once made a "shrill roar," their sound has been silenced.

The early people of North America gave close heed to the migratory lives of birds. This attention is given mute witness by a site called Poverty Point, as far downstream from the Upper Iowa as you can go, near the mouth of the Mississippi on Bayou Macon in northeastern Louisiana. There, 3,200 years ago, several thousand residents built a town on an octagonal plan of concentric embankments, with a large open square at the center. This community depended on trade going up and down the entire length of the Mississippi and the Missouri. A bird-shaped mound over seventy feet high was completed on the western edge of Poverty Point in the direction of the setting sun. An unfinished mound of similar shape lies to the north. Because the bayou heavily eroded the area east and south of the town, it is impossible to know whether similar bird mounds existed in those quadrants, but it is possible that they did.[7] An orientation toward the directions that mark the coming and the going of the sun, the sources of warm winds that dominate the summer and the cold winds that dominate the winter, is ancient. Its earliest remaining North American markers, positioned near the mouth of the river into which the Upper Iowa flows, are in the shape of birds. The Mississippi River is one of the main seasonal flyways for birds and was a flyway for the passenger pigeon. Noticing over generations the trustable accuracy of movement among birds like *Ectopistes migratorius*, native peoples used them as a guide for their own movements.

The world, Heraclitus observed, is a shifting place, "known by what is in motion." The movements of birds were a window into the hidden meaning of the natural world for a people who also lived on the move. Like the passenger pigeons, Native people along the Upper Iowa lived a semi-migratory life for thousands of years, right up to the time of European settlement in 1849. They clustered at sites of plenty. They dispersed in seasons of relative scarcity. Like the people of Poverty Point, people on the Upper Iowa followed and attended to the yearly movement of animals. Though these people moved around, they also claimed home ground on a patch of river bottom near mounds or hillsides that held the bodies of their dead. On archeological survey maps of the Upper Iowa, these sites cluster like flocks of birds along the mouth of the river and the mouths of the smaller tributary streams that enter into it. The river's people moved out in pursuit of game and returned to the rich bounty at the stream's mouth. This cycle went on with only minor variations for over two thousand years, although today those people, "the old ones," like the pigeons, are gone.

≋ "The old ones" is a phrase Pete Fee uses for people of the past. "They're still with us," he maintains, "but in a different form. They're watching, and the women trill when you do something good." Fee points down at the round wooden surface of the table where we drink our cups of morning coffee. "You know. I'm sure, around this circle, if we could hear them right now, they'd be . . . ," and in a quiet, ghostly voice he gives a trill. "Those are the old ones." Fee has moved around a lot in his life, but today lives in a brown house that tucks into the bottom of the last bluff north of the Upper Iowa before its waters mix into the muddy flow of the Mississippi. Fee's house was the family home of his wife Alana, and across the road live his children and grandchildren. I sit at his kitchen table on a sodden October day because I've come to see if Pete and Alana Fee can help me in a task as difficult as hearing the celebration trill of the dead: the task of understanding the old world of the river.[8]

The people who were living on the Upper Iowa when prehistory became history were some of Pete Fee's ancestors. Until their story becomes part of the written record of European eyewitnesses, those old ones are called, by scholars, Oneota. When priests and traders showed up in the late 1600s, they gave these residents the name the Winnebago used for them: Ioway, the sleepy ones. The Ioway, however, call themselves *Baxoje*, the people whose noses are covered with ash.

Fee is an enrolled member of the Ioway tribe. The majority of his family still live on and around the reservation of the Northern Ioway in White Cloud, Kansas. He respects the old ones who lived here long before him and the stories his ancestors passed along. On the other hand, his children and grandchildren attend New Albin schools. He is a veteran of two tours of military duty, belongs to an electricians' union, and reads *Mother Earth News*. He respects the world he has experienced with his senses as well as the information learned from anthropologists, some of whom he calls friends.

≋ The person who contributed most to understanding prehistory along the Upper Iowa had no formal training in anthropology or archeology. Ellison Orr, who collected the last passenger pigeon egg in northeastern Iowa, kicked up arrowheads as a boy on a farm along the Yellow River. His passion for true archeology was awakened in a campaign trip by buggy down the lower valley of the Upper Iowa in the fall of 1878. Only twenty-one, Orr had been convinced to run for county superintendent of schools on the Republican ticket. Roads were bare earth tracks. As he reached the river bottom where Bear Creek enters the Upper Iowa, Orr noticed pot fragments, grinding stones, and mortars in the dirt of the roadbed and its shoulder. Stopping to pick these up and gaining new additions as he canvassed from house to house, Orr had filled the back of his buggy by the time he reached New Albin. This abundance suggested to Orr the richness of the valley's prehistoric past. Fifteen years later, when an older man named Wilbur Dresser offered to dig artifacts for five dollars and a share of the finds, Orr agreed. Dresser dug in several of the hundreds of mounds in the valley that Orr had traveled. Dresser returned, Orr reported, with "a nice lot of pottery, pipes, knives, arrow-heads and bone and copper beads."[9]

The pots and pot fragments Dresser dug up along the Upper Iowa River mark the separation of Woodland culture from its Archaic cultural past. With pottery, Woodland people could contain, carry, and heat water and mix and contain food far more easily than their ancestors. Woodland sites, like the Oneota sites that succeeded them, are scattered with pottery remains. Tempered by fire, a pot came from earth but did not become mud when it came in contact with water. Fired earthenware offered a new power. The fusion of fire, water, and earth in one circular vessel may have also fixed "the old ones" of the Woodland period more in place because, though they provided better storage, pots broke more easily in transit than skin bags or woven baskets.

Ellison Orr ran the Waukon office of the phone company from its earliest days, a job that included putting in the lines that eventually crisscrossed the countryside of Winneshiek and Allamakee counties. In his spare hours he dug, making notes and cataloging his finds. Orr distinguished himself from other amateur diggers in the Upper Iowa Valley by his meticulous method and by putting together a picture of the cultures whose artifacts he uncovered. Many of the landowners on whose property burial sites were situated had little sympathy with his passion. One farmer told him that when a pot, eighteen inches across, turned up in the soil of his barnyard, he smashed it because it was "haythen." Orr was careful with his finds. When he retired in 1930 from the phone company, he prepared his extensive collection to donate to the State Historical Society. At a 1933 academic conference, the culture of Oneota that had made its home in the Upper Iowa was given the name "Orr Focus."

The bulk of the materials in Orr's collection were Oneota, deposited between 1000 and 1670 C.E., but a number of finds didn't fit. Some smaller pots were tempered with sand rather than the pieces of shell that characterize an Oneota pot; many stone points had shapes far different than the triangle favored by Oneota craftsmen. Orr believed that another culture had also made its home along the river. He guessed that this culture was earlier, that it was Woodland, and that it was responsible for the creation of some of the mounds, but he had not produced hard evidence. When the Iowa State Planning Board began using Works Progress Administration (WPA) money to further cultural projects in the state, Orr served as field supervisor of an extensive archeological study of the river valley to answer the question about this second culture. In the summer of 1934, at the age of seventy-seven, Orr began the full-time project that consumed the remaining fourteen years of his life.

There was urgency to the project's timing. When the antiquities of northeastern Iowa had been studied as part of two national surveys in the late nineteenth century, complete maps were created to mark the locations of Indian mounds, village sites, bank enclosures, rock shelters, and painted and carved rock. By the time Orr wrote up the reports of his own surveys, he recorded that 972 mounds along the Mississippi in Allamakee County had been totally obliterated by farming, construction, or erosion. Along the Upper Iowa, close to a hundred mounds had been totally erased. Of the eight recorded sites of banked enclosures, only three remained.[10]

In the summer of 1934 the county relief officer assigned men to do the digging. One was in his seventies. Another had bad lungs from a gas attack during World War I. Due to a childhood illness, another required braces to keep his back straight.[11] But all, Orr was relieved to find, were good with a shovel. On June 11 the group began its first excavation at the New Galena mound cluster on an oxbow in the Upper Iowa. Near the lead-mining region of the 1850s, called New Galena, the mounds were on a high flat terrace that looked east toward the most important juncture of streams in the lower Upper Iowa: where Bear Creek enters the river shortly after joining Waterloo Creek. Orr had entered the river valley near this spot in his electioneering buggy ride fifty-six years earlier. Twenty-five years earlier Orr had surveyed the site and found thirty-two mounds, some five feet in height. When Orr and his crew arrived to dig, they found only fifteen mounds, the highest rising two feet. The plowed site was growing young corn with bits of human bone evident among the rows. Selecting the center of what had been a large mound, the workers delineated a square. In the first day they uncovered bits of Oneota pottery, bone fragments, and an Oneota spear point.

The second day, however, Orr and his supervisor, Charles Keyes, found a burial that confirmed the theory they had set out to test. Having cleared away the black soil to the gravel of the terrace, they discovered a pile of gravel next to a similar-sized pit of black earth. After two and a half feet of slow digging, they uncovered in the pit of black earth the upper ridges of bone in five bundled skeletons. One skeleton was accompanied by copper button earrings. In the center of the group burial was a small, grit-tempered Woodland Indian bowl, exquisitely decorated with a design of incised lines and points. Woodland people had constructed the mound by first clearing away the earth to the gravel substratum. That done, they dug a pit in the gravel and heaped the displaced gravel next to the pit for the burial of the bone bundles. A mound of earth was raised over the entire excavation. The Oneota materials had been deposited higher and later in a mound of Woodland origins. The chief mound builders of the Upper Iowa Valley were the Woodland people, whose culture emerged fifteen hundred years before the Oneota. Though the WPA archeological project continued to map out the contents of sites for five summers, the accuracy of Orr's guess was clear at the end of that second day.[12]

The uneasiness early people along the river felt about the powerful forces of water and soil may be signaled by the construction of the mound Orr and his WPA diggers excavated. Woodland mound builders chose ground that was safe from angry floods, and they cleared away the fertile and acidic topsoil, placing the bones in the buried subsoil. Bones were buried in a bundle after the body had been left to weather in a tree scaffold. Other mounds contained bones cremated by fire. The transforming powers of air and fire intervened with the substance of the flesh before the body and its spirit could be properly interred within the earth. Intrusive burials in some mounds suggest that in subsequent years, the Woodland people who made them or the people of later groups returned to enact ceremonies and place new bone bundles in the ground. Elaborate construction techniques suggest that the dead were respected, feared, or loved and that their proper passage from the world of the living into that of the dead required proper ritual. With hoes fashioned from the shoulder blades of elk or deer, Woodland people excavated a pit up to one hundred feet across. They shoveled sand and dirt with animal bone spades or clam shells into skins or baskets, carrying load after load to create a mound four or five feet deep.

≈ Pete Fee has long known about his tribe's ancient connection with the Iowa soil. As a child he knew the federal government had underpaid the money promised to the tribe for Iowa territory. He says, "All the time I was growing up, at tribal meetings I'd hear about these lawsuits and how they were going." The lawsuits were settled when he turned eighteen. Though he knew of that legacy, he grew up unmindful of much of the tribe's history and tradition. "You see, my grandpa's family, they didn't want to be Indians. In their days, Indians were getting shot, and hung, and killed. They were looked down upon." Fee's parents and their generation "wanted to get off the reservation and to get away." His best connection with the old ways was his grandmother. "She told me old stories and, you know, she made me proud to be Indian," he says, "whereas my grandpa wouldn't have done that."

Beyond his grandmother was a great-grandfather whom people on the reservation called "The Squire." Fee's grandmother's father was "as traditional as they come. He was a drinker and mean. He was tough. And in those days people would come from a long ways to whip you if you were tough." In the 1880s a division arose between the Ioway who wanted to maintain the traditional way of communally owning land and those who wanted to assimilate by adopting private land ownership. The traditionalists moved to Oklahoma. During that move, Pete's great-grandfather, The Squire, went along to help with the horses. "Well," Fee says, "he told me that when they were on the way down there a big storm came up, and he said the holy men had everybody lie face down on the prairie and the holy men sat up and prayed. And what they prayed was, that if they were to continue, then let the storm stop. If they were doing the wrong thing, they'd turn around before it was too late. And the storm stopped. So they got back on their horses and went on their way."

≋ The clans of the Ioway tribe today are the Bear, the Buffalo, and the Eagle/Thunder. The clan unique to those Ioway who went south to Oklahoma is the Eagle/Thunder. Possibly those holy men who prayed to let the storm stop on the trip to Oklahoma were speaking to their Thunder ancestors. In the oral legends of the Ioway, the origin story of the Eagle/Thunder clan is also the origin story of the now defunct Pigeon clan. This story gives some sense of how people who lived on the Upper Iowa thought about the totem spirit that resided in the dark flocks of passenger pigeons. The story, related by an Ioway to J. Owen Dorsey in the 1880s, says the "Eagle and Pigeon people came to earth in the form of birds," warriors who came "to hunt men." The story continues: "They met the Bear and the Wolf people. After leaving them, they journeyed until they reached a certain place, where they made a village. They surrounded this with palisades, calling the settlement *Maⁿcú Joe*, Hill or Bank of Red Earth."[13] Bear, Wolf, Eagle/Thunder, Pigeon, Elk, Owl, Beaver, Snake, and Buffalo are the nine traditional Ioway clans. In the old story, the people of the air, Pigeon and Eagle/Thunder, meet the people of the earth, Bear and Wolf. Together, their village makes a whole people. Some of the traditionalists who moved to Oklahoma have kept alive the bird half of that whole through their Eagle/Thunder clan. Spiritual relation with the animals and elements is the modern Ioway's most crucial piece of heritage from the world of the old ones.

≋ In the last phase of Woodland culture, beginning fourteen hundred years ago and lasting until nine hundred years ago, a bird mound and bear mounds, honoring sky and earth, were constructed along the Upper Iowa. The single bird-shaped mound is cradled in a semicircular bend of the river. Ellison Orr measured the effigy: three feet high at its center and close to eighty feet across from wing tip to wing tip. It was, he wrote, "well proportioned, representing a flying nighthawk."[14] Downstream from the bird mound, a bear effigy was constructed at a site called Voll farm. In the Sand Cove, behind the last set of bluffs along the Mississippi just south of New Albin, three bear mounds were created. In the Black Hawk Shelter, in the outcrop just above these mounds, Indian remains and a large number of bear bones were found.[15]

≋ Fee's clan affiliation is Bear. The ceremonial names of the people in his family connect back to the origin story of the Bear clan. "When that person being named makes his spirit journey, no matter how old he is, you want the people on the other side to say, 'There he comes, the one with that name. That's so-and-so's relative. Come on over, and we'll help you get through this spirit journey!' That's what it's for. So people will recognize you on the other side, in the spiritual world," Fee says. One of his granddaughters was given the name Comes With Them. This name "means that down through time she comes with them, comes with those bears."

≋ The bird and bear mounds were important fixed points in a world of regular change. During the harsh winters, these Late Woodland people dispersed to camps along the upper reaches of the streams emptying into the Mississippi, where the competition for game was less intense.[16] People returned to the river's estuary even as the passenger pigeons returned. Late Woodland groups used effigy mounds as territorial markers, but also as sites for ceremonies such as funerals, marriages, alliances, and hunting agreements that may have been accompanied by feasts and other rituals.[17] Tribes came together at the mounds their ancestors had placed, located where streams came together.

The lifestyle of Late Woodland people was intimately suited to the Upper Iowa River region of broadleaf forests, floodplains, and prairies. It is likely that the men hunted and produced the implements of hunting, including, for the first time, bows and arrows. Men also engaged in religious activity. The women most likely cared for the very young, harvested foods, prepared food, processed skins and fibers, made pottery, and perhaps built shelters and practiced their own religious rites. Late Woodland people also practiced limited cultivation.

As hunters and gatherers, Middle and Late Woodland peoples needed to know when the paddlefish and drum moved into the Upper Iowa to spawn, when the leaves of the wild potato appeared on the forest floor, when cattail shoots were big enough to eat, and when elk holed up among cedars. Seasonal opportunities determined when a family stayed and when it moved, where the next camp would be, when the nighttime hunting would take place along the marshy bottoms, or when hunting would take place on the upland prairies during the warm morning. The Ioway have a word, *Madadanyida,* for the time when people and animals spoke together.[18] Animal signs spoke as meaningfully to people as their own human words. Since Late Woodland people did small-scale gardening and had limited ability to store food, they stayed as near as possible to fresh and adequate food sources, including animal sources, and were expert readers of the signs through which the plant and animal world spoke.

The effigy mound builders of Iowa lived on the outer edge of a culture that extended east into more forested terrain. The economy of the forest not only defined the Woodland people's place on the landscape; it defined their sense of time, social organization, and cosmology. Landscape lacked fences, and yet had boundaries established by custom, discussion, or war. The end of the Woodland and the beginning of the Oneota period show signs of an unusual scale of violence along the river. Some communal memory of this turmoil is lodged in the Pigeon clan origin story where Pigeon, Eagle/Thunder, Wolf, and Bear live together in a village surrounded by palisades for protection. In the period between thirteen hundred and eight hundred years ago, warming climate may have encouraged the expansion of horticulture in the Upper Mississippi Valley, along with an influx of southern, more agricultural peoples.

Hartley Fort, a roughly square depression 150 feet across, surrounded by an embankment of earth, sits on a high bench of land above the spot where French Creek empties into the Upper Iowa. In 1964 an archeological dig uncovered evidence that the embankment had been heaped against a stockade of logs, six inches thick, set at eighteen-inch centers, with an entry on the side opposite the river.[19] The enclosure seems to have been a fortified village constructed around one thousand years ago by Late Woodland peoples to maintain a territory contested by outsiders, or perhaps threatened by factions from within. Hartley Fort marks a cultural midway, where the Woodland culture was becoming Oneota.

Ellison Orr's excavations showed that Woodland sites like Hartley Fort later became homes of the Oneota, ancestors of the Ioway. On the same bench of land as the Hartley Fort is another site, Grant Village, one acre in size. Here, Orr and his crew did their third set of excavations in the summer of 1934. Since the site included evidence of Woodland mounds, a nineteenth-century archeologist, Colonel Norris, guessed that an early residential site must have been later set aside for burials. Orr's dig proved the opposite: later Oneota people occupied a place earlier used for Woodland mounds.

≈ Pete Fee has a story about the demands that the dead place upon the living.

Winter time is coming up. That's the time we tell stories. I keep thinking about that, that we ought to do that more. You know, tell those stories: how we got here, clan stories. I can give you an example. My great aunt Pearl and a friend, an old lady named Irene Foster, would go into town for a bender. Now those people believed that when you went to the other side you would need things, and it was the job of people here on this side to make offerings to give you what you needed. Well, Pearl and her friend were walking down the street. It was Nemaha, which isn't a town more than a few blocks long, but it was dark. And it seems they would walk along and they'd hear footsteps coming along behind them. And so they'd stop, but when they'd stop, the footsteps would stop. Then they'd start walking again, and they'd hear those footsteps, and stop and they'd hear nothing. So finally they stopped, and my aunt Pearl said to her friend, "Give me that jug!" And she took it and she unscrewed the cap and she poured a little whiskey right there in the dirt and then put the cap back on. When they started walking again they listened, but those footsteps just stopped. And Pearl said, "You see, it was just somebody from the other side. They needed a little drink too."

Of this and the other old stories he's heard throughout his life, Fee says, "To me it's all about relationships. If you keep those old stories coming down, then you understand how we are related, not only to each other but to God, to the earth, to all that we know about. You know we *have* to be related. That's what's missing today, everywhere. We've forgotten how we're connected."

≋ Though Oneota lived up and down the Upper Mississippi and the Lower Missouri rivers, those who made their life along the Upper Iowa classically express the culture. The Oneota tended to bury their dead in mounds that already existed, in cemeteries, and occasionally in new mounds. Over twenty feet across and up to ninety feet long, the Oneota houses at Grant Village along the Upper Iowa used a scaffolding of saplings covered by lighter material such as bark or woven mats. The walls were thin. Inside the houses, platforms were constructed, probably for sleeping, sitting, and storage. Pits were dug in the floor or just outside the walls for the storage of food. One of the storage pits excavated at the Lane Enclosure was lined with big bluestem grass from a nearby prairie, and still contained the charred remains of beans.[20] Once the harvest season was over, the village probably dispersed to other sites along the river valley where families occupied smaller, easier-to-heat houses.[21]

The people at Grant Village cleared the rich bottomlands of the Upper Iowa by girdling trees that grew in their field areas and cultivated small plots of land with sticks and shoulder blade hoes. They practiced mono-culture, introducing a single species and cultivating away its competition. They raised corn, beans, squash, and pumpkins. Remains of catfish, drum, buffalo fish, turtles, beaver, elk, deer, and bison were found in the Grant Village excavation.[22] If the Oneota came from the east, it is possible that their new proximity to the prairies tempted them to develop a special dependence on bison and elk hunting. The culture found its classic expression along the Upper Iowa, and for this reason was named Oneota. But Oneota pots, weapons, and house remains are found in similar environments of wooded river and lakeside bottomlands bordering on prairies along the Big Sioux, the Des Moines, the Iowa, the Missouri, and up and down the Mississippi River.

The lives Oneota knew are inferred from archeology and anthropology. It is possible that the long houses at Grant Village each housed fifty to sixty-five people in a settlement of 200 to 250 people.[23] These bark structures might have each housed a clan, or two associated clans. The Ioway of later times would, during their buffalo hunts, divide the tepee circle of their hunting camps into two sections, the spring and summer clans, like the Buffalo, in one half, and the fall and winter clans, like the Bear, in the other.[24] One of the sandstone petroglyph crevices along Bear Creek, likely created by the Late Oneota people, is dominated by carvings of vulvas; another is covered with images of male thunderbird impersonators. The separation suggests a different sacred site for each gender. One of the most remarkable images of a hawk man that was made during the Oneota period is a five-sided tablet of Catlinite. Orr described the figure as "the thunder god or spirit . . . the body and limbs of a man with the head of a bird, facing the left."[25] From the hawklike head, a zigzag of lightning flares down across the belly.

≋ The lives of birds speak to the way that the sharp seasons on the Upper Iowa promote a life of migration. Bird movement is not bothered by fences, roads, or dams. Though bird numbers continue to decline, their migratory habits are less affected by settlement than those of other animals. Their life on the move persists much as it has for hundreds or thousands of years. Nighthawks, whose form served as model for the effigy mound on a bend in the Upper Iowa, leave their nests on the gravel roofs on the business buildings in central Decorah to fly, each evening, mouths open, scooping moths and fish flies from the air above the city street lights.

They flock on August evenings, while the weather is hot and the bugs are at their thickest.

In flying groups ranging from ten to ten thousand, nighthawks of the Upper Midwest follow the plentiful supply of insects until they are as far south, for the southern summer, as they were north for the northern summer. Having fledged their nests on the Upper Iowa, they might spend the other half of their year on the Paraná River or the Paraguay. The bobolinks that still nest in the dwindling remnant grasslands along the Upper Iowa River spend a southern summer in the pampas. Cliff swallows swoop over the Upper Iowa River all summer from nests daubed onto the girders of bridges, but they winter in Argentina and Brazil. The most colorful or melodious summer birds in the parks that fringe Decorah—Baltimore orioles, rose-breasted grosbeaks, and scarlet tanagers—flit each winter through the foliage of forests of Amazonian countries like Ecuador in the company of trogons, sylphs, cock-of-the-rocks, parakeets, quetzals, and fruiteaters. The most common migratory warm-season birds on the river—robins, red-winged blackbirds, and killdeer—edge their way south along the Mississippi corridor with the cooling of the season as the passenger pigeon once did. Then they follow the thaw north in the spring. These birds are hunters, dependent on catching insects or worms that disappear completely for part of the year on the Upper Iowa. Their piece of the river basin habitat and the menu it provides indicate the place they must seek elsewhere before the season cools.

≈ The names given to the months is an example of the way traditional hunting peoples were attuned to the habits of their place. For example, the Winnebago and the Ioway share a common origin, but the tribes divided. The Ioway moved west of the Mississippi to the forested river corridors bordering the prairie. The Winnebago settled in the more extensive eastern forests around Lake Michigan. The Winnebago called the fourth moon of their year "fish become visible," a name the Ioway did not use. The Ioway, who believed their ancestors came west to pursue bison, called their eighth month "bison rutting moon." The Winnebago, who placed less emphasis on this animal, did not use this name.

An image that helps me understand the *Madadanyida* world of the Upper Iowa is the picture of a bison, carved in the sandstone of a petroglyph crevice along Bear Creek. The bison is drawn in naturalistic style, but superimposed on its body are two symbols. On its flank is a sign that indicates killing, while emanating from its head is a sign that may indicate speech.[26] Before traditional hunters took an animal, they had a ceremonial conversation with its spirit. Their hunt would only be successful if the spirit of the animal they hunted gave them the authority to take its life. Understanding the Oneota habit of the place is to envision it as a matter of kinship and common language that connected people to the animal, plant, and mineral world.

≋ Pete Fee has a story about how the place spoke to him, reminding him of a clan obligation he had ignored.

> I'm Bear clan. So all the people I can give names to are Bear clan, my descendents. A younger relative of mine in Kansas wanted a name and talked to me about it, maybe two years ago. And I said, "sure." But then I forgot about it. The next year he brought me some tobacco and asked again for that name, so then I started thinking about it. I was working in Dubuque and about every week when I went to Dubuque I'd go past Effigy Mounds and cross the Yellow River. It seemed like every time I crossed the Yellow River I'd think about him. And I couldn't think of why. As the time went on I got to thinking about that yellow clay that's in that river. That's an old Bear clan name, Yellow Earth—*Máyan Dhí*. I put the connection together in my mind that *Máyan Dhí* should be his name. I told him that, and he liked that.

Fee explains the name's connection to the clan's origin story: "When they first came up out of the earth, those bears, they came into different stages of the earth's crust, the yellow earth and then red earth. Those names, they take you back to the beginning. Naming ceremonies are important. Even after I'm gone, the younger people in my family will know their names and where they came from. That's a start to keeping that old world alive if you can."

≋ Orientation is a basic requirement for a scientific archeologist. Ellison Orr's manuscripts make it clear how natural it was for him to orient his work and his knowledge to local landmarks like the river, a notable bluff, or a substantial oak and to describe the location of objects on a clear directional grid. As a surveyor for the telephone company, he would have at least once tramped close to nine hundred miles through ridges, valleys, and prairies, establishing exact map locations for phone lines in the county. It was also part of Orr's passion to put together in his mind a living sense of the ancient people along the Upper Iowa.

≈≈ The annual Ioway powwow takes place in a clearing above the river at White Cloud, Kansas. At the powwow in 2003, Pete Fee finally carried out the clan obligation of bestowing an Ioway name on the nephew that he had neglected. Pete says his nephew

> was at Winfield, Kansas, at a big bluegrass festival. But the next morning he showed up and wanted his name. I asked if he had someone to cook for him. He said, yes, his mom and his aunt could cook for him. So they were all ready to go. They cooked and fed everybody, because any time when you invite people, you feed them. Then the family gathered around and we did the ceremony. You make your prayer; it's to the spiritual world. And you call on God, *Wakanda*, and you ask for a blessing, and the relatives that are gathered around, you ask their blessing, and you give that name. We gave my nephew his name, *Máyan Dhí*.

Another Ioway took his formal place in the Bear clan.

Living in New Albin for the past five years, Pete and Alana Fee are only seasonal visitors to the reservation at White Cloud, where most of Pete's relatives live. The Fees live in a house where Alana's father laid up local stone for the fireplace chimney. "It's *his* turn," Alana says, thinking about the two decades they spent on Pete's reservation, away from her family. Pete affirms this: "We lived at White Cloud for twenty years. Now we're surrounded by Alana's relatives." He pauses for a minute and adds, "That's the most important thing: relatives." Fee's work as an electrician took him to jobs in different states and other countries, but family gives his life bearings: the family living and the family passed on.

Conversing about relatives in the quiet of his kitchen, Fee tells about the morning his granddaughter got the name Comes With Them. "It was just a small ceremony, and we had it at our house. And when we pronounced that name, people were looking up. We were praying. And we saw, coming from the river, two eagles. They came and they made one circle, and they went back to the river. Everyone went, 'Ahh!' " Fee still thinks about that morning on the reservation at White Cloud while he is in Iowa, hundreds of miles away. "That's what is supposed to happen," he explains, thinking about the old ones. "They sent a messenger for that name!"

≈≈ For centuries people recognized kinship with the elements. These people also defined themselves by their relation to animals. The richest sites of ancient habitation cluster where the waters and valleys are greatest, and the effigy mounds there represent creatures of two different elements: earth and sky. The Oneota are gone, and their descendants have mostly moved away, but the Bear, Buffalo, and Eagle/Thunder clans of the Ioway remain active. The animals with whom the old ones traced a kinship also remain only in part. Eagles and owls still nest along the river, but bears, wolves, elk, and bison were long ago displaced to the north and the west. With the passing of the human way of life that revered these animal relationships, the animals also disappeared. The sacred pipe of the Pigeon clan, decorated with the skins of seven ivory-billed woodpeckers, now rests unsmoked in climate-controlled storage at the Milwaukee Public Museum, and the river islands of the Upper Iowa will never again know the shadow of a migrating passenger pigeon.

Unknown World

1634–1832

The spring at the source of Coldwater Creek pours forth at the bottom of a one-hundred-foot limestone grotto, hung in summer with ferns and blue harebells. Mist rises from the stream at daybreak, the rush of water shutting out most other noise. Standing by Coldwater Spring on a July morning, it is easy to imagine yourself the first person to have stumbled into paradise.

A portion of the landscape at Coldwater Spring *did* remain unknown until 1967. That fall Steve Barnett put on a face mask and dove into the dark at the base of the rock. Water, rushing toward him at over eight thousand gallons per minute, spun him until he was disoriented. Thinking he was swimming to safety, he pushed further into the channel of the spring. When he came up he found air, but also total darkness: an underground room over five hundred cubic feet in volume. On a second visit to the spring, Barnett and his friend Dave Jagnow dove in with wet suits and scuba gear. They pushed forward into new rooms and passages. On the third trip they swam through almost a quarter mile of water-filled passages before emerging into a space in which they could stand up and walk. The stream's channel had led them to a corridor wider than their reach and taller than their heads: Coldwater Cave, a chilly place where no light had ever shone and no person had ever set foot.

≋ A cold shift in climate began after European discovery of the Americas. One hundred years before the French arrived on the Upper Mississippi, growing seasons shortened and annual temperatures lowered. Perhaps this cooling climate in the Little Ice Age helped begin the shift, along the Upper Iowa River, away from horticulture and back to an economy of hunting, a shift soon to be accelerated by the European demand for furs and the Indian desire for trade goods.[1] Europeans began unmindful of the very existence of America. In 1634, when Jean Nicolet stepped from his canoe onto the western shore of Lake Michigan wearing a brightly bro-caded Chinese robe, with a pistol in each hand, he hoped he had discov-ered the Northwest Passage to a port of China. The water route he had discovered led not to porcelain, silk, and tea, but instead to a Mississippi basin rich with the pelts that French businessmen would come to call "soft gold." The cold of the Little Ice Age had also increased the European mar-ket for beaver felt hats at a time when European beaver had been hunted to near extinction.

The first indication to the people living on the Upper Iowa that dis-ruptive forces on the ground were making their way west was the after-shock of events further east: a visit by eastern Indians looking for a new home. An Iroquois military offensive armed with English guns drove sev-eral tribes, including the Ottawa and Hurons, out of their traditional Great Lakes territories. According to Nicholas Perrot, in 1656 displaced Ottawa and Hurons surveyed the Upper Iowa,

> which is named for the Ayoës [Ioway]. They followed this stream to its source, and there encountered peoples who received them cordially. But as they did not find, in all that region which they traversed, any place suit-able for a settlement—since the country was entirely destitute of woods, and contained only prairies and level plains, although buffaloes and other animals were found there in abundance—they retraced the same route by which they had come; and, having again reached the shores of the Loüisianna [Mississippi] River, they continued to ascend it.[2]

These refugees, used as they were to the eastern woodlands, were not happy with the prairie expanses they discovered on the Upper Iowa.

The first European to meet the Indians who had greeted the Ottawa and Hurons on the Upper Iowa was a French priest. In 1676, when Louis André was proselytizing among the Winnebagoes along the Fox River near Lake Michigan, he reported that seven or eight families came east, speaking the same language as the Winnebago. Father André called them "*aiaoua* or *mascouteins nadoessi,*" prairie Sioux, and said they came from a distant vil-lage that was large "but poor, since their greatest wealth is in buffalo hides and red stone calumet pipes." Without any comment on his success, Father André concluded, "I preached Jesus Christ to them."[3]

The next French explorer to the Mississippi, Michel Accault, came to trade rather than save souls. Accault's boss, La Salle, envisioned a new world empire for France. La Salle enthusiastically painted for his monarch a picture of French wealth in the Mississippi basin drawn from fur, leather, wood, agricultural products, minerals, and fruit. Louis XIV, France's Sun King, had already elsewhere awarded the patent for trade in beaver skins, but in 1678 he gave La Salle the monopoly on the New France trade in bison skins, the commodity in which the Ioway were rich. To secure these, La Salle sent a group of traders west toward the Mississippi under Michel Accault in 1678 and 1679. Accault reported as early as the summer of 1678 that he had traded for a large quantity of hides from these people.[4] In 1680 La Salle sent a group of explorers, including Accault, up the Mississippi to probe its upper reaches.

In a 1681 letter, La Salle praised Accault's knowledge of the language of Upper Mississippi tribes "by whom," he said, "Accault was liked, because he had spent two winters and a summer there, during which time he had seen several of the largest of the villages."[5] In 1682 La Salle fretted in a letter that the Jesuits operating around Green Bay had shut him out of the beaver trade and that now another Frenchman, DuLuth, had designs on the Wisconsin River trade in bison skins "on which alone I rely, owing to the great number of buffaloes killed every year, which is greater than one can believe."[6] The Ioway's buffalo hides probably brought Accault to their Upper Iowa home and soon had other Europeans competing for their trade.

A French observer said of the Ioway who brought bison skins to the French in the late 1600s, "They are extremely courageous and good-hearted. They often kill cattle and deer while running after them. They are howlers."[7] Hunting the bison with stone tools and no horses required courage. A bull buffalo can weigh one and a half tons, with horns in a spread that can measure up to three feet across. It can sustain a speed of thirty-five miles per hour for a stretch of at least half a mile and also wheel nimbly, like the fighting bulls of Spain. The Ioway used the approach of quietly surrounding a herd and then charging into the press to fire off arrows at close range, a dangerous technique that worked better once they had horses. Even so, prior to the importation of the horse, Indians successfully arranged situations that diminished the bison's great advantages of size, power, and speed. In the winter, for example, they hunted in deep snow, when their snowshoes bettered their chances. They herded buffalo onto thin ice, where the animals broke through and drowned.

The wealth of the bison, beginning with its skin, pervaded Ioway life. The dried stomach, bladder, and intestines of buffalo could be used to store food. Its sinews went for thread or the string for bows and snowshoes. Its fat was a popular hair grease, as well as a medium for paint or as insulation for the skin. The hide was used in robes, shields, and boxes. An Ioway tepee covering required the skins of ten bison, providing snug winter shelter against the cold and serving as a portable house, taken on the hunt. Bison wool was spun, braided, and woven. The bones made tools, and the hooves cooked down into glue. The bile of bison gall made yellow paint. Dried manure was the most readily available fuel on the prairie and was used to smoke the meat that needed drying after the hunt.[8]

For the Ioway, the practical usefulness of the bison was matched by its importance to their cultural imagination. The Buffalo Doctors of the Ioway wore buffalo horns and head skin, with a strip of back skin all the way down to the tail. Wearing this in healing dances and ceremonies, they shook rattles made from the dewclaw of a buffalo and employed medicine that included the fat, meat, or manure of the animal, practicing a form of healing called "the buffalo's ways."[9] The powerful Buffalo chief ruled the village in the summer months and planted the first kernels of corn in the ritual that began spring planting. The Ioway had dances that imitated the buffalo's movements, songs that described its hunt, and myths and stories that celebrated its long association with tribal people. Pieces of its hide and wool were symbolically incorporated into the pipe stems of several clans. The buffalo bull faces danger and foul weather head-on and butts heads in the mating season with little sign of suffering. Such bravery was emulated by Ioway braves and demonstrated when, howling, they killed bison "while running after them."

≋ On a fourth trip into Coldwater Cave, Barnett, Jagnow, and a friend spent over two days mapping close to 3.5 miles of underground passageway. They began to chart what would eventually prove to be the largest cave in either of the states in which the Upper Iowa flows. The process of mapping is still going on, driven in part by the threat of pollution. The state of Iowa owns Coldwater Spring and the creek immediately below it because it is a good trout stream. Trout swim up to a mile inside the cave. Occasionally, however, the water turns lethal. In spring runoffs, the level of bacterial contamination in Coldwater Creek has jumped to a million colonies of bacteria per liter, roughly the strength of raw sewage. Cave explorers in Coldwater, on one occasion, hacked their way through a cylinder of pesticide foam twenty feet wide and twenty feet high, filling the passage for eighty feet. Contamination in Coldwater threatens trout, water quality in the river, and drinking aquifers in the river basin.

The person contracted to map the pollution stream in Coldwater was Pat Kambesis. As a spelunker, Kambesis had explored the inky reaches of

Coldwater Cave on and off for sixteen years. When her graduate school adviser gave her the choice of studying the hydrology of any cave in the world for her degree, she chose Coldwater. In the summer of 2002 she came from her home in Cave City, Kentucky, to trace the sources of the creek's contamination using chemical dyes to map the channels of water flow beyond which cave explorers could crawl. She thought she would be charting the underground reaches of one tributary of the Upper Iowa. To her surprise, in monitoring the flow of water through the familiar cave, she charted not one, but five Upper Iowa feeder streams.[10]

≋ Nicolas Perrot, the first French visitor to the Ioway on the Upper Iowa, came down the Wisconsin River in 1685. He established a fort on the Mississippi, probably near the present site of Trempealeau, Wisconsin. To pay respect to the newly arrived European, a delegation of Ioway arrived "weeping hot tears, which they let fall on their hands along with saliva, and with other filth from their noses, with which they rubbed the heads, faces, and garments of the French." For the French, "All these caresses made their stomachs revolt."[11] The next Ioway to visit Perrot brought along a man who could speak Algonquin and who explained that the Ioway were returning east from their prairie bison hunting to set up their village near Perrot's fort. A few days later Perrot visited them. Claude La Potherie said in summary of this visit, "Never in the world were seen greater weepers than those peoples; their approach is accompanied with tears, and their adieu is the same."[12] After their visits with Perrot, the Ioway were fired to spend their winter hunting beaver. "For this purpose," according to La Potherie, "they penetrated far inland."[13] The tribe of bison hunters who farmed along the Upper Iowa had entered the European trade in beaver.

When La Potherie said that the Ioway ranged "far inland" in their pursuit of beaver pelts, he reflected the orientation of European traders who entered present-day Iowa by a pathway of water that extended from the northeast, when "inland" Iowa was an uncharted fringe of New France. These encounters, during the reign of Louis XIV, gave the river the name by which it is still known, the "river of the Ioway." The larger expanse of prairies and scattered woodlands over which the Ioway traditionally ranged was eventually called Iowa, too, as was a major river to the south.

Perrot's meeting with the Ioway, on the bank of what very likely was the Upper Iowa, took place in the winter of 1685–1686. The Ioway now had beaver pelts and were ready to trade. When the Frenchman arrived, the Ioway asked if they could "sing for him" over a tobacco pipe. The ceremony lasted "a great part of the night" and involved three men holding Perrot, as he sat on a bison skin, while a fourth sang to him, holding a smoking pipe. The whole group sang and took individual turns standing before him singing, before giving him the pipe.[14] With this significant gift, the Ioway were also formally initiating their side of the exchange that, for the next 150 years, would pull the French inland along river routes where their lives would mimic and mix with the Indians on whom they now depended.

The most sought-after pelt in the fur trade was beaver. In Perrot's time the Ioway had a Beaver clan, the members of which were known as "water people." Beaver was their spiritual ancestor, sought in visions by the keeper of the medicine bundle of the clan. On shore a beaver leaves a print that, like a human's, has five toes. Of all the animals hunted by the Indians, the beaver is most like people in its social life and habits. Beavers reshape their environment to make it suitable to their needs. Beavers in still water construct mounded lodges of sticks and mud, into which they dig their den. In undammed water, beavers create bank lodges. Beavers are monogamous, pairing for life. Left undisturbed, with an adequate supply of food and an unsilted pond, they maintain the same family lodges and dams for generations. In the pool behind their dams they sink a winter supply of bark-covered poplar, willow, young cottonwood, and other gleanings, such as corn ears, to a depth where it will not freeze. These ponds allow the entrances to their lodge to open into clear water year-round.[15]

When the Ioway residents of the Upper Iowa winter hunted beaver, they broke holes in the ice and placed nets or sentries over the underwater entrances to the lodge. Then, using heavy stone hammers, they broke into the lodge, scaring the beavers into the water. Some were caught in nets. Others were impaled by a waiting hunter as they swam into the clear water of the pond. Beavers in a bank lodge were sniffed and sounded out by dogs. The earth above the lodge would be broken in, the animals inside speared or clubbed. A French priest reported in 1683 that on winter hunts, "Indians sometimes work with undiminished energy from morning until night without taking a single beaver, and they often take only three or four."[16] In times of open water, beaver could be hunted at night by bow and arrow as they went up on the bank to gather food, or they could be killed by a deadfall, where a heavy log was propped up by a stick that would be pulled away by the feeding animal.[17]

Once killed, the beaver were skinned. Musk glands containing castoreum, the oil that maintained the dryness of beaver fur under water, were near the anus of the animal. Indians and Europeans prized castoreum for medicinal qualities as either a stimulant or antispasmodic, and Europeans used it as a necessary lure on their beaver traps, as well as a fixative in perfumes.[18] Pelts made their way to a trading station on the Mississippi, up the Wisconsin River, across Lake Winnebago, downriver to Lake Michigan, up to Michilimackinac, across Lakes Huron, Erie, and Ontario, down the St. Lawrence to Montreal, Quebec, and the Gulf of St. Lawrence, across the Atlantic to the English Channel, and up the Seine, all by power of muscle and force of wind. The Parisian hatter bought the raw pelt at public auction, pulled off outer guard hair, and brushed the readied pelt with a mercury nitrate solution to help the fur begin to felt. The half- to three-quarters pound of underfur shaved from the pelt was carded, spread into a batt, pressed into a cone shape, compacted and waterproofed in a hot bath, blocked into shape, dyed, stiffened, finished, and lined.[19] No competing material provided the same luster, feel, and warmth as beaver felt. The hand-processed fur of an Upper Iowa beaver now allowed the Parisian man of means to step forth in the Faubourg Saint-Germain, his head covered in perfect practicality and style. Before stepping out thus attired, he splashed on some scent, its fragrance fixed by a tincture of the castoreum of beaver.

Around 1700, horses from the Spanish Southwest became available to tribes of the Upper Mississippi. The speed, mobility, and power of these animals opened the prairies to the Ioway as nothing had before. The tribe moved west, and the Upper Iowa became nobody's river and everybody's river. Indian populations plummeted as diseases to which Europeans were immune emptied out villages. The river basin remained part of New France, renamed Louisianna by La Salle. The French trader and explorer Le Sueur produced a map, reprinted by Guillaume De L'isle in 1703, that demonstrates why, without a resident tribe or navigable waters, the Upper Iowa was disregarded. Le Sueur's map and many that followed it showed an overland trade road from the west bank of the Mississippi River across from the mouth of the Wisconsin River to Ioway villages on Lake Okoboji and the mouth of the Big Sioux. This path, the Chemin des Voyageurs, beginning south of the Upper Iowa, was the shortest route for trade coming from the Great Lakes to the tribes along the Missouri River.[20] The fur trade relied on that road, rather than on the shallow, cascading waters of the Upper Iowa.

Deciding I need to see, firsthand, the Coldwater mapping project, I meet Pat Kambesis in April 2004. She has offered to drive me around the countryside that feeds water into Coldwater Cave. Kambesis is a pale, dark-haired woman with a cave bat on her bumper sticker. As we drive into the country, she tells me about cultivating the goodwill of landowners. A cave in Iowa belongs to the owner of the property above it. Coldwater Cave begins in domes that fan out beneath a landscape of plowed fields, meadows, and wooded draws. As we drive the country gravel, tractors inch like beads of condensation on glass across the land. Farmers are working the newly opened soil. In the karst topography through which the cave winds, surface water disappears through cracks in the bedrock into sinkholes or through swallet holes in streams. Kambesis tells me that landowners let her walk their property and, eventually, pour containers of bright red and green liquid into their creeks. In the first of her dye traces, Kambesis put dye into a swallet hole in Elliot Creek, a stream that flows into Coldwater Creek. The dye never showed up at the mouth of Coldwater. "I had to go back onto the river and look for another spring," she says, "and sure enough, there it was. We called it Serendipity." Eventually, she found water that went into the cave reappearing in three additional springs.

To further complicate the mapping of the underground course of water that runs through Coldwater Cave, Kambesis ran one of her dye tests during high water after a rain. She put the dye in a source that normally fed nearby Pine Creek. In the congested flood of underground water the dye did not appear in Pine Creek. It re-emerged at Coldwater Spring. Cave explorers had already discovered that the Cascade Creek passage of Coldwater Cave led to a divide where the water running through the cave came out in Pine Creek. The divide occurs at a place with a name inspired by its smell: Pig Trough. In high water, Pine Creek Cave passage overflows through Pig Trough into the Coldwater Creek passages. Such high water events produce the highest bacteria readings in Coldwater Creek. Kambesis's unlooked-for conclusion was that if people want to stop the worst of the pollution that emerges from the cave into Coldwater Spring, they have to do their main cleanup in the farmyards and septic systems of the Pine Creek watershed.

≋ Two European nations besides France eventually established their presence in the region of which the Upper Iowa is part. Since the British were granted Canada and French lands east of the Mississippi in the Treaty of Paris in 1763, their trade interests legally extended to Prairie du Chien, where they took over the French trading outpost.[21] Though the Spanish worked to extend their influence up the Mississippi, the English illegally dominated trade on the Upper Iowa side of the river.[22] An English trader, arrested by Spanish authorities around 1770 while working in Spanish territory, lost goods such as blankets, metal tools and utensils, gunpowder, beads, and jewelry to his captors.[23] Pelts from the Upper Iowa basin procured these valued items during this period. In 1766 Jonathon Carver left Detroit to survey British interests on the Upper Mississippi. His journal entry for October 23, 1766, notes that in ascending the Mississippi above Prairie du Chien, he "passed some small rivers falling in on both sides."[24] One was the Upper Iowa. Connecticut trader Peter Pond provided another glimpse of the region when he described a 1774 trade rendezvous at "Planes of the Dogs" (Prairie du Chien). The Indian encampment there stretched a mile and a half. Besides trading and counsels, the Indians engaged in tremendous games of lacrosse. Traders from Mackinac, like Pond, came in canoes that could transport three or four tons of goods. From Mackinac came 130 such canoes, returning east with 150,000 pounds of furs. In addition, Pond said numerous trading boats came up from the south, the boats from New Orleans being rowed by thirty-six oarsmen and carrying wine, hams, and cheeses.[25]

The Spanish claim to the territory that included the Upper Iowa was based on Hernando De Soto's discovery of the Mississippi in 1541. Once the Spanish decided the region offered no mineral resources worth despoiling, they let it slip away. However, after the French lost Quebec, Montreal, and Detroit to the British, France attempted to create a stronger ally in Spain by secretly, in 1762, ceding to that country its claims to all lands west of the Mississippi. In 1780 a party of Spanish traders arrived in Prairie du Chien. In 1781 Francisco Cruzat, the Spanish governor of the Illinois territory, wrote from St. Louis to the Sac and Fox living south of the Upper Iowa: "Yes, my children, your fathers, the French and the Spanish, have always been but one; as you have heard it said, so you now see it."[26]

After Napoleon's rise to power, the Spanish returned Louisiana to France in 1800. To augment his flagging resources, the French ruler sold the land to the United States in 1803. Thomas Jefferson's representatives in Paris, Robert Livingston and James Monroe, had been authorized to spend ten million dollars to purchase the Spanish lands of Florida and New Orleans. Instead, Napoleon's minister, Talleyrand, offered them eight hundred thousand square miles of land, which at fifteen million dollars came to about three cents an acre. The Upper Iowa River basin became a possession of the U.S. government at a cost of about $3,500. Its future to whites involved the exploitation of far more resources than fur.

≋ As we drive back to Decorah, Kambesis says, "Though karst has similar features wherever you find it, each karst cave has its own distinctive geology." For years, one of the mistakes made by Coldwater Cave explorers was pursuing what they now call "the myth of the upper level." As the first cave divers like Barnett and Jagnow shone their miners' lamps upwards in some of the domed chambers, they saw shadows. David Jagnow developed a theory which assumed that the modern cave had descended from an older passageway above, the same process that had formed Mammoth Cave in Kentucky. Jagnow guessed that the shadowy areas at the tops of domes were the entrances to old channels, and that another, older cave, spread empty and dry above them. Years of exploration with climbing gear and careful later inspection with incandescent, rather than carbide, lamps finally dispelled the myth of the upper level. Coldwater begins in sinkholes and cracks that carry the water into widely separated domes. These are the terminal points in the gradual, but steady, descent of water into the cave. Kambesis made a similar mistake in her theory about most of the water in Coldwater flowing through Coldwater Spring as its path to the river. "Be careful not to assume anything," her research adviser cautioned. "You'll end up wasting time trying to prove the wrong idea, and overlook the reality." As we return to town at dusk in Kambesis's sedan, she says that the reality of the cave is far more complex than she dreamed. She also says that the only way I will understand Coldwater Cave is to experience it. I am not a person who gladly seeks out enclosed dark spaces, but I can see that she is right.

≈ When America bought the most current European claim to the Mississippi corridor in 1803, it had done no negotiating with the people who lived there. Whereas the Spanish, French, and English had seen the area as a foreign region from which to extract raw materials at a handsome profit, its new American owners saw it as real estate. After 1803 it was real estate they had already purchased. Before they could take possession, they needed to explore it, find out who lived there.

For this reason, the first government explorers in Upper Iowa country were only half occupied with exploration. The rest of their work was to improve relations with Indian tribes who lived all along the Upper Mississippi. Zebulon Pike was the government's first emissary. President Jefferson sent Pike and twenty soldiers up the Mississippi from St. Louis on August 9, 1805. They were to assess the extent of the territory, plan for the establishment of trading posts and forts, and purchase full rights to the lands on which a fort could be constructed near St. Anthony Falls. Pike encamped "about 3 miles below the River Iowa."[27] When he came across the Mississippi to the Dakota camp on the south bank of the Upper Iowa, he was saluted with "what might be termed three rounds" of fire. Pike returned the salute. As Pike's boats neared the bank of the Upper Iowa, he noted that some braves "tried their dexterity, to see how near our Boats they could make their Balls strike: so that they may literally be said to have struck on every side of us." Thus greeted, the first presidential representative of the United States government stepped onto the banks of the Upper Iowa with pistols stuffed into his belt and "sword in hand."[28]

As the Ioway had done for the French trader Nicolas Perrot one hundred and twenty years earlier, Wabasha, the village chief, prepared a peace pipe to give to Pike. Seated in the chief's lodge, Wabasha, whose name in Dakota meant "the Leaf," told Pike that he "was happy to see one who knew the Great Spirit was the Father of all; both the White and the Red people." Wabasha offered Pike a meal of wild rice and venison. Pike accepted the meal and pipe "with pleasure," he said, "as the Gift of a Great Man, and a Brother."[29] Before he left in the late afternoon, Pike presented Wabasha with tobacco, knives, vermillion, salt, and rum. The strange new ritual of handshaking had a comic novelty for the Dakota. In a mood of great levity, Wabasha's braves insisted that, since Pike had shaken hands with Wabasha, they would line up to shake hands with Pike's soldiers as they departed.[30]

American officials also pursued diplomacy with the Dakota in the new capital of the nation, Washington, D.C. Thomas Jefferson met with Dakota representatives on January 6, 1806, and he assured them, "In establishing trade with you we desire to make no profit. We shall ask from you only what everything costs us and give you for your furs and peltries whatever we can get for them again."[31] Though the Americans, he said, were "as numerous as the stars in the heaven" and were "strong men," they sought peace with other nations, and hoped the Indians would do the same. "My Children," he concluded, "I have long desired to see you. I have now opened my heart to you. Let my words sink into your hearts and never be forgotten."[32] Jefferson's visitors did not forget his promise of peace and fair dealing. The government in Washington, however, remembered the part about being strong and "numerous as the stars" better than the promise of equal exchange. Jefferson's own dream of America was for a nation of planters. That dream had more power in the development of unexplored western lands than the immediate aim of trading fur.

After Pike's expedition, the federal government lapsed into a sleepy, unmindful attitude about its Mississippi frontier river lands. The American government was slow to live up to its promises and to develop its interests on the distant reaches of the Upper Mississippi. The British still traded furs in the region as a natural extension of their interests in Canada and maintained the allegiance of their Indian trading partners. Once the War of 1812 broke out, almost all of the Dakota sided with the British. Wabasha, whose father was a celebrated hero on the British side of fighting in the Revolutionary War, apologized to a British representative for entertaining Americans like Zebulon Pike. He said the Dakota had been "amused for some time by bad birds."[33]

The War of 1812 stirred the U.S. government to be aggressive in securing its interests along the western frontier. A new fort, Fort Crawford, was built in Prairie du Chien, and in 1817 Major Stephen Long sailed up the Mississippi to further scout the river for sites of trading posts and forts. Long's journal shows that a small Fox village was on the Upper Iowa, and he met a party of Fox in twelve canoes who had just been hunting there.[34] Near the mouth of the "Little Ioway River" he saw a small village of Dakota who raised an American flag as the skiff was oared past. Long "returned the compliment by discharging a blunderbuss."[35] To further consolidate the government's hold on the Mississippi, Colonel Henry Leavenworth went up that river in the summer of 1819. Major Thomas Forsyth, the Indian agent accompanying Leavenworth, reported that they stopped along the banks of the Mississippi at the mouth of the Upper Iowa to greet a chief named Tamaha, or Rising Moose. Forsyth gave Tamaha gunpowder, tobacco, and whiskey, which in his official government diary he recorded as "milk."[36] When Stephen Long ascended the Mississippi again in 1823, his party noted a village of Wabasha's band near the mouth of the Upper Iowa and recorded two acres of corn planted near the spot.[37]

≈ Though I am hesitant to try the adventure, my trip down into Coldwater Cave takes place on a Saturday morning in April 2004. With the car trunk full of neoprene wetsuit gear, my friend John Moeller, his son Daniel, and I pull up at a café on the main street of Harmony, Minnesota. The Coldwater Cave survey group members, gathered for their monthly day in the cave, are eating breakfast. They have driven here from all over the region. At the table next to ours, a caver is showing off photos from a trip exploring lava tubes on Mauna Kea volcano. A group from the Iowa Geological Survey is, like us, going to tour the cave, but the people to whom we are introduced are going to do survey work. Mike Lace, a cancer researcher from Iowa City, Iowa, who also coordinates the cave mapping, has volunteered to use part of his day to accompany the Moellers and me. Lace is a slight man who claims that his size sometimes makes him the canary for the first push into the cave's tighter spaces. I am heading, under his guidance, into a claustrophobic's nightmare, so I am happy to see a gentle expression in his eyes.[38]

≈ In 1825 James Monroe publicly announced a presidential policy by which all Indians would be forced to settle in a permanent Indian territory, closed to white settlement. This territory would begin west of the Mississippi. In August 1825, 1,100 Potawatomi, Ottawa, Winnebago, Dakota, Ojibwey, Sac, Fox, and Ioway were brought together for a council at Prairie du Chien. The purpose was determining the boundaries of lands in the territory west of the Mississippi. Since the federal government decided to relocate some eastern tribes to the western side of the river, tribes like the Dakota had to move to make room.

The 1825 treaty council in Prairie du Chien was a grand display. The Dakota and Ojibwey, coming in a flotilla of two hundred decorated canoes from the north, were brightly dressed and painted. They arrived at the council site in tight formation to the beating of drums and with a discharge of firearms. The Ioway, Sac, and Fox arrived from the south in a formation of seventy canoes, singing war chants and passing the entire village of Prairie before sweeping around to return from the north.[39] General William Clark, the acclaimed explorer who was governor of the Missouri Territory and superintendent of Indian affairs for the region, was the council's main organizer. Clark opened with the false claim that the United States wanted "not the slightest piece of your land." Continuing more truthfully, he said he hoped that "all should live in peace."[40] Indian orators were bothered by the idea of setting up boundaries and ownership. Cut Ear, an Ojibwey, could see the logical outcome, that "in running marks round our country or in giving it to our enemies, it may make new disturbances and breed new wars." Walking Turtle, a Winnebago who would later camp on the Upper Iowa, said to the federal representatives, "My Fathers I did not know that any of my relations had any particular land—It is true every one owns his own lodge and the grounds he may cultivate—I had thought that the Rivers were the common property of all Red Skins and not used exclusively by any Particular nation."[41] The assembled chiefs were forced to establish boundaries. The line dividing Dakota lands from the lands of the Sac and Fox stretched over 150 miles beyond the Mississippi, beginning on the east with a natural landmark they all knew: the first twenty miles of the Upper Iowa. The only other landmarks the signers all knew enough to agree upon were rivers: Trout River (which still had no name), the Red Cedar, and the Des Moines.

≋ To prevent unpoliced public access to Coldwater Cave, the state of Iowa placed bars across Steve Barnett's water route at the spring and drilled an entrance hole with a lockable lid at one of the farms that sat over the cave's main passageway. I am happy not to have to swim a quarter mile against a strong current of frigid water in total darkness to reach my destination. Instead, in our quest to see Coldwater Cave for ourselves, the Moellers and I follow Lace's pickup down the gravel road from Harmony to the wooded draw where a shed houses a ladder to the cave. Cars, pickups, and tents cluster in the draw at the base of a large pasture. Small groups of people discuss their plans for the day, stripping off their street clothes. They take their time, savoring the brisk air before squeezing into blue and black neoprene that droops from them like a sloughed-off skin.

Inside the shack, Lace opens up a field notebook to show us how he maps sections of the cave. Using a compass, a clinometer to measure inclination, and a measuring tape, Lace can sketch the cave passage in pencil on the graph paper of a pocket-sized yellow notebook. "These are pretty rough," he apologizes as he opens the field book. I look down to see an expert drawing of angular limestone slabs jutting upwards from the stream bed. Stalactites point, like sharply nailed fingers, from the ceiling. This is the tiny vertical section. The larger horizontal section shows the cave floor: slabs laid flat, with small and rounded boulders between them. Lace scans such pictures into a computer file that puts together the map of the entire cave. As he is explaining his work, others enter whose conversation is peppered with the names of landmarks in the dark landscape below our feet: Beaver Boneyard, North Snake, Brothers Grimm. Having touched base with the other groups, Mike has us walk into a brightly sunlit side room and sign in for a trip down the ladder.

≋ Because steamboats sped up the arrival of settlers, in the late 1820s the government began to pacify and lay claim to its Upper Mississippi territory. Miners illegally took lead from Indian lands on both sides of the Mississippi, forcing the Indian agent, J. M. Street, to take Henry Dodge to court over these encroachments in 1827–1828.[42] To eliminate conflicting claims, Caleb Atwater, an Ohio man, visited Prairie du Chien in 1829. In accord with the 1825 treaty that Clark had secured, Atwater acknowledged the Upper Iowa as the southeastern corner of Dakota lands. In a book he published after his return, Atwater said that Dakota territory extended "from the upper Ioway river, to the Frozen ocean in the north, and to the Rocky mountains in the west." It was a country, he said, "filled with wild animals."[43] Atwater's duty was dealing with the Dakota and other regional tribes to gain access on both sides of the Mississippi for lead miners. An emissary of white empire, he believed in the nobility of its aims. He envisioned a free and settled America "laid off by its Author, for one people." In dreamlike terms, Atwater's book promotes a vision of an independent country stretching from coast to coast, sharing its resources and manufactured goods. To the skeptical, Atwater pointed to America's rivers: "Here, then are the rivers, which are to the body politic, exactly what the arteries and veins are to the human body, in them, and through them, circulates the commerce, which is the life and blood of this vast country."[44] Atwater's writing reflects the enthusiasm of a man who traveled seven hundred miles by river without putting hand to a paddle. He sailed by steamboat from Maysville, Kentucky, to Prairie du Chien. Steamboat access gave lead miners more lucrative prospects for extracting mineral wealth, the rights to which Atwater was to secure.

Putting an Upper Iowa dividing line on the map between the Dakota and the Sac and Fox did not slow the accelerating war between the two sides in the 1820s. Each carried out raids that disrupted the fur trade. In the winter of 1819–1820, before tensions accelerated, the Sac and Fox sold the skins or pelts of 2,760 beaver, 922 otter, 13,440 raccoon, 12,900 muskrat, 500 mink, 200 wildcat, 680 bear, and 28,680 deer.[45] With constant raids, these numbers had fallen. In 1829 Robert Stuart, of John Jacob Astor's American Fur Company, wrote the Indian Bureau that increasing fear and violence would cause "a great loss in the Fur Trade," and Astor's son directed his representative in St. Louis to allow the territorial governor "no peace night or day" until the intertribal hostilities were settled.[46] In response, a council was held at Prairie du Chien in the summer of 1830. This time, in a plan approved by President Andrew Jackson, the government proposed to buy lands west of the river. At this meeting of Oto, Ioway, Sac, Fox, Winnebago, Dakota, and Menominee, the government convinced the Dakota on the one side and the Sac and Fox on the other to sell a twenty-mile corridor of their lands adjoining the neutral dividing line specified by the 1825 treaty. This created a Neutral Ground that the government hoped would provide enough of a buffer to end hostilities.

The Dakota chief Wabasha, whose band had long lived and hunted the region, was angry about the government's 1830 purchase of land north of the Upper Iowa.[47] There was wisdom as well as selfishness in his objections. Forsyth had said, on his tour of the region in 1819, that Wabasha "is no beggar, nor does he drink."[48] Whiskey was like smallpox, an evil to which Dakota had no resistance. Those who drank it became dangerous, easy prey for sharp traders. Though the French had lubricated their trade with brandy and rum, they used enough restraint for their own welfare and the minimal welfare of the Indian hunters on whom they depended. The English and Scots were less scrupulous, offering whiskey to give themselves a quick advantage, especially between the 1763 defeat of the French in the Seven Years' War and the 1803 Louisiana Purchase.[49] When the Upper Mississippi was thrown open to the easy access of Americans, the whiskey trade became epidemic and burned through Indian lives like fire.[50] The second new evil for which the Indians were unprepared was the American money they now received for land. Traders loved federal annuity money because Indians were unused to wealth; they spent it quickly and freely, often on whiskey. Depending on money, they also depended more than ever before on the traders. Wabasha was angry at the 1830 treaty council because Dakota were beginning to starve on increasingly overhunted lands. The Mississippi Valley was being emptied of game, yet the lands his band had long hunted and farmed north of the Upper Iowa were productive and rich. What was the sense in exchanging them for money which would be most readily converted into liquid poison?

The American negotiators said Wabasha and his band would still be able to hunt in the Neutral Ground, though they could no longer live there. In the end, Wabasha joined fifty-nine other Dakota representatives in signing the treaty, in return for his band receiving immediate gifts, a $2,500 annuity for each of the next ten years, a blacksmith, and schooling for children who wanted it. Two years later a Dakota chief named Lark explained the ban on villages and war parties in the Neutral Ground as a symptom of white greed for land and trade. Pointing to the western bank of the Mississippi, he told the Prairie du Chien Indian agent, "My father, we had a little piece of land over there which we wanted to keep for hunting; but you gave us a great deal of trouble about it." Then pointing to the fur trader, Rolette, Lark said "he told us he wanted rats [muskrat pelts], and not scalps."[51]

≋ The ladder to Coldwater Cave descends from a light-filled room of the cave shed into darkness and the sound of cascading water. The first person down, I climb the long ladder in a thick wetsuit and boots. At the bottom I shout "off ladder!" and shuffle backwards across a wooden platform into the dark. A half-moon of dim light wavers at the bottom of the ladder shaft as Daniel Moeller climbs down. Away from the ladder there is only darkness so heavy it pushes in at me and the air fills with the reverberation of cascading water. Switching on my flashlight, I see Coldwater Cave: a vigorous stream running down a gravel bed, pocked walls of stone rising up twenty feet apart, and a smooth ceiling of sandy-looking bedrock streaked with brown and red. When Lace and the Moellers are down, we step into the creek and wade upstream. "This cave," Lace says, "is essentially in pristine condition: the way it was several hundred years ago or even longer." Though the main life in the cave is microbial, occasionally something bigger washes in. Beaver Boneyard, for instance, got its name from remains explorers found there. In one sandy stretch of water, the beam of my flashlight lights up a ghostly filament: a seed sprouting from the sediment. When I reach to touch it, it twists and floats away like smoke. Where a small cascade of water and flowstone enters in from the right, Lace stops us. "That's North Snake Passage," he says. "Looks friendly enough, but it doesn't stay that way. It's eight hundred to nine hundred feet of belly crawling, then another 250 feet to the dome." "Friendly" is not the word that comes to my mind as I shine my flashlight up to a small and shadowy crawl space at the top of the flowstone. Surveyors had pushed into this space as far as ingenuity would let them. The water we see trickling over the flowstone was the mappers' clue that they could find more to survey. "It's axiomatic," Lace says, "the cave follows the water."

We also follow the water. We need wetsuits in the cave because almost all of the passage has water at its base. Sometimes the water is waist high. In a stretch called Pothole Country, John Moeller twists sideways ahead of me as he steps into a hole. I lurch forward into a depression where the water is up to my chest. Having mapped the entire bottom, Lace knows where to place his feet in the muddied stream. Where the path leaves the stream to travel over rock, the cave surveyors have marked out a walkway in yellow plastic construction tape. "We've tried to keep people to the path that's going to do the least harm to the cave," Lace says. "We try to be good stewards." That stewardship includes using wire and epoxy to repair broken flowstone and washing off slabs of rock tracked over with mud. It also influences decisions about cave exploration. "If there's a place where we can't get further without damaging some beautiful flowstone, we'll say 'no.' It's just not worth destroying something this beautiful to get there," Lace says, gesturing to a curtain of white calcium carbonate.

≋ In the spring of 1832 William Clark, the territorial governor in St. Louis, appointed an old friend, Nathan Boone, to survey the Neutral Ground. Born in 1781, Nathan Boone shot his first buck while hunting with his father, Daniel Boone, in western Kentucky.[52] The year of his marriage, Nathan Boone moved into the Osage River country of Missouri. In one of his first years in the Osage territory claimed by Spain, he and his brother, on a winter hunting and trapping expedition on the Kansas River, two hundred miles from home, were robbed and stripped by a band of Osage. The frost and exhaustion of the trip back home nearly cost him his life. In the War of 1812 Boone fought Sac Indians. In 1832, at age fifty, his life in Missouri had become too settled, so he took a series of jobs at the edge of the frontier. The Upper Iowa survey was the first of these. He put together a survey team of seven other men, including his assistant, two chainmen, a flagman, a horseman, a camp keeper, and an axman. To keep the nature of the territory and its boundaries clear to the two tribes involved, the government also sent along an Indian agent and tribal representatives from the Sac and the Dakota. This group arrived at the mouth of the Upper Iowa on April 19, 1832.[53]

Boone's charge reflects how unfamiliar the treaty land was to whites. Using only the rivers mentioned in the 1825 treaty, he was to survey and mark the borders sketched out by the 1830 treaty. The new owners of the Upper Iowa River valley also asked that he keep a record of streams, timber, soil conditions, and the mineral potential of their unexplored property.

Beginning the survey on that April day in 1832 was difficult. The Upper Iowa fed into a maze of sloughs, lakes, and ponds that made up its river plain delta. Boone reported that they began "at a point inaccessible in the middle of the main channel of the Upper Iowa and its confluence with the Mississippi."[54] The crew measured over forty miles of meandering Upper Iowa from that point until they came to a stream, about thirty feet wide, entering from the left. Boone decided that this was the "left fork" mentioned in the 1825 treaty "by the road leading from Prairie du Chien to the Red Cedar crossing it as the only fork or branch of the Iowa River that the road crosses."[55] At this, the mouth of Trout River, Boone scrawled down the first written description of a point on the upper reaches of the Upper Iowa: "On the lower side of the fork is a cliff about 20 feet high. Immediately in the forks stand three elm trees within a few feet of each other."[56] The team measured its way to the source of this fork and struck off toward the Red Cedar and the Des Moines to create a straight line to the western border of the Neutral Ground. By the time the crew returned to the Upper Iowa basin on their way back east, they had surveyed the Neutral line, its west border on the Des Moines and 117 miles of the north border of the Neutral Ground.

On June 3, 1832, on their return journey east, they entered a part of the watershed that was "gently rolling," its soil "second rate" but "fit for cultivation" near the current site of Lime Springs, Iowa. On June 4 they struck the river and took three days to cover the eighty miles of territory they needed to measure to "prove" their accuracy against the point where they had left Trout River in late April. They surveyed five and a half miles north along the Upper Iowa through country that varied from oak savanna, with scrubby hazel underbrush, to heavy timber. At the point where they struck east again, toward the Mississippi, Boone, who had left off his schooling at age thirteen, wrote that the country was "Roling Barony land timber scattering and scrubby white Oak—Undergrowth Same."[57]

On June 12 they left Upper Iowa land and entered the drainage of the Winnebago River to the north. In all of the survey team's journey into the interior, the only landscape points to which they could give name were the major rivers and a spot where, the Sac representative said, a battle had taken place in 1831 between the Sac and the Dakota. Though they skirted Clear Lake, they could give it no name. The area had been lived in and hunted for ten thousand years, but for this first official delegation, the place was largely unpeopled and unknown. They left a line of blazed trees and earthen mounds with charcoal centers marking the northern border of a new stretch of U.S. government territory: a land of streams, untilled soil, and uncut timber.

By the time Nathan Boone reached the banks of the Mississippi again, the federal government needed him for a job other than surveying. The Boone surveying party reached the Mississippi on June 16, 1832, finding the river flooded. Boone must have gone down the river to Prairie du Chien anyway, because that same day he was made a captain of the U.S. Mounted Ranger Battalion. Two days later, on June 18, 1832, Congress authorized the formation of six companies of Mounted Ranger volunteers to help quell Indian troubles.[58] Boone crossed the Upper Iowa and found the point near Painted Rock, twenty miles south, from which he would begin the southern boundary, but on June 26 he terminated his survey work with the following statement: "Quit work . . . in consequence of the hostilities of the Indians."[59] While Boone was surveying to help pacify the Sac and the Dakota, the Black Hawk War broke out. Boone returned to Missouri to enlist a company of volunteers that was mustered into service on August 11, too late to be of help in the short-lived war.[60]

In the last battle of that war, Black Hawk's band ended up trapped at the mouth of the Bad Axe River, just across the Mississippi from the Upper Iowa. Black Hawk and several other leaders fled north and east, leaving the sick, starving, old, very young, and a few loyal braves behind. Troops under General Atkinson, called White Beaver by his Indian guides, had overtaken Black Hawk's band by land. In the early morning of August 2, 1832, the steamboat *Warrior* arrived on the river, carrying troops and cannon from Fort Crawford. At daylight, Atkinson attacked. Black Hawk's people were shot on land, shot in the water as they tried to swim, or drowned in the current. The American soldiers killed women, children, old people, and warriors. The steamboat *Warrior* sprayed the woods with grapeshot and rifle fire to drive out survivors and then crossed to the western shore. Some of the members of Black Hawk's band who made it to the Upper Iowa side of the river had already begun to escape south. The Sac refugees were caught by Wabasha, who had been deputized by an army captain named Loomis. Of the persons Wabasha and his band of 150 Dakota warriors overtook, they spared 22 women and children. They killed and scalped 68 others.[61] When soldiers on the *Warrior* arrived at the Upper Iowa side of the Mississippi, they sprayed the islands and the shoreline with grapeshot and rifle fire. In their charge through the islands, they found few to take as prisoners: elderly men, women, and children. Though Black Hawk was not there to witness the massacre of his followers, the first prominence below the Upper Iowa has since been called Black Hawk Bluff because of the killing that took place there.

≈ In talking about repairs to stalactites on our hike through the subterranean waters of Coldwater Creek, Mike Lace uses a word that gives me pause. "Some of the speleothems we repaired a few years ago," he says, "are already healing over quite nicely." The cave is chiefly stone, water, and air. "Healing" suggests how much it is alive, a living system into which people have only recently pushed themselves. As we splash into the upstream edge of Pothole Country, Lace points out a perfectly circular depression, ten inches deep. At its center rests a round black stone: a dark nucleus. "Boulders like this get rounded as they dig their way down into these potholes," he explains. Looking down at the cabbage-sized rock nesting in its pool of water feels like looking over an unexpected precipice. The geologic life of the cave unfurls before me. This round rock in its round hole started as a squared-off block of limestone in a tight, square bed. Years of water, moving the rock, has dug out this new cave space. The pothole is like a single cell in a plant that has spread its limbs sixteen miles, the flow of water essential to its continued life.

To gauge the climate of the world above over the last ten thousand years, researchers have used the growth rings of stalactites in Coldwater. Ground-water seeps through the Galena limestone above the cave, absorbing calcium from the rock, leaving behind a microscopic film of calcium as it drips from the stalactites, new growth to cover the old or to heal a break. The rate of growth and the mix of carbon and oxygen in the calcium carbonate of the stalactites changes, depending on whether the climate is damp and marked by forest growth or drier, hotter, and marked by prairie.[62] While the life aboveground grows and decomposes, passing from chill winter into blazing summer, the cave lives and grows in steady darkness and temperature. The cave began growing when ground sloths pounded the turf above. It grows with the steady interplay of water and rock, even as I slosh through it. It will still be growing with quiet slowness in the dark when our impatient species passes into extinction. Exploring the cave is arduous, but I realize, as my friends and I trudge tiredly to the ladder, that the cave is insulated from much of the world above: a sanctuary as well as a frontier.

≋ In the fall of 1833, James Craig completed the survey of the southern border of the Neutral Ground that Nathan Boone had quit the previous year due to the war. Because the federal government planned a new use for the territory, J. M. Street, the Prairie du Chien Indian agent, went along to examine the southern edge of the Neutral Ground. He reported to Washington that the hunter who accompanied him "expressed his astonishment at the abundance of all kinds of game except buffalo." They observed elk, deer, and bear. "The sign of fur animals, particularly rats and otters," Street reported, "is considerable on all the streams and ponds." Street was particularly excited about beavers: "I saw, for the first time, a beaver dam in progress, on which there had been two new logs put during the night previous to our visit, and every appearance that the ingenious animals had been at work until disturbed by our approach."[63]

The government's new plan for the Upper Iowa basin and the rest of the Neutral Ground was this. It would push the Winnebago to the west side of the Mississippi, as had already been done to Black Hawk's Sac. The government would make a home for the Winnebago in the Neutral Ground it had bought from the Sac, Fox, and Dakota. Having surveyed its potential, the federal agent deemed it a place where the Winnebago could settle, hunt, learn to farm like European Americans, and learn English. The Dakota, who had been granted Neutral Ground hunting rights in 1825, would hunt elsewhere. Though Thomas Jefferson had assured his Dakota guests that the government only wanted to trade in furs at "no profit," thirty years later the Upper Iowa basin was part of a government plan that would extend Jefferson's dream of a nation of farmers beyond the Mississippi to the banks of the Upper Iowa.

We Have Never Sold Any Country
1833 – 1848

The October morning was still dark as a wiry man, comfortable on his horse, rode up to the trading post of Antoine Grignon on the Trout River. The man, Coming Thunder, likely viewed the mission ahead of him with some repugnance. He was to accompany John Seymour, a representative of the Indian agent Jonathan Fletcher, on a surprise inspection to see whether chiefs were living inside the agreed-upon boundaries of their territory along the Upper Iowa. Fletcher suspected Coming Thunder's fellow chiefs had moved either north to the Root River or east, too close to the Mississippi. The agent would withhold annuity payments until he was sure they were living in the territory stipulated by their treaty. In this spying mission, Coming Thunder would serve as the tribe's witness. Though Fletcher had recently named him head chief of the Winnebago tribe, Coming Thunder was unhappy to be a part of the vise that was squeezing his people out of their mobile way of life.

Coming Thunder and Seymour rode hard. In barely over a day they made an eighty-mile circuit, leaving no time for warnings. Filing his written report, Seymour would produce the most thorough description of the Upper Iowa and its villages in the decade the Winnebago lived on the river. Mounting their horses, the group left two hours before sunrise for a "brisk" eight-and-one-half hour ride downstream. They forded the Upper Iowa four times. Seymour, with an eye for future development, said they passed four "beautiful mill streams." One came in from the south, perhaps Trout River, and three from the north, perhaps Canoe Creek, Patterson Creek, and Bear/Waterloo Creeks. Thinking about settlement prospects, Seymour said that in the thirty miles they rode downstream he saw "no timber . . . fit for building." What he saw were "bluffs two hundred or more feet in height many places perpendicular showing limestone on the top and sandstone basis, sparsely sprinkled over most of the way with stunted oaks seen to approach the river as you descend." The river was "a clear rapid stream, the fords were generally above two feet in depth and from forty to sixty yards in width." The eastern point of their ride was a village that Little Decorah (One Who Stands and Reaches the Skies) had established five years earlier. Two miles upriver, on the north side, Seymour examined the villages of Elk and Young Walking Turtle. Three miles further upstream and on the same side were the villages of Waukon Haga Decorah (also called Rattlesnake or Snake Skin) and Old Walking Turtle.

At the village sites Seymour found wigwams covered with reed and hay matting in which were stored pumpkins, guns, and cooking utensils. As Coming Thunder looked on, Seymour thrust his hand into the sand in Elk's village. Wiggling his fingers downward, he felt the hard surface of a container of corn, cached elbow-deep beneath the ground for the winter. Leaving at midnight, the group rode hard upstream, arriving about sunrise, seven and a half hours later, at Coming Thunder's camp on the south side of the Upper Iowa, near Trout River. Though Seymour did not take time to visit, since Fletcher had already done that, he reported that Big Canoe (also called One-Eyed Decorah) and Black Hawk had villages four miles further upstream on the north side, near the mouth of Trout Run and what would later become the site of Decorah. Seymour concluded that Coming Thunder's camp looked the most permanent of any he had visited. "Here everything indicated a disposition to comply with both the letter and Spirit of . . . regulations, which I am sorry to say I cannot say of the others."[1] Seymour's ride offers a glimpse of a river largely still unknown to whites, with Winnebago villages clustered at its midpoint and again near the mouth of Bear and Waterloo creeks, with completely uninhabited country in between that was almost entirely prairie or oak savanna. The river was running clear at a volume where, today, its waters would run silty. Seymour's record is the best picture we have of the river just prior to the basin's shift to agriculture.

John Seymour's account also testifies that the lifestyle of the Winnebago on the river was not settled in the way whites demanded. The reason for Seymour's visit was that Coming Thunder, Waukon Haga Decorah, and Walking Turtle had all been known to live on the Root River. Antoine Grignon, at whose trading post Coming Thunder met Seymour, later recalled about Waukon Haga that he "was camped on the Iowa river [Upper Iowa] when I knew him. . . . He did not remain in that section long."[2] Grignon used the word "camped" to describe the band's residency on the river. That Seymour had to be dispatched by Fletcher suggests that village occupation was impermanent. Fletcher's campaign to convert hunters to settled farmers had a long way to go.

Not only might a band move its summer village site yearly, but it moved during the course of the year. The village where most of the band spent much of the summer planting season was abandoned for hunting camps and winter camps. Moses Paquette, describing the life of the traditional Winnebago who stayed in Wisconsin, said, "Most of them are seldom at home. In the spring they scratch up the ground a little with hoes—very few of them use plows—plant their corn in a crude fashion, and then go off into the woods, hunting and fishing, until time to hoe the crop. This task over, they go off until gathering time, and then are away for the most of the winter until spring again." The "winter hunt," Paquette observed, might last from the end of September to the end of April.[3] Hunting and gathering drew the bands to the sites favorable to each throughout the year. This means that the "villages" Seymour visited may have enjoyed only a few months occupancy in the warmest months of the year, being deserted for the rest. The Winnebago who used them lacked a farmer's attachment to a single plot of ground.

In the 1840s the forty-mile-wide strip of land that centered on the eastern half of the Upper Iowa was called the Neutral Ground. Coming Thunder's people were living there because they had given up their claim to a large part of Wisconsin and Illinois, lands that stretched east to Red Bank on Lake Michigan, their ancestral home. The tribe would have preferred to stay on the east side of the Mississippi. The understanding at a treaty signing in 1832, agreed upon by all sides, had been that the Winnebago would move to a new home in the Neutral Ground, bordering the Mississippi, but that they would still hold claim to some of their even-more-valued land in Wisconsin. The mission and agency in the Neutral Ground constructed in 1833 to carry out that agreement were located near the mouth of the Yellow River on the Mississippi, with easy river access to Prairie du Chien and Wisconsin.

This 1832 agreement was soon altered. In an 1837 treaty signed in Washington by a handful of minor tribal members who were coerced and tricked by government officials, the eastern twenty miles of the Neutral Ground (including the agency site) were declared off limits, the last Wisconsin land was signed away, and the government was given the right eventually to find a new home for the tribe someplace other than the Neutral Ground.[4] The agency and mission on the Neutral Ground were moved from the Yellow River to the Turkey River in 1840 to help ease the tribe into accepting the twenty-mile exclusion zone along the Mississippi dictated by the 1837 treaty. The site on the Turkey was over forty miles west, up a river too shallow and steep to navigate.[5] The 1840 move was calculated by the federal government to sever the Winnebago from the Wisconsin land that had been their home.

The same year Jonathan Fletcher was ordering Coming Thunder to help police the narrowed boundaries of the Neutral Ground, New York journalist John O. Sullivan coined the phrase that made President James Polk's policy of federal expansion seem divinely sanctioned. Sullivan told his 1845 white audience that it was the "fulfillment of our manifest destiny to overspread the continent allotted by Providence for the free development of our yearly multiplying millions."[6] Coming Thunder was not alone in disliking the direction American progress was taking his tribe in the 1840s. The Neutral Ground was hospitable: unsettled, open, filled with familiar game and plants, and partially protected by government soldiers from intrusion by other tribes and from white settlers. But it was not home. Some Winnebago resisted and eluded the initial move out of Wisconsin. The result was division. A trader whose fortunes were closely tied to the tribe on the Neutral Ground later wrote: "Wisconsin was always the region they desired, and it is doubtful if the generation of that day would have ever been content elsewhere."[7] Whirling Thunder, a chief who moved to the Upper Iowa, lamented to a trader who represented him there: "our people is broken in many pieces." From a frontier to which many Americans looked for a promising future, Whirling Thunder saw nothing ahead but a holocaust: "our old men . . . see nothing but death, and when they are gone they must leave their children fighting one another and separated forever." The move to the Neutral Ground represented compliance on the crucial tipping point of land ownership. "Our brothers on the Mississippi will never meet us as friends," Whirling Thunder explained. "They call us cowards and *pale faces* because we fulfill our treaty stipulations."[8]

≈ The division over compliance with the treaties of the 1830s still persists. Descendants of those who stayed in Wisconsin or returned there call themselves, today, the Ho-Chunk Nation. The ancestors of today's Ho-Chunk Nation insisted more resolutely on their traditional views, their traditional land rights. The ancestors of the Winnebago Tribe of Nebraska complied with the move to the Neutral Ground and subsequent land treaties. The Winnebago understood that their way of living on the land made lighter use of it than whites, and they felt the force of Manifest Destiny at work on them, making resistance difficult. Though they spent close to a decade camping on the Upper Iowa, they did little to change its landscape through their use of it and left with scarcely a trace. Today, their descendants live east of the Mississippi and west of the Missouri, with the state of Iowa and over 150 years of separation between them.

≈≈≈ In the 1840s the Winnebago and their white brothers disagreed about whether to use land for modern farming or to use it predominantly for hunting and gathering. The government began pushing the Winnebago from limited horticulture to plowed-ground agriculture during their residency in the Neutral Ground. When the largest group of Winnebago were moving to the Neutral Ground in 1840, tribal agent David Lowry ordered that ground be prepared for hay on the Red Cedar to feed Winnebago ponies during the winter hunt. In 1843 a metal plow, drawn by draft animals, broke ground along the Upper Iowa for the first time. In the agency report of 1843, David Lowry wrote that the hands hired by the agency had plowed forty-six acres on the Upper Iowa: twenty-three for Winneshiek (Coming Thunder) and twenty-three for Kara-mani-ga (Old Walking Turtle).[9] These fields would have been near the mouths of Trout Run and Trout River, respectively. In 1844 Lowry joined Captain Sumner from Fort Atkinson in a May sweep through the Root River and the lower part of the Upper Iowa to police settlement sites, as Seymour would again do in 1845.[10] Though Lowry thought he would find Waukon Haga Decorah and Old Walking Turtle on the Upper Iowa, he found them on the Root where, by May 17, 1844, they had planted corn. Coming Thunder and Big Canoe were also on the Root. Lowry ordered teams to plow ground further up the Upper Iowa to help the bands resettle there for the summer.[11] The steel coulter blade of the plow was, for a second year, cutting sod. In agent Jonathan Fletcher's report of 1846, he said, "Three additional fields have been ploughed and fenced this season, for the bands who moved from the Mississippi and the Root rivers and located on the Iowa."[12] For four years running, fields had now been plowed for cultivation in the river basin. Lowry and Fletcher hoped that agriculture such as this would help the more resistant bands of the tribe settle into the American mainstream.

Corn was the field crop traditionally favored by the Winnebago, but the agency farm on the Turkey also produced wheat, buckwheat, oats, hay, potatoes, turnips, and beans. In 1842, for example, twenty acres of agency land produced between three thousand and five thousand bushels of turnips.[13] The federal government, however, sought to push the Winnebago ever beyond the frontier of settlement, isolated from European Americans. While Washington and the territorial government urgently

wanted to move the Winnebago further into the frontier, the agents working closest to them realized that this was no permanent solution. In the
1840s the United States was fighting a war with Mexico, discovering gold
in California, and acquiring the Oregon Territory. Eventually there would
be no more frontiers beyond which to push Indian tribes.[14] The agents
preferred converting them into farmers.

In part they succeeded. The year the Winnebago signed an agreement
to move to a tract in Minnesota, Jonathan Fletcher reported that of 2,400
Winnebago in Iowa, living in twenty-two bands, over 2,000 had taken up
farming. The majority of bands, he wrote, "have applied to be furnished
with harness, waggons [sic], and plows." Until that time, almost all Winnebago field work was done by women, according to the traditional division of labor. Now, however, "Some six of the Chiefs, and several of the
head men of the tribe have gone into the field, and held the plow, in a
farmer-like manner, from day to day."[15] The leader in this was Chief Little
Hill, whose band lived near the agency. Fletcher said that Little Hill "turned
his attention chiefly to farming, and has done more than any other chief
to advance the civilization of the tribe."[16] David Lowry reported in early
1848 that "the wife of a chief observed, not long since, that it was not now
thought a disgrace for a man to work."[17] In accepting the nobility of agricultural labor for men, the Winnebago shifted toward the Jeffersonian
dream of an America of independent farmers and landowners.

Though many chiefs began to assimilate to agriculture while living on
the Neutral Ground, those associated with the Upper Iowa maintained traditional values.[18] These held sway among the Winnebago during the transitional period of the 1840s. Some of the chiefs who settled on the Upper
Iowa (Waukon Haga Decorah, Coming Thunder, and Whirling Thunder)
were the most frequent speakers for the tribe at treaty sessions in the 1840s.
They were truculent. Coming Thunder, for example, was furious when the
government allowed a white man, Joel Post, to erect a halfway house
between the river and the army fort. He complained to Fletcher. The agent
explained it was "a convenience to the Officers of the Fort, and to the people of the Sub Agency to have a house of entertainment there." Coming
Thunder looked Fletcher in the eye and responded, "It is a convenience [to
the Winnebago] to hunt game in Wisconsin."[19]

Coming Thunder resolutely stuck to the old ways and avoided putting
his hand to the plow. When he spoke during council his manner was "bold,
commanding," and charismatic.[20] He turned no visitor to his lodge away
hungry, a custom especially important for the ceremonial head chief of

the Thunder clan.[21] His life on the Upper Iowa would have been very mobile, his waking hours occupied with what an acquaintance described as "hunting, gossiping, gambling, and listless loafing."[22] He had no interest in putting hand to the plow.

Jonathan Fletcher, who was responsible for counting the members of households at annuity payment time, said Coming Thunder had four wives.[23] Because he chose to live at a far remove from the agency, none of his children would have attended the school that was, after agriculture, the agents' main way of pushing assimilation. Fletcher was so optimistic about the prospect of education reaching resistant tribal members that he subserviently proposed in 1846 that "if it is considered probable . . . the Winnebagoes would long occupy their present home, I shall deem it my duty, respectfully to suggest to the Department, the expediency of establishing . . . additional schools at a point on the Iowa River and also on the Red Cedar."[24] Introducing plowed fields was the first step in assimilating the Winnebago along the Upper Iowa, followed, in Fletcher's plan, by a school on the river.

In the mission school, offered as part of treaty agreements, Winnebago children were taught "reading, writing, arithmetic, gardening, agriculture, carding, spinning, weaving, and sewing, according to their ages and sexes."[25] Setting up the original school and mission in 1833, President Andrew Jackson appointed David Lowry, a minister of the Cumberland Presbyterian Church, to supervise. Charged with teaching the Winnebago how to assimilate, Lowry developed a policy against continued removal. "Keep the Indians," he wrote, "on their old worn-out hunting grounds—surround them by settlements, and . . . the savage hunter is forced to become a tiller of the soil and the way is opened to the introduction of the arts and sciences."[26] Surrounding Indians with the society of farmers was better, he argued, than isolating them on a frontier populated by whiskey sellers and "all the vice and depravity of the filthy scum of civilization which everywhere floats upon its border."[27] The Winnebago saw from the beginning what Lowry had in mind. Waukon Haga Decorah, the chief orator of the tribe, explained the tribe's skepticism at an initial conference with him in 1833: "The Winnebagoes are asleep, and it will be wrong to wake them," he warned. "They are red men and all the white man's soap and water cannot make them white."[28]

Though designed to tear children away from their traditional culture, Lowry's school was promoted by some chiefs such as Little Priest. The number of children who attended the school ranged from 2 students in

1834 to 170 in 1844. Entering the school, children were given English names. Martin Van Buren, Henry Clay, Walter Scott, and W. H. Harrison were among the boys registered in 1844.[29] The writing of a pupil who assumed the English name of Margaret Porter was printed by a visitor in 1846. It gives a sense of the divided lives the schoolchildren lived: "I like to go and live in a new bark wigwam. When all the children come back from hunting, they are glad to come in school again. A great many School children have died. When any one dies, they paint their face, then put every thing new on; then dress them very fine, and bury them. . . . They say the white people when they die go to one place, and the Indians go to another place."[30] Margaret Porter wrote about the smell of the wigwam in her newly acquired English, but entering the wigwam she resumed her Winnebago name, clothing, and language. Had she died there, she would be buried in the face paint of her clan and age group. Moses Paquette, whose handwriting sample, "Beautiful writing is a speaking picture," was on display in the 1842 school report, later said that in the school "the children were very good Presbyterians so long as they remained at the mission: but most of them relapsed into their ancient heathenism as soon as removed from Mr. Lowrey's care."[31]

Besides being a man of the gospel, Lowry also emphasized the tenets of mainstream culture. Youthful handwriting from an 1842 school report reads, "Money commands many comforts."[32] In "Moral Questions Relative to Practical Plans for Educating and Civilizing the Aborigines," written during the last year of the Winnebago residence on the Neutral Ground, Lowry wrote, "The more of the articles of food, clothing, &c. consumed by the whites we can introduce among the Indians, excepting of course those whose tendency is debasing, the more readily can we convince them of the propriety and benefit of a corresponding change in their habits."[33] Visitors to Lowry's school and independent observers like Governor Chambers were impressed with his pupils' progress.

≋ I decide in 2001 to visit the tribal headquarters of the Ho-Chunk Nation in Black River Falls, Wisconsin. The tribal representative who meets me in the light-filled atrium of the headquarters building is Samantha House, a friendly young woman doing an internship in the Department of Heritage Preservation and taking care of her grandmother before starting law school in Colorado. The internship, she says, is allowing her to "get into the legal aspect of tribal life." For example, the tribe is currently fighting a mineral water company that has developed a well on the site of a sacred spring. In another case, a developer is planning a housing addition on the site of a Ho-Chunk cemetery. Though House has grown up on the Oneida reservation, the daughter of an Oneida father, her mother is Ho-Chunk. She has spent her life visiting her mother's family, members of the Deer clan. She is excited to be part of an office "charged," she says, "with protecting and preserving the cultural legacy of the Ho-Chunk." Today, with new wealth from gaming revenues, the Ho-Chunk Nation is funding projects that help reconnect tribal members to the resources and lifestyle that were part of their history on the Upper Iowa through a bison ranch in Muscoda, Wisconsin, and the reintroduction of peregrine falcons into the wild on the cliffs of the lower Upper Iowa and the Mississippi. The Nation is also developing a camp where its children can get the horseback riding experience that came naturally to Coming Thunder's generation. Since House likes horses, she says, "I get *particularly* excited about that one!"[34] Samantha House's internship, her plan for a career in law, and projects like the horse camp show that her mother's tribe is attempting to nudge Manifest Destiny in a different direction.

~~~ In addition to agriculture and education, capital provided a third path by which the Winnebago along the Upper Iowa began to assimilate. Some trade in the 1840s came, as it had for generations, from fur. Traders' records for the period tally up purchases by village, and annuity payments were made to the chiefs of the villages. Some show the fur trade still in operation. The Dousman firm that represented John Jacob Astor's American Fur Company dominated trade with Indians around Prairie du Chien, including fur trade on the Upper Iowa. David Lowry reported in 1848 that most furs traded by the Winnebago ended up for sale in London.[35] The goods seized from an illegal trader on the Red Cedar edge of the Neutral Ground in December 1843 show that Indians had brought in the furs of elk, beaver, deer, coon, wolf, and bear, and that in return the trader had come stocked with calico, yarn, mirrors, socks, bells, ribbon, vermilion, combs, earbobs, blankets, and knives.[36] Beginning in October 1841, Henry Sibley joined the Dakota among whom he traded for a winter hunt in the lands between the headwaters of the Upper Iowa and those of the Red Cedar. His account is the best record of a traditional hunt in the area in the 1840s, a peek into the world of migrating hunters that would be gone by the end of the decade. Starting at the Cannon River, Sibley and the Dakota moved southwest ten miles a day until reaching their camping site, forty miles east of the Red Cedar. At the end of four months of hunting, Sibley reported

they had taken "2,000 deer, 50 or 60 elk, many bears, and a few buffaloes.... To these may be added five or six panthers."[37] As time passed and more Winnebago hunted the region, however, people noticed the disappearance of game from the Neutral Ground, particularly bison and beaver.

Though pelts and hides provided a kernel of trade, treaty agreements shifted the Winnebago away from fur. Annuity payments, a twice-yearly mortgage payment of cash from the federal government after 1832, encouraged improvidence. Though the Winnebago had been trading with the French, British, and Americans for two hundred years, the federal annuity system lured the tribe more and more away from subsistent self-reliance toward more total dependence on the capital economy. The Dousman record for trade on the Upper Iowa in 1842, for example, shows sales, on credit, of blanket cloth and shirts to two women and a calico shirt, lead, and a laced frock coat to the Winnebago chief Le Petit Garçon.[38] Most credit purchases were repaid not in furs but by annuity money. Other annuity payments were made directly in goods. The order for annuity goods in 1843 included 1,600 blankets, 5,400 yards of cloth, 60 dozen shirts, 1,000 knives, 2,880 awls, 4,520 clay pipes, 1,200 mirrors, 100 pounds of vermilion, hundreds of rifles and shotguns, and the gun flints to supply them.[39] Under the annuity arrangement Indians had more wealth, but they became more dependent on trade, often with traders whose honesty was dubious.

The Winnebago, the military force, and the Indian agent had no direct legal authority over traders who set up operations just across the border between the Neutral Ground and Iowa Territory with the aim of preying upon alcoholism in the tribe. Over that line, where the town of Luana eventually developed, a frontier entrepreneur named Taft Jones built a cabin from which he sold corn liquor. The place quickly earned the nickname Sodom. Unwilling to let Jones reap all the profits, a former soldier named Graham Thorn erected a competing establishment down the road. With evil pluck, Thorn named it Gomorrah. These whiskey dens were just out of military jurisdiction, near the military road that connected the Winnebago Agency and Fort Atkinson with Fort Crawford on the Mississippi. Gomorrah was the site of one of the first recorded murders of whites in the area. In 1840 Jones traded a Winnebago man whiskey for the blanket off his back and let him stagger half naked from Sodom into the winter cold. When the man's son discovered his father's frozen corpse the next morning, the young man fired into the nearest whiskey den, Gomorrah, and killed a young Irishman named Riley whom he saw sitting on a bench inside. He assumed his target was Jones. Jones eventually died from drinking too much of the liquor that also killed his Indian customers. Graham Thorn killed a Winnebago customer and fled to safer parts.[40]

Winnebago usually directed their alcohol-related violence at each other. In 1842 David Lowry reported that in a population of just over two thousand, forty-nine had been murdered in twelve months, mainly by each other. In 1843 Lowry came to the defense of three Winnebago sentenced to be executed for murder. Though they had killed a family with the innocuous name of Teagarden, Lowry pointed out that Mr. Teagarden had invited the Winnebago braves into the house to get them drunk on whiskey, a practice that invited violence.[41] Waukon Haga Decorah summarized the situation in 1843: "The whiskey sellers cheat us out of our blankets and horses and guns, and everything we have. We cannot keep away from them." But he added, "It would not do for us to destroy these shops, as it would make great trouble. For our Great Father told us once, that if an Indian killed a white man he should not have any friends to talk for him."[42]

The trader who made the most from his connection with bands of Winnebago on the Upper Iowa was Henry Rice, an associate of Hercules Dousman. In a trial held in the spring of 1845 to determine Jonathan Fletcher's fairness in his position as agent, the chiefs most connected with the Upper Iowa were described, by the testimony of several witnesses, as "Fur Company chiefs," or "Mississippi chiefs" because they traded with Rice and Dousman.[43] As an example of the control afforded to traders, these fur company chiefs trusted Rice to pick out a new territory for them, to sign the 1846 agreement as a fellow chief, and to visit Minnesota, accompanied by their own head chief, Coming Thunder, in 1847 to examine "the interior of the Sioux country."[44]

Henry Rice had a trading post on the Upper Iowa, a few miles south of the current site of Decorah, between Dry Run Creek and Trout Run. Here, legend has it, the Winnebago brought him some brook trout, which led him to try out the fishing in Trout Run Creek—the first white man recorded to have fished the area.[45] In 1845 Rice operated trading posts near the agency and also on the Red Cedar. He applied to have a trading post on Canoe Creek, then called Big Canoe Creek, but was turned down because Coming Thunder and Big Canoe were afraid that their people "would be tempted to commit depradations."[46]

The bands that made their camps on the Upper Iowa and most closely befriended Henry Rice were among the Winnebago factions that clung hardest to the old ways. It paid traders like Rice to encourage their traditionalism:

dependent on trade rather than on cultivation, fuzzy on arithmetic, loyal in alliances, and living the mobile life. The main hunting in the Neutral Ground took place on the prairies to the west, on the Red Cedar River, where the town of Charles City is located today. The longest hunt took place in the winter. Coming Thunder complained at a November 1, 1844, treaty session that federal negotiation was keeping him from leaving for the hunt. Two months later, in January 1845, Major Dearborn reported to Governor Chambers that the "Indians are mostly out a hunting."[47]

The geography of the Winnebago in the 1840s, and the place of the Upper Iowa in that geography, was negotiated according to the contest between the dictates of the treaties and the dictates of tradition. The chiefs who chose to live on the Upper Iowa liked moving around and kept their distance from whites who wanted to run their affairs. One of the first chiefs to move his band to the Upper Iowa in 1840 was Little Decorah, followed by his brother, Spoon. Spoon Decorah recalled that they were denied their annuity in 1841 because they had not gotten permission to live on the Upper Iowa, a sign of the way the agent, David Lowry, extended the hand of his control beyond his mission and agency on the Turkey to the next river to the north.[48] A census by the agency in 1842 showed 554 Winnebago living on the river in four different villages.[49] The river became home to a limited number of Winnebago, under such chiefs as Coming Thunder, Whirling Thunder, Yellow Thunder, Old Walking Turtle, Little Thunder, Elk, Young Walking Turtle, Little Decorah, Spoon Decorah, Waukon Haga Decorah, and Big Canoe Decorah. Whirling Thunder's request to move his band to the Upper Iowa provides the best single clue to the kind of place it was. "I want to move from where I now live to the Upper Ioway River" he told David Lowry in February 1842. "A part of my Indians are very troublesome—always drinking."[50] The Upper Iowa was the most neutral territory in the whole Neutral Ground. That ground belonged to the tribe by treaty, unlike the Root River to the north, where the most traditional Indians moved to stay near the still-traditional Dakota and to stay clear of the agency. Unlike the agency on the Turkey, however, it provided distance from the interference of the agent and from the assimilating forces he represented. It was also a long ride from the liquor traders. It was middle ground: a place largely unvisited by whites but approved by government for the Winnebago. The chiefs who moved there attempted to abide by the minimal letter of their treaties while keeping a safe distance from white culture, or at least from the meddling of the government's agent and the ready temptation of the whiskey dens.

The government's removal policy in the 1840s was based largely on a desire to keep Indians permanently separated from whites. When John Chambers was sent by President John Tyler to the Winnebago in 1843 to get them to agree to move elsewhere, he gave, as one of his first reasons, "it is becoming dangerous for you to remain longer; the whites are surrounding you."[51] Once the Winnebago began to settle into the Neutral Ground they voiced a strong desire to stay there, fearing that the next move might make their lives even worse. As Whirling Thunder said to commissioner Henry Dodge in a hearing about the territory in 1845, "The eye of the Great Spirit is upon us both. What we say is the truth. We are poor and have been driven from our country into another. We hope that our Great Father will suffer us to remain on the Neutral Ground."[52] As settlement in Iowa crept northward toward the Neutral Ground, however, the government saw the Winnebago's position as increasingly impossible for white voters and lobbyists to tolerate.

≈≈ Seeking out the story of the Winnebago's brief stay on the Upper Iowa, I am excited to hear that David Lee Smith, tribal historian of the Winnebago tribe of Nebraska, will tell stories at Rendezvous Days, the yearly festival that celebrates the 1840s beginnings of Fort Atkinson. The fort in Fort Atkinson is a state preserve. At stalls inside its high log walls, men in loose shirts, canvas pants, and moccasins sell fox furs, beaver pelts, and Indian tacos. The mix of heat and September dust in the air is oppressive. Smith sits on a temporary stage beneath the squared stone walls of the north barracks, wearing blue jeans and a white t-shirt. He tells a story of creation. The story features the success of a heroic underdog: Turtle. Smith runs his hand over his graying hair, trying to concentrate in the heat, squinting into the bright sunlight. "Creator pulled dirt out of his left eye, and made the earth, but it was dead. His tears covered the earth with water," Smith says. "Then Creator asked, 'Who will go down to bring up dirt from the water world?'" The proud Hawk and Eagle fail. Creator's other companions are too scared to try, but they laugh when Turtle, a humble character sometimes viewed as the ancestor of the Winnebago, volunteers.[53] Turtle gets tossed, screaming, into the depths. When he returns to the surface, long after the others have given up on him, he has mud on his claws. Because of that mud, Creator can stretch out the body of Turtle and make islands big enough for all the creatures living today. Creator charges Turtle with teaching people the right path. Like the rest of the Rendezvous Days audience, I grow restless in the heat, but I am excited by the message of the story. A descendant of Waukon Haga Decorah, the chief orator of Coming Thunder's day, has given breath to a tale that lets me know that the earth is not inert but alive and charged with soul and character.[54]

≈ The resistance that clan leaders on the Upper Iowa voiced against further land deals expressed their deep religious conviction that the world is in the hands of a Great Spirit "whose eye [was] upon them." No point of disagreement more deeply underlines the differences between their people and European-Americans. The Winnebago who made their home on the river believed the earth and its waters to be their spiritual mother, created by the Great Spirit as a source of nourishment to them and to other creatures.[55] To their thinking, claiming the right to sell a piece of their mother earth was repugnant. They were new to the river basin, but found the place attractive. European-American explorers arriving there agreed. In 1835, when the army sent Stephen Kearney on the first cross-country military survey of the Upper Iowa, Kearney penned in his notes: "Country hilly. Plenty of wood & water. Good encampment. This country is romantic and abounds with many picturesque appearances such as high hills & deep Vallies [sic] with here and there a fine cascade caused by the water of the Prairie tumbling into the creeks below."[56] When the government asked Winnebago leaders to sell this land in 1843, Waukon Haga Decorah replied on behalf of his fellow chiefs: "We do not call it ours—for we did not make it nor could we make it so pretty and fair a land. The Great Spirit made it, and we cannot sell it. We have never sold any country, but have given up our homes to our Great Father to make room for his white children."[57] When pushed to reconsider, he repeated this point twice: "We told you that we did not own this land, not any of it, even the smallest willow island in the Mississippi, and that the Great Spirit made it, and gave it to the red man for a residence, but the oldest of them never claimed it, though they lived on it and hunted all over it."[58] For Americans whose forefathers drafted the Constitution, the right to buy and sell land was fundamental to their definition of citizenship, an ancient and sacred right. For the Winnebago, the idea of having the right to sell any piece of land along the Upper Iowa disturbed the familial universe.

Winnebago such as Coming Thunder kept the past alive in their memory, attempted to maintain all their old agreements and promises, made all their major decisions in egalitarian council, and lived on the move across a land to which they denied ownership out of respect for its life and for the life it gave them. As Coming Thunder said at the time of the Winnebago removal from the Neutral Ground in 1848, "The Winnebagoes do not write their words like their white brothers, but they remember them much better, and here, upon their great mother earth, they say they will go, and they will keep their word. The Great Spirit ha[s] heard them say it."[59] Later, in 1855, he told a commissioner: "I am an Indian, a naked Indian. The Great Spirit has made me as I am. My flesh is as it will be, my hair as it will be, my eyes as they will be. . . . We will not [do white man's] work, or wear white man's clothes."[60]

Coming Thunder's dislike of white government did not dissipate. When the tribe was removed from Iowa in July 1848, he was undoubtedly among those who confronted soldiers as they neared the Mississippi. One soldier said they were "all painted and ready for war. They looked as if they had dipped their hands in red paint and then spattered each other all over open handed with their fingers spread apart. Their hair was painted as red as blood and set straight up on top of their heads; and some of them, especially the chiefs, had plumage stuck in their hair, some of it of considerable height."[61] Coming Thunder later called this placing "brush in the road to the new lands" and building "a wall upon the Mississippi to stop the Winnebagoes."[62] Though Coming Thunder and his people would not have chosen on their own to leave Wisconsin and move to the lands along the Upper Iowa, they found the land congenial and were right to fear the consequences of moves that placed them at ever further distance from their home and their traditions. Moving once again in Minnesota, the tribe was then abusively forced to a Dakota Territory reserve where they starved and froze. Coming Thunder led other Winnebago in an attempt to return by river to their homeland. He died on the journey. The departure of Coming Thunder's people from the river basin marked the end of the semi-nomadic lifestyle of hunting and gathering that had been in place there for thousands of years and left the river basin open to a nation of farmers jostling to acquire new land.

The Great Improvement
1849–1869

On the day after Christmas 1853, a small group of Norwegian settlers celebrated a religious service in a log building between Dry Run and the Trout Run basin where, five years before, Henry Rice had traded with the Winnebago. Their Lutheran pastor from Norway was conducting one of the first services in his New World parish. The country was new to all of them. That night the pastor's wife, Elisabeth Koren, wrote in her diary describing the river valley she had first seen that day, "It was very beautiful, though only sparsely settled."[1] Vilhelm Koren had begun to minister to the members of what eventually became dozens of church parishes. For the time being his congregation was defined by three rivers: the Turkey, Paint Creek, and "the Little Iowa." His core parish, where he would remain until he died, had at its heart the Little Iowa, a river the Yankees in Decorah, five miles distant, called the Upper Iowa.

Two months later, the Reverend Koren sat down with the leaders of this parish to organize it. They divided the Little Iowa Congregation into six parts, defined partly by township lines and partly by the flow of two branches of the same stream: Trout Creek and Little Trout Creek. The townships had been established in 1848, when government surveyors came in with axes and shovels, notebooks and chains. They marked the coordinates with slashes of an axe on convenient trees, mounds of earth and stakes where the ground was open, and oak posts and charcoal at section corners. Like a surgical team preparing for an operation, the surveyors plotted out a land surface that would soon be pricked with fence posts and incised with the coulter blades of sod-busting plows. The survey men made a corresponding record in their notebooks for the eventual use of the land office in Dubuque. In their notes they described the land surface they surveyed. For example, in the second week of May 1849, surveyor Joseph Moorehead and six chainmen and markers surveyed the section lines where the Korens would eventually build their church and parsonage.

Their notes describe a rolling landscape of oak woods, savanna, and prairie. Moorehead wrote, "This township very broken. The bluffs are of silicious limestone." He further noted, "The timber is scattering and inferior. The soil is generaly [sic] thin and but little of it 1ˢᵗ rate."[2] Mrs. Koren's diary would eventually describe outings in just such terrain.

The land had been opened for sale in 1851, in sections one-mile square. Some parcels were set aside for the siting and financing of schools, and others were traded for warrants given to soldiers. Other parcels were bought up by moneymen who knew that as neighboring parcels were improved, the price per acre of their undeveloped land would rise. Some of these men moved to the area to become land traders and bankers; in the late 1840s, money in Iowa was often loaned out at 40 percent.[3] Others, never setting foot beyond the Ohio River, acted through agents. Other sections were purchased immediately by men and women who settled and improved their parcel until they could sell for a higher rate and move on, or dug in to make a piece of the river valley their final home. Everyone banked on the land drained by the Upper Iowa to improve his or her fortune.

In the minds of the area's newest settlers, the unchecked free fall of water toward the Mississippi begged to be improved through impoundment. Dams raised water in a pool. Channeled from its new height through a flume, the urgent cascade of impounded water moved a wheel or turbine, powering machinery that cut logs, ground grain, or twisted wool into thread. For centuries, the Upper Iowa had been important as a source of water, as habitat for hunting and gathering, as a point of reference and identity, and for occasional transportation. The river's new importance was as a source for power. No amount of dredging would make the Upper Iowa a river fit for moving grain, lumber, or wool to market. Its improvement would be through its dam power. Eventually, fifteen dams would obstruct the river. Water, falling over those dams, powered the machinery that converted raw commodities into more usable goods. When settlers talked about the "improvement" of water, they were talking about harnessing a stream to drive the engines of capital.

≋ The only dam on the Upper Iowa that still has its engines in place is located in Old Town, a quiet spot with several houses, a public park and campground, and a bridge. The spillway forms a long sparkling wall. The pool behind it ripples with the darkness of its deep waters and the upside-down images of cottonwoods. Below the spillway the water quickly narrows again into a tail of current, winding away toward the Mississippi. The fall of water, drowning out every other sound, lends the place a strange peace. In 1857, however, it was the busiest spot in a distance of many miles. Irish masons joked as they labored to lay stone for M. M. Marsh, a man whose mill would become the district business center.

When I call the museum in early spring 2004 to find out about Lidtke Mill, Anna May Davis answers the phone. Davis is ninety-seven years old. She instructed both my mother and me in music. The descendant of one of the mill owners, she is at the museum to look after some of the exhibits. Davis's ancestors were some of the industrious, principled Welsh who dominated the area around Lime Springs in the first fifty years of settlement. She learned music at an early age in a little community that had hosted Eisteddfods, or Welsh singing contests. Back in my school days in Decorah, she kept a sharp proprietary eye on me and other restless boys who lacked her Welsh zeal for singing instruction. She is still, to me, Miss Davis, and I have not heard her voice in over thirty years. When I pause and stumble she replies, "I know why you're surprised; you thought I was dead. But I'm glad you called. I've been thinking about you. I think one of your ancestors might be buried up around here!" Davis may be nearly one hundred, but she is charged to the brim with questions about my family tree.[4] When I visit the mill, however, April Cheeseman is the guide in the miller's house. April's house tour includes a quick look out the window, built into the kitchen wall, that would allow the miller to sit at his lunch table while keeping an eye on wagon traffic at the mill. "I'm glad you showed up," Cheeseman tells me as we finish. "Anna May told us a few months back to watch out for you."[5]

≈ The nearest improved water for the Norwegians who gathered just after Christmas in 1853 was in Decorah, six miles away. Even with the slow pace of oxen pulling the wagon, on a good day the Norwegians could bring their grain to town and return before evening with flour. Decorah was a Yankee town in the 1850s. Nathan Parker, in his *Iowa as It Is in 1856: A Gazetter for Citizens: and a Handbook for Immigrants* (1855), wrote of it, "The society for the most part is made up of eastern people; and strangers in search of elevated, polite and refined society can find it here."[6] Mrs. Koren, though polite and refined, spoke uncomfortable English. She did not, in her first year, ever go to Decorah, though men ran errands for her there. Towns on the Upper Iowa frontier that flourished were usually on an upland site near a main road or located where waterpower for industry was abundant. Decorah had the double advantage of a location on the overland stage route between Dubuque and St. Paul and a wealth of river and spring power. By the time the Korens arrived, two dams were there. One diverted water from Dunning's Spring to a mill for grinding flour. The other diverted a stream from the river toward the sawmill and the big new stone gristmill near what would become the town center. Within a few short years, dams were built up and down the tributaries of the river.

The earliest of my ancestors to settle along the Upper Iowa were a group of German Americans who moved west from Pennsylvania. My great-great-great grandfather, Conrad Brandt, bought land along the Canoe Creek in 1852 to farm and to erect a mill. He bought nearly a full section of land and put a few dozen acres into cultivation. On the creek he built a mill with his sons Eli and Joseph. From the rest of his land he harvested timber to saw in the mill. Perhaps while harvesting timber on a piece of that land, another great-great-great grandfather, Jeremiah Hochstetler, the father of Conrad's young second wife, was killed in 1864 by a falling tree.

Decorah became a funnel for a frontier that was expanding north and west. In March 1854, three months after her own arrival, Elisabeth Koren met an immigrant wagon on the road, heading northwest as the spring began to arrive: "I met a prairie schooner," she observed, "from which projected here a face, there the leg of a chair or some other article of household furniture. It was drawn by three or four pairs of oxen and led by a large, tall Yankee, who marched ahead with his gun on his arm."[7] The restlessness of the American population was horrifying to Koren, who missed the settled culture of her Norwegian life. "I think the whole population of Wisconsin must be moving west," she commented when she heard of a traveler passing three hundred parties of Norwegians in transit from that state. "There is no land for them here," she guessed, so they moved to the north and west, "where they can easily pick up large tracts at lower prices."[8] A land office opened in Decorah, however, on Christmas Day 1855. The waiting crowd was so elated they drank themselves silly. To save their intoxicated selves from their own stupor and potential violence, they consigned five hundred thousand dollars to a grocery box, watched over until morning by a banker, Leonard Standring, newly emigrated from New York state.[9] The land office did such brisk business that fist fights broke out in the waiting line, and people waited through the night for the next day's opening, even when the temperature was thirty-five degrees below zero.[10] When William Beard, who farmed in the uplands of Trout River, came into town on January 5, 1855, he noted the effect of the new land office in his diary: "Go to Decorah with load of corn, worth 50 cents per bushel," adding, "Town is full of strangers looking for land."[11]

Even past the end of the Civil War, immigrants continued to arrive, not just singly but in groups. As farmers were seeding their fields in 1866, the local paper reported "scarcely a day passes but from half-dozen to fifteen to twenty of the white covered wagons of immigrants appear in our streets; some stopping hereabouts and some pushing further to the northwest."[12] William Beard, a Yankee farmer with a more mercantile outlook on life than Mrs. Koren, moved west with capital he hoped to improve. He began hiring Norwegian laborers as soon as he arrived in 1852. "Can get anything done for money," he boasted in a letter to his in-laws, "lots of Norwegians here who are great fellows for work."[13] The census of 1860 showed a Norwegian girl, Hannah Jacobson, to be living with the family, helping Mrs. Beard take care of the house and six children.

Water figured heavily in the value of land settled by people like the Beards or the Korens. A site needed a spring within walking distance, a creek in the bottomland, or a hand-dug well that could provide a steady supply of water. Beard, when he arrived in 1852, chose a building site "near one the best springs in the country." But failing to get the house done before winter, he had to move into a log cabin three-quarters of a mile from water. He hauled water by the barrel to serve the cabin and his cow. Well-watered bottomlands, in contrast, could provide year-round grazing for cattle. The Korens, in their first year in America, were guests on farmsteads that strung out within convenient distance of a little tributary of Trout Run. The Day family, in what became Decorah, chose a protected depression fed by a hillside spring within sight of the river, a site earlier used by Big Canoe's band, as graves on the hillside above them showed. When the Korens picked an upland spot for their parsonage, it required not only digging but also blasting by the men of the congregation to complete the well they needed for their home.

Though there were benefits in locating at the edge of a stream, there were also threats. Eli Brandt, one of the family who built the mill on the Canoe Creek, built his log cabin on the Upper Iowa very near the mouth of the Canoe. In a bad flood, high water caught the family unaware and Eli, my great-great-grandfather, had to carry his children on his shoulders through the floodwaters to higher ground. The river flooded extensively again in 1859, and floods washed out bridges in Decorah in 1865 and 1866. The March flood of 1865 broke up the winter ice, carrying it through town. The newspaper reported that it swept out the West Decorah Bridge "as though it had been so much cob-web." The editor noted that the Dry Run, which ran through the middle of town, had become "a perfect sea of water" and washed away the wagon, team, and two passengers of a rig that attempted to cross it in one of its narrower spots. "We are perfectly satisfied," he wrote, "with the power *Dry* Run has to get very *wet.*"[14]

The same grim surprise of high water awaited the earliest settlers of Old Town, who built their cabins on banks of the river where timber and water were both within easy access. A spring flood in 1858 surrounded cabins on both sides of the river, trapping a family on the south side. A man named Collins braved the high waters in a boat to allow the family to escape from a window in their loft.[15] The Lidtke Mill stands on that same side of the river.

≋ I particularly want to see the engines of the mill driven by the power of the river. Gerry Robinson, a retired telephone worker, shows me around the mill after Cheeseman finishes the tour of the house. Standing on the bank of the mill pond beneath a large cottonwood, Robinson points out the gate that opens fifteen feet of water into the box where the current turns the turbines. Pointing back to the building, he says, "The water this spring was clear over where we're standing. It was gushing out just under that window on the mill."[16] Floods still shake the foundation of the mill on the river.

≋ It would be the early 1870s before any settler child born on the Upper Iowa frontier would come of age. Until that time every adult saw the place largely in terms of someplace else: the spot they originally called home. William Beard continually compared Iowa to Indiana. Arriving after the fall prairie fires in 1852, he wrote to his wife's parents, "Sarah Maria thinks there is finer places in the world than this—The prairies are all still burnt over & look rather gloomy."[17] Elisabeth Koren fought her bleak nostalgia for friends and family, the settled community of Norway. The Korens, in Springfield Township of Winneshiek County, lived in the uplands between the sources of Trout Run and Trout River at the transitional point between woodland and prairie. To get from place to place they traveled, in the cold December of 1853, on a road that Mrs. Koren said was little but "stump and stubble": a pathway only partly improved over the original wood and prairie.[18] Trying to get from one farm to another in those first frozen days of December, the Korens got tangled in hazel brush, turned back by dense wood, and daunted by a trackless expanse of prairie. When they went by sleigh to a new farmstead, they had to ask directions at every inhabited crossroad and still got lost. Koren was filled by dread when, a few miles from home, they found themselves surrounded by prairie. "It is not beautiful in the western settlements; here and there the landscape is cheerful enough, but generally there is one great desolate prairie after another without lovely lines. The horizon at times looks so much like a distant, peaceful sea that it would be impossible to believe otherwise if one did not know the land's physical characteristics. We thoroughly enjoyed surrendering ourselves to the illusion for a little while."[19] Having been raised in a coastal city in the rugged country of Norway, only fantasy could relieve Mrs. Koren of her desolation.

When it came time to site their parsonage, the Korens chose an upland spot, near the protective edge of the woods. Mrs. Koren wrote of the property, "It is not hard to find pretty sites. There is one elevation from which one has as lovely a view as I have seen here—across field and meadow, woods and ridges. The house is not to be there, however, but on a slope nearby, closer to the woods. I shall be happy if it is placed there; it will be some distance from the spring, but that always happens if the building site is to be at all attractive."[20] Though it meant hauling water a long way until their well was dug, they chose a site with a prospect. By the time they moved in, they had hired a boy and a girl to fetch and carry their water. On the prime prospect, the highest point between Trout Run and Trout River, their Norwegian congregation would later build their church.

Until cultivation formed a band and patchwork of firebreaks, prairie fires still burned through the open grasslands that Beard's wife and Elisabeth Koren found depressing. Elisabeth Koren describes eight different occasions of watching such fires in the course of her first year in America. There were, however, more than that, for she wrote in March 1854, "Hardly an evening passes that we do not see a prairie fire."[21] Several of the fires were visible for days. On the Ides of March, 1854, she followed the progress of a fire that was mild enough so that she could stroll beside it as it spread through the leaf mould and grass of a forest without affecting the trunks and branches of the trees. She marveled to find herself feeling that a sea of fire, lighting up a spring night, provided "a rarely beautiful scene."[22]

Some of the fires were set deliberately to burn off a field or to create a firebreak. In 1860 Wesley Bailey, the new editor of the *Decorah Iowa Republic*, complained about the carelessness with which local farmers set prairie fires, which often resulted in loss of crops and buildings. The practice was well established already when the Korens came. At the end of March, the Reverend Koren helped their host farmer set fire to an open hay field in preparation for the growing season ahead. In late October, settled on their own place, Mrs. Koren asked a neighbor to burn a firebreak around their house to eliminate the dry, end-of-the-season grass that grew in their yard, and then she worried twelve days later when a fierce fire, fueled by high winds, burned through the neighborhood. But her feelings changed to keen alarm in November, when she ran from window to window of her own house to watch a raging fire that burned haystacks, terrified the deer in the woods, and spread to the forest itself. "It was sad to see the flames lick through the woods and set fire to the trees," she confided to her diary the next day.[23]

Mrs. M. M. Barnes, living down on the river bottom a few miles away, near the mouth of Trout River, did not have the luxury of watching the fire through a window. The men in her settlement went to the hay fields near the river to protect their stacked hay, leaving the women to protect the houses. With damp mops and brooms they fought the flames until, she wrote, "Our dresses nearly burned off, our eyes were full of smoke and cinders, our faces black and our hands torn and bruised." The fire came "crackling and running as if Satan were after it." Mrs. Barnes was undaunted, however, and commented to her friend in a letter describing the conflagration: "This, Em, is a part of western life, but as a whole I like it. Excitement abounds, everyone is alive and doing, no drones in the hive and room for all the ambitious ones."[24]

Other than burning off a small area around crops and buildings, the main way of stopping such fires was to plow. Mrs. Barnes didn't have to worry about the stacked wheat and hay by her stable, because a protective strip had been plowed around them, turning fuel for fire safely underneath the earth. Plowing was so central to the project of improvement that, in the early years, it went on far into the summer. In July of her first year, Elisabeth Koren complained of the shouting at the neighbor's farm as they broke the prairie sod: "It is shameful the way they whip the poor oxen."[25] It took up to twelve oxen to draw the plows that broke prairie.[26] Though perhaps spiced with colorful expressions, the shouting Mrs. Koren complained of would be centered on the basic commands of "haw, gee, and whoa," right, left, and stop. Oxen were slow, but they were also strong and gentle. The heavy wooden plows designed to break sod had a cutting knife or coulter at their front edge. The single iron plowshare behind this was long and sharp. It turned over a row of sod anywhere from sixteen to thirty-two inches in width and half a foot in depth. The grasses, the broadleaf plants, the hazel brush, sumac, and softwood seedlings were trampled by oxen, broken at the root, and turned upside down into darkness as the man or boy walked behind on the earth exposed to sunlight and cultivation for the first time.

The chief crop for the new settlers was wheat. After plowing, wheat could be cast by hand into newly turned sod and raked with a harrow, a wooden frame studded with iron points. Until the mid-1860s, the wheat was harvested by hand. Mills custom ground the wheat for farmers or bought the wheat, milled it, and then marketed the flour. The mill at Dunning's Spring advertised in 1859, "Wheat wanted, for which CASH (the highest market price) can always be obtained at the Spring Mills."[27] Though oats produced a smaller yield, the price and the local market were good, since horses did best on them. In his last year of farming in Indiana, William Beard noted in his diary that he had "sowed 11 acres of oats, sowed on corn stubble plowed 5 1/2 inches deep, harrowed twice and rolled." By 1854, his second summer of farming in Iowa, Beard had planted twenty-five acres of oats.[28] Oat straw that wasn't strewn back on fields or burned was set aside as bedding for animal stalls and as stuffing for mattresses.

≈ The current mill at Old Town was rebuilt after a fire in 1894. From the scale that weighed the farm wagons as they came with their load to the area at the back where sacks of flour were sewed shut, the workings are still in place. Though the original mill was designed to grind wheat, this newer mill processed oats, corn, and buckwheat. As we pass through the inside of the mill, Robinson has me peer into a dark opening to see rollers that were used to press oats into oatmeal. On the downriver side of the building sits a blower. "That's where they would throw the corn cobs," he explains. "And when the stack almost reached the ceiling, they'd turn on the blower, and the cobs would fly out the window and into the river, where they would be washed away."

≈ Called "Indian corn" by settlers from the East, corn continued to be raised by white settlers, just as it had been raised by Indians here for over a thousand years. Though the field was plowed for corn, the seeds were usually planted in hills and hoed into place, also a continuity with Indian practice. In his first two years of planting in Iowa, William Beard's corn sprouted poorly. He blamed this on the harsh winter ruining his seed. Replanting the first year on May 29 and the second on June 15, he was surprised to find out that his June corn ripened well. "Done as well as any I had, it got ripe and sound," he recorded in his account of the year. He was perhaps learning that he was planting in too much haste. Farmers who had learned their business elsewhere adjusted, slowly but of necessity, to the harsher climate. Fifteen of the forty corn acres Beard planted the second season went directly into newly broken sod and, he reported, "done vary well."[29] Corn went to the mill to be ground into corn meal. Wesley Bailey, at the *Decorah Iowa Republic*, wrote in 1864, for example, that the new Trout Run mill would soon be turning out corn meal "good enough for an editor."[30] If the market looked better for hogs and beef, corn was fed by the ear to stock. Landowners who favored a more leisurely approach sometimes simply turned their animals loose in the field.

Farmers raised potatoes for market and home use and depended on other kitchen crops. Founding settler William Painter harvested melons growing on the future site of Decorah from seeds introduced by the Winnebago.[31] Early experiments showed that low winter temperatures and the late and early frosts would make it difficult to introduce fruits. Testing what could grow in the new climate took patience and perseverance. Wesley Bailey, the transplanted New Yorker who edited the *Republic*, reported that an August frost in 1863 killed his grapes and "took the conceit out of us."[32] He was happy to discover in 1864 some concord grapes that had survived in Freeport, just down the river. Joel Dayton, a businessman who began in Waukon but then expanded and later moved to Decorah, made his living on nursery stock, advertising for sale in 1860, "Apple trees—grafted, seedlings, and Siberian Crab—Cherry trees, currant and gooseberry bushes, lilacs, mammoth pie plants, and grape roots." He concluded his ad with a statement meant to assure customers of the local winter hardiness of his stock: "My Trees were all raised in Allamakee County, Iowa."[33]

Other important staples grew wild. In her diary, Elisabeth Koren expresses no deeper passion than her near ecstasy with the first wild strawberries of spring. On one excursion in mid-June, she wrote, "I . . . found so many berries that my tongue became quite raw; at any rate it smarted very much."[34] Although strawberries and black-cap raspberries grew wild throughout the region, in some places they had also been cultivated, like Mr. Painter's melons, by previous residents. On the lower river, in Allamakee County, Porter Bellows settled in 1851 to farm and to build a mill on French Creek. At the time of his arrival, the pole and sapling frameworks of a number of round, dome-shaped Winnebago dwellings were still standing on a terrace above the Upper Iowa. Just across and up the river was a place early settlers called the "Indian Thicket," where wild grapes, wild plums, gooseberry bushes, and crab apple trees grew in dense profusion. Settlers considered this to be one of the orchards of Coming Thunder's tribe.[35]

Getting farm produce to the Mississippi was a challenge. During the sugar shortage in the North caused by the Civil War, James Bucknell, in

Decorah, invented an evaporator that allowed him to convert the sorghum cane raised by local farmers into molasses and sugar. Partly because it was a condensed commodity, sorghum, the northern "sugar cane," was three times more profitable than wheat.[36]

Trees figured heavily in people's decisions about where to settle. Most, like Mrs. Koren, preferred some closeness to timber, fearing the open prairie. The people who came to settle on the Upper Iowa tended to use the word "openings" to describe much of the woodland they found: openings of oak sometimes mixed with hickory. J. C. Fredenburgh, for example, described Canoe Township at the time of settlement: "With the exception of along the streams, timber was scattering, with openings here and there. They called them white oak openings. In these openings the blue grass grew to the height of many feet."[37] Fredenburgh is describing what, today, would be called oak savanna: scattered hardwoods that survived the regular torrents of fire, surrounded by prairie vegetation that grew head high. From Elisabeth Koren's point of view, trees were essential for beauty in the landscape. She was angered at how quickly the Norwegian farmers around her cut down trees. She and her husband lectured their neighbor, Ingebret Sørland, about cutting his "pretty trees." He continued to cut, however, and blamed his wife: "She wants to see the fields." Mrs. Koren, still far from adjusted to farmers, didn't buy this excuse, commenting, "really it is just on account of those wretched cattle, which always must come first."[38] Trees had come down, of course, to build each of the houses in which Mrs. Koren stayed. Trees furnished fuel for her heating and cooking. Trees made the posts and rails for the fences that kept the cattle out of the corn and the pigs away from the house. A few miles away from her, William Beard hired a man full-time to cut fence rails during his first year on Trout River. The man charged him seventy-five cents for every hundred rails he cut and split and took care of his own room and board. These fences, called "rattlesnake fence," zigzagged across the pioneer landscape, the ten-foot rails stacked without posts, stabilized by their z-shape pattern. These fences made prodigal use of wood, but the labor cost little, and farmers were often happy to clear woodlands to open new fields and pasture.

Most of the log cabins that housed early settlers were made from oak, not because working oak was easy or desirable, but because oak was plentiful. In advertising the area to settlers back east, Aaron Street wrote: "In some portions of the county, we have what are here called oak openings; in which is some of our handsomest and best farming land. The oak, of different species, is the prevailing timber here, though we have many other varieties."[39] William Beard built his first house from sawed lumber. The wood cost, he reported, between ten dollars and eighteen dollars per thousand feet, and for the inside woodwork and cabinetry, "I have to go to lansing for some pine lumber."[40] Pine, imported from the evergreen forests further north by floating down the Mississippi, being sawed on the river, and being hauled by wagon to the new settlements, continued to fetch a premium price. In 1860, for example, pine flooring fetched twenty dollars per thousand feet in Decorah, while flooring made from local oak was twelve dollars.

The first brick maker in Decorah didn't arrive until 1858; in the meantime, the demand for sawed lumber remained high. In the first sawmill in Decorah, on the diverted millstream William Painter shared with Philip Morse, just one of the blades cut three thousand feet of lumber a day.[41] In July 1862 the local paper reported that Greer and Marsh, in their building just above the south bank of the river in Decorah, had a steam planer "doing the work of fifty men . . . every piece of board passing through . . . need[s] no touch of the plane or joiner afterwards."[42] The engines for converting trees into lumber had to be fully in place before settlement could begin in earnest.

The forested landscape began to change. As the threat of prairie fires gradually diminished, trees grew where they had not before. Joel Dayton, setting up his nursery showplace just a mile north of Decorah on the road to Locust, planted long avenues of soft maples, brought in from Allamakee County. He promoted these as just the thing for quickly getting wood, shade, and wind protection out on the open prairie. Some of the roughest forest land was subdivided into five-, ten-, and twenty-acre woodlots where the trees were harvested sustainably for fuel and other needs. Because of the difficulty of importing coal by wagon, wood remained the fuel of choice for heating, cooking, and steam generation. In other places the trees disappeared acre by acre, both for the value of the timber and for the sake of increasing the amount of land under cultivation or in pasture. When the town of Decorah's first resident minister, Ephraim Adams, gave a Thanksgiving sermon in 1867 to take stock of how far the town had come in eighteen years of settlement, he invoked the "bluffs, now becoming so bare, then covered with their forest."[43]

The early farmers plowed with little sensitivity to the lay of the land. They had so much land at their disposal, so well enriched by millennia of green manure, that they abused it. Their up-and-down-hill furrows created perfect channels for transporting soil. In February 1859 a visitor to the Spring Mill, Decorah's first mill dam, wrote, "Just now surface water from remote sink holes, rushes in and makes it turbed."[44] Decorah soon had implement makers who provided residents with the machinery for any kind of landscape rearrangement. The Ammon company in downtown Decorah manufactured "wagons, plows, cultivators, drags, scrapers, etc." for residents trying to convert wild land into farms, drives, and roadways.[45] By 1860 the local paper was promoting the use of subsurface plowing, that is, adding an additional ten inches of depth to better loosen the soil. Looser soil, however, was even more apt to erode. A newspaper article in 1865 reported that crowds gathered to see a new machine, recently purchased by Judge Williams, "that does the work of fifty men and several teams using only two men and three spans of horses. Removes, cuts, deposits between sixty and seventy cubic feet of earth per minute."[46] The settlers were equipping themselves for even greater improvements.

Even as settlers dammed the river and the streams that fed it, they drained the water reserves that once covered much of the region. Wetlands posed great challenges to settlers, especially the poorly drained prairie areas to the west. The state of Iowa passed laws in December 1852 and January 1853 for eliminating swamps and wetlands. One of the county officers elected in 1853 was the Drainage Commissioner, an office won by J. F. Moore in Winneshiek County. The state felt obliged to see wetlands eradicated in the name of efficient transportation and better farming. W. J. McGee, who surveyed the land surface of northeastern Iowa later in the century, looked back somewhat nostalgically on the surface conditions that existed on the prairie in the 1850s:

> The slough is a characteristic feature of the region; it stands midway between the swamp and the upland prairie; in pioneer days, when the prairie surface was heavily grassed, these tracts were thousands of square miles in extent, particularly in the springtime, and were impassable to vehicles for most of the summer; muskrats and crayfish inhabited them, and they were dotted with the houses of the former and perforated by the chimneys of the latter; but with the incursion of settlers some of the sloughs dried up spontaneously, others were drained, and now nearly all have been invaded by the plow, or at least converted into pasture lands.[47]

Many noted a drying up of the entire countryside as settlement progressed. Springs disappeared or became more intermittent. The river itself changed. George Bellows, who came with his family in 1851, remembered in old age that the level of the entire river had gone down, running less full than it had when his family operated a ferry near French Creek because there were so few areas suitable for fording the river in those days.[48]

≋ For boggy sections of prairie or for late planting or replanting, buckwheat was an ideal crop. A flowering herb that produced a rich harvest of tiny seeds, buckwheat was easy to plant and held its own on any kind of ground. Buckwheat flour made the mill at Old Town famous. Empty bags hang on the wall near the display of oats. A blue stag's head is pictured on the center of the white flour sack. "The quality was so fine, and so well known that almost all the buckwheat flour ground at Lidtke Mill went out East or to Europe," Robinson explains. "And of course, buckwheat flour is bitter, so it has to be mixed with sugar. The miller's wife came over and got flour from each new batch, and cooked it into pancakes to serve the men at the mill for lunch. Those men wanted to be darn sure they had the mixture right, because they were the first people who were going to be eating it."

≋ Life on a frontier left the early settlers feeling exposed. In their first winter cabin, William Beard's family on Trout River hung horse blankets on the wall that faced into the wind. "In the morning," he reported one day, "we found pretty good sleighing upstairs."[49] During his first February in Iowa, in 1853, Beard froze his face on a trip to Dubuque and lost two hired men in succession because they froze their toes. Settlers had come to the Upper Iowa at the tail end of the Little Ice Age and the winter of 1856–1857 gave them a taste of what an arctic air mass could do in the middle of a big continent. Beard kept a diary that included the following entries:

> Jan. 24th, 1857—Thermometer frozen up again; out of wood; snow 4 to 6 feet deep; can't get a horse out to the state road; dug some logs out of drifts near house for wood.
> Feb. 5th.—Road in places banked up 7 or 8 feet high.
> Feb. 6th.—Snow 6 inches on top of crust.
> Feb. 10th.—Shut in; cannot get out to state road; burn fence posts.[50]

The "crust" Beard noted in his diary was formed by freezing mist and rain on top of two to three feet of snow. As a result, horses, oxen, deer, and elk broke through and floundered belly deep in snow, while people wearing snowshoes could walk over it. Many of the deer, all along the river, and elk in the western reaches, were easily killed by settlers in that hard winter when they wandered or were chased into ravines where they were trapped.[51]

Once summer came, cabin rooms crowded with people and a cooking stove became stifling in the heat. "This is really a disgusting climate," Elisabeth Koren complained to her diary after getting a sunburn on the first day of July.[52] People moved their stoves to a makeshift cooking camp outdoors to find a slight relief. Though most settlers seemed to believe the place had a healthy climate, they had to stiffen themselves to its extremes.

Because settlers had come from elsewhere, they were partly deaf and partly blind to their new environment. Settlers who had spent several springs and summers along the Upper Iowa complained of the birds not singing, even though they lived in meadows populated by larks and song sparrows or at woodland edges that were home to wrens, brown thrashers, and catbirds. While on her way from Norway to Decorah, Mrs. Koren was told by a fellow Norwegian that in the older Norwegian settlements in Wisconsin, "there are plenty of birds, but they do not sing as they do at home."[53] The unfamiliar songs of birds in the American Midwest went unrecognized by immigrants, and the depth of mid-continent winters made the summer nesting season slow to arrive. The woman who first shared her home with the Korens complained that the only sound one could expect in the spring was the croaking of frogs.[54] By the end of her first May, Mrs. Koren could write home and say of the birds from experience, "although there are said to be many that sing beautifully ... most of the time we must be content with chirping."[55]

The process of slow awakening to the New World is obvious in Elisabeth Koren's diary. Though she did not know their names, she watched out for birds new to her. Koren started by noticing the birds with the brightest and most obvious coloration. Living as she did on the edge between woodland and prairie, the first to captivate her were the brilliant yellow goldfinches and the bright indigo buntings. "The little bird of indigo blue," she decided, "wins the prize."[56]

The birds most obvious, because of sheer numbers, were the passenger pigeons. Hamlin Garland, who eventually made his name writing novels and memoirs, spent one spring of his childhood standing in newly seeded fields in the uplands above Canoe Creek with a double-barreled shotgun to ward off the "pigeons, in clouds which almost filled the sky."[57] Open country at the time of settlement was also thick with prairie chickens that threatened newly seeded cropland. Elisabeth Koren wrote of walking down a lane, in July 1854, and "flushing prairie chickens at almost every step."[58] Anxious for a bit of fowl in her diet, she chided her neighbor for not having his gun when he reported having seen twenty prairie chickens on his walk to her house.

Besides dam power, the rivers and streams attracted settlers because of fish. Elisabeth Koren, having grown up along an ocean, missed the regular diet of saltwater fish she had known in Norway. However, she cheerfully informed her father in a letter, "There are fish in abundance, mostly pike and other fresh-water fish . . . three to four English miles from here."[59] Aaron Street, who lived at Springwater on the Canoe Creek, wrote an article in the 1855 *Friends Review* to encourage other Quakers to move west and join the little Quaker settlement there. "We have sure evidence of pure water," he told them, "the speckled trout abounding in our small streams."[60] In three days fishing on Bear Creek, five fishers brought home thirty pounds of brook trout apiece.[61] At eight cents per pound, fresh trout were the same price in Decorah in 1860 as preserved cod. George Bent and his friend Silas Brace recalled catching chubs and brook trout in Silver, Canoe, and Pine Creeks, often on hooks fashioned from a pin.[62] In his first month of printing his newspaper in Decorah, Wesley Bailey reported eating a flavorful breakfast of trout caught in Bear Creek, and that pike, "splendid fellows—from three to four feet long,"[63] were being regularly caught in the Upper Iowa. To impress the new editor with the quality of these pike, a local hotel keeper, Ira Protheroe, gave him "a part of a pickerel, the whole fish measuring three feet and five inches and weighing fifteen pounds. It was shot in the river near by, and was a fine specimen of the finny tribe."[64] No pin hook would hold such a fish; apparently only a shotgun would do.

Some wildlife was killed not for food, but out of fear. The fiercest defensive attitude was directed against the larger predators: prairie wolves (coyotes), timber (gray) wolves, bear, bobcat, and cougars. In 1865 the Winneshiek County board of supervisors set bounties: five dollars for a wolf, three dollars for a wildcat.[65] In a time when a dollar was, for many, a full day's wages, such bounties show how seriously settlers sought to clean out predators. In just the first half of 1871, for example, Allamakee County paid out a bounty fee on forty-seven wolves, thirty-seven wildcats, and forty foxes.[66] Smaller nuisance animals, too, found their bounty. Pocket gophers, long the residents of the tallgrass prairie, created mounds that disrupted fields and holes that threatened to break the legs of cattle and horses. Their 1865 bounty was twenty-five cents.

Less common, but equally untolerated, were bears. Whenever a bear happened to lumber its way into the northern edges of the new settlement, it was quickly hunted down. George Bent remembered two being killed around Burr Oak in his childhood.[67] In Canton Township of Fillmore

County, Minnesota, a bear was tracked to a sinkhole cave where it had begun to hibernate in the fall of 1856. A group of men tried smoking it out and prodding it awake before one of the party finally shot it twice and then distributed bear steaks to his friends.[68]

From the settlers' point of view, a chief improvement in the river basin was replacing its wild animals with domesticated ones. On the way back home from the church service at the old Rice trading post building, Mrs. Koren's party stopped at a Norwegian farmstead where to enter the cabin, she reported, "One has to cross an area something like a dunghill, where horses, oxen, cattle, swine, hens, and all kinds of four-legged and two-legged creatures wander about amiably together."[69] Though crops were the early mainstay of farmers, stock supplemented them as a cash resource. In 1860 the local paper in Decorah criticized wheat farmers who were "'one idea' men and devote all of their resources to a single purpose." The editor encouraged them to also raise sheep for meat and wool.[70] Eventually, Decorah would have two spinning mills to process wool. The first was opened by an Englishman in downtown Decorah in 1865, just at the tail end of the booming market, created by the Civil War, for wool cloth. The other opened later on Trout Run.

More common than sheep were hogs. The earliest settlers depended heavily on their pigs. Mrs. Koren, who came across country by wagon from Lake Michigan, was already tired of the frontier diet of pork before she arrived in Decorah. A later Decorah settler from England, H. H. Horn, concurred. However well cooked it was, pork "eaten three times a day," was a meal plan "hardly to be recommended."[71] A pig could be slaughtered in cold weather, its meat salted and preserved in a large wooden barrel. A single sow could deliver a litter of ten or twelve piglets. At market weight, these could be slaughtered in winter and hauled as frozen carcasses by sleigh to McGregor on the river. Thriving on corn, hogs were much in evidence on the Upper Iowa frontier. Elisabeth Koren, accustomed to a carriage in Norway, rode with her farmer hosts in an ox-drawn wagon, accompanied on one February trip by "three of Ingebret's pigs galloping after us like a pack of hounds."[72] Chickens brought even quicker dividends than hogs. Elisabeth Koren, who knew nothing of raising livestock, had, by her second year in America, begun to tend a growing flock of chickens. For the Korens, eggs and an occasional rooster, steamed in the pot, provided the most dependable relief from the monotony of "this land of pork."[73]

Cattle on the earliest frontier were important as draft animals, as well as for milk and beef and for breeding ever-expanding herds. When William

Beard arrived, he bought the cow that would be the start of his Iowa herd: a three-year-old heifer about ready to calf that cost him seventeen dollars.[74] The cattle on the frontier were small, all-purpose animals of no particular breed distinction; the settlers called them "scrubs." Moving cattle to and from market meant driving them. For example, having assembled a herd of one hundred fat cattle, the Day family drove them to McGregor in early February 1865. Their plan was to walk the animals across the Mississippi on the ice and sell them at the railhead on the other side of the river in a market where commodities had been made scarce by the war. The ice on the McGregor bank was weak, and forty broke through. Luckily for the Days, only two of the animals drowned. "This will take off a trifle of the profits on the drove," Bailey commented in the Decorah newspaper, "but then the Days can stand it."[75]

The most valuable animals were horses, worth from two to six times the value of cattle. Horses pulled the seven different stagecoaches that left Decorah to connect with McGregor, Lansing, Dubuque, St. Paul, and points west. They pulled buggies, sleighs, wagons, and carts. They carried riders. As farm machinery became more labor saving, they provided the fast pulling power needed for efficient operation. The Reverend Koren, who needed to attend to far-flung gatherings of Lutherans, bought a horse to get him there. Because of their cost and importance, horses inspired settlers to band together in neighborhood patrols to stop horse thievery. A tributary of the Upper Iowa, Staff Creek, helped cover the tracks of one of the more notable horse thieves of the late 1850s. Oren Goff stole horses in Winneshiek and Howard counties. After stealing the animals, he drove them up the creek so they would leave no tracks and hid them in a cave. In early May 1860, a party of vigilantes surprised Goff while he was sleeping, tied him up, hauled him to a hilltop near New Oregon, stripped him to the waist, whipped him, and strung him up from a bur oak, with the threat that they would hang him unless he confessed. Wesley Bailey, newly arrived on the frontier from the settled East, wrote an editorial condemning the rough injustice of "Judge Lynch."[76]

Besides importing the farm animals on which they had long depended, settlers introduced new insects that would "improve" on the native ones. A man named Smith advertised in the Decorah newspaper in February 1863 that he had Italian bees, ready to "sell on reasonable terms with the hives they are in."[77] There were no honeybees in America, and the other imported strain, bees from Germany, proved less winter hardy than the Italian ones: a decided disadvantage in northern Iowa.

≈ In the engine room, Robinson demonstrates what I have been waiting to see: turning a large wheel that opens the gates to the flume. The gears and axles that take up most of the room moan, creak, and start to turn. The engine that once converted the raw materials of the region into marketable products speeds up with a guttural roar. But the belts that carry power to three different floors and two buildings are unhooked. Today, the monster is only awakened for a few minutes at a stretch, a spectacle for idle gawkers like me.

≈ The frontier that the Korens found at the end of 1853, where creeks were the prominent reference points, year by year looked more platted, fenced, and plowed. People grumbled about the parcels of land bought on speculation that still maintained their wild appearance. When Wesley Bailey looked over the countryside on arriving in the spring of 1860, he was pleased to find, on the prairie west of Decorah, a 240-acre farmstead where, he reported, "The grounds around the house are beautifully graded and planted, in order, with trees and shrubbery—looking precisely as though the owner had rural taste, and was in fact fitting up a permanent home for himself and family."[78] Heading out toward William Beard's part of the county, Bailey had mixed feelings. On the one hand he saw "large fenced farms, with neat and commodious dwellings." On the other, he felt that the farmers in that direction had "*too much land.*" The result, in an area where other farmers, like Beard, had each taken up nearly a square mile of land, was too much open space. "We have an idea," Bailey wrote, "that smaller farms are better cultivated, and have less soil running to waste."[79] The abundance of property had allowed the early settlers to buy extravagantly and let much land go unmanaged. But for good and for ill, the face of the landscape was changing.

≈ In its first twenty years, the Upper Iowa frontier made steady improvement in the eyes of its settlers, becoming a new and sometimes better version of the places they had left behind. When William Beard said goodbye to Indiana in 1852, he sold a 135-acre farm for twenty-five dollars per acre. On Trout River he bought 600 acres and had a cow, two pigs, and four horses. By 1870 he had thirty-nine cattle, seventy-five pigs, twenty-three horses, four hundred sheep, two mules, and over seventeen hundred acres. The value of each Iowa acre was still only one-third of the price for which he had sold in Indiana, but his farm home was called the "showplace of Winneshiek County." He had a twelve-room house, two barns, outbuildings (including a blacksmith shop and cabins for his Norwegian workers), an orchard, gardens, and an apiary.[80] The days of sleighing in the loft of his drafty log cabin were over. Pastor and Mrs. Koren improved the landscape with the construction of Norwegian Lutheran institutions such as Washington Prairie Church and the Norwegian Luther College, overlooking the Upper Iowa from a steep hilltop north and west of Decorah. As with Yankee settlers like William Beard, they had come to appreciate the place in its own right, but their life work was mainly bent on transforming the basin of the "Little Iowa" into the kind of place they had left behind.

Steam, Wind, and the Powers of Earth

1870–1918

When the railroad arrived in the Oneota Valley in the 1860s, its effects were revolutionary. Towns were born, died, or moved wholesale. The rail link to either coast converted an isolated frontier to an accessible piece of a nation being newly reconfigured. That high-speed link gave farmers the freedom to reverse two decades of bad agricultural practice by shifting to dairy and livestock, ending the area's original dependence on wheat. Steam, and later electricity, allowed the region in the years between the Civil War and the beginning of the First World War to reach its peak in population, to speed up its use of resources, and to help produce food for the nation. Though exploitation of the area's resources was ratcheted up in these years, fed by the speed and power of steam, people also showed a dawning sense of stewardship.

Farmers, millers, and investors of the 1860s were anxious to get their crops to populous eastern markets cheaply and quickly. Transporting wheat and flour in railroad boxcars that held three hundred bushels of wheat was an improvement over the wagon boxes carrying thirty to forty bushels that bumped over dirt and rock roads to the river. Samuel Wise, who was building a new house on a tributary of Canoe Creek, began his diary for February 1869, the year the railroad would come to Decorah, with "went to Lansing with wheat, got load of lumber 800 feet, snowed in morning." The next day he wrote, "came home from Lansing, very stormy, got home early, did not stop for dinner."[1] The trip to the Mississippi River was dangerous and took two days. Wise made two more Lansing journeys over the next ten days. One of several companies that tried and failed to bring a rail line to the area, the Northern Iowa Railroad Company, claimed in June 1861 that the countryside through which it had planned the railroad's route had "raised in the last year upwards of two million bushels of wheat, and of this probably eight hundred thousand bushels remain in the hands of the farmers."[2] Farmers could not get their produce to market. The

McGregor Western finally reached the Upper Iowa basin, buying what land rights the Northern Iowa had purchased and receiving grants of land to bankroll the rest. Howard County voters ceded their swamplands (originally intended to fund schools) to help McGregor Western pay for the line's construction. The tracks from Postville kept to the upland between the Upper Iowa and Turkey rivers. The point on the railroad closest to Decorah was Conover, a hamlet created by the railroad because of location and named after a company official. William Wallace Cargill, newly turned twenty-one, arrived in Conover in 1865, the year the trains arrived. Cargill built a grain warehouse in Conover with an older investor who could share the cost. When the rail and its station moved west to Lime Springs, Cargill moved his operation there and became partner in a second business in which he could buy and sell commodities: a lumberyard.[3] Cargill, Incorporated, today the nation's largest private corporation, got its start in these raw towns where the railroad was first connecting the commodity-rich agricultural frontier to markets and industry in the rest of the nation.

≈≈≈ The Granger Farmers Co-op Creamery is the last creamery in the state of Minnesota to accept milk in cans. The members who deliver their milk in cans are Old Order Amish, restricted by their religious faith from using electricity. The twenty-first-century farms that produce this milk are not unlike the farms of the 1880s. People and horses do the main work. These Amish farms are also not unlike late-nineteenth-century farms in needing to sell their cash produce to a larger national market requiring a highly mechanized system of transport. The Granger Farmers Co-op milk that begins this journey in cans has been cooled down by spring or well water, the cooling on the farm being supplemented in hot weather by Upper Iowa River ice. I would like to see some of that ice.

≈≈≈ The railroad reoriented the frontier. The Lime Springs where W. W. Cargill opened his doors to the lumber trade was not the same town that had begun thirteen years before by the side of the Upper Iowa River. The route of the railroad, pushing directly toward Austin, Minnesota, missed the river town. The residents moved from the mill site, which then became Old Town, to the rail line—Lime Springs Station, or Glen Roy—rather than be bypassed. Capitola Smith Booth recalled her family's move to the new railroad town: "Father tried to explain that we would see the same stars and moon, the same canopy of blue sky at The Station, but it was hard for us to believe."[4] LeRoy, Minnesota, moved from its mill site on the river as well; the mill remained where it could grind wheat into flour, but other businesses and homes migrated southeast to the rail line. Small villages on the Upper Iowa such as Forreston, Plymouth Rock, and Kendallville failed to grow when the railroad missed them completely. The first two eventually disappeared. Chester, where the railroad bridged the Upper Iowa, shifted south and east. McGregor Western made Chester a station town in repayment for angling north out of Howard County in violation of the contract it had made with the voters who gave it the grant of swamplands. Cresco, in the upland between the Upper Iowa and the Turkey, was created like Conover as a convenient spot for a station. Because of its importance to the railroad, it became Howard County's biggest and most prosperous town and county seat.[5] At the mouth of the Upper Iowa in 1872, the Clinton, Dubuque, and Minnesota Railroad created a new town at its northernmost point in Iowa. The new village was christened, as Conover and Cresco had been, by a company official. He named it New Albin.[6]

This reorientation of residential centers to the railroads was the beginning of a revolutionary shift away from the river edges, which had been the homes of people for thousands of years. The same steam that drove the engines of trains also drove engines of manufacturing. In 1869, between the water-powered Heivly Mill and the water-powered Decorah Woolen Mill, the Ammon, Scott, and Greer factory converted to steam power to run its saws and engines. An 1870 map of Decorah shows a black smoke stack rising between the two water mills. An 1875 survey of Allamakee County, whose main town, Waukon, was located on the high ground between watersheds, showed sixteen water-powered wheels in operation, generating 240 horsepower of energy. Seven steam-powered engines, generating a disproportionately high 156 horsepower, turned the wheels of the county's other factories.[7] Though waterpower figured heavily in the business of the day, the portable power of steam was freeing people from their link to rivers and streams, just as the steam drill increasingly freed them to live on upland sites where they could dig to any depth in the earth to tap into a ready supply of water.

Citizens of Decorah were not about to be left off the railroad map. They raised money to help pay for a trunk line and waited impatiently while the McGregor Western Company changed hands to become part of the Chicago, Milwaukee, and St. Paul Railway Company. The rail arrived in Decorah the same year that the golden spike, linking East Coast and West by rail, was set at Promontory Summit, Utah. When the city gathered in September 1869 to celebrate the pounding of the last spike in the Decorah branch of the railroad, the speaker, E. E. Cooley, connected this event to the one in Utah: "When, on the 10th of May, 1869, the last rail was laid and the last spike driven in the Pacific Road, we all felt a thrill of pride and gladness over what seemed to us a national success. We feel it no less today, aye more intensely as a matter of local advantage. Our own enterprising, beautiful and much loved town, from being just outside the lines of commerce and high civilization, is now brought by telegraph and rail into the most intimate relations with them."[8] Though the rail linked Decorah to St. Paul and Chicago, the first point of "commerce and high civilization" was Conover, a four-year-old railroad town with thirty-two saloons. Sixteen-year-old George Bent, whose father was a pastor in Burr Oak, was among the anxious crowd that rushed from the county fairgrounds to be treated to a ride on the first train trip to Conover. He said, "It was beyond all doubt the greatest train in the world—composed mostly of box cars."[9] The Decorah leg was meant to haul goods more than people. Samuel Wise could now cut his hauling time in half and do more of his business at the nearer town of Decorah. Still working on his house in December 1869, on the 6th he wrote, "To town with wheat and brought lumber back with me."[10] His new link to markets was only half a day each way instead of the old full-day trip each direction to Lansing.

≋ The Granger Farmers Co-op Creamery has been the collection point for local dairy farmers since 1911. Standing in the office, I look at a display from the creamery's history, assembled on a shelf above the office desk. A cardboard box for a pound of the creamery's butter shows a grassy meadow where a stream winds its way. The logo says "Riverside Creamery Butter." Lauren Applen, a gray-haired man who wears a black seed corn cap, plaid shirt, and blue jeans, stands to welcome me. Applen, who now manages the co-op, grew up on the first farm upstream from the creamery. His father belonged to the co-op and farmed 140 acres. Applen was a dairyman and member of the co-op as well. His farm, just upriver from the creamery, was located on the only loop the Upper Iowa takes back into Minnesota after flowing south into Iowa at Chester. Leaning back in his desk chair at the co-op office with his hands folded behind his head, he recalls, "The river flowed right through our dairy pasture. In a flood we had a hard time fetching the cattle home to milk." In the hot days of summer, he says, "I swam in that river morning, noon, and night." From the impoundment of a dam that extended into the water just north of the creamery, Applen's father harvested ice to cool the co-op's Riverside Creamery Butter. Today, Applen says, the pool above Granger is still the favorite site for the co-op's Amish members to harvest the winter ice I hope to see.[11]

〰 Getting the branch line to Decorah was not easy. Besides convincing railroad company officials that a dead-end line would pay for itself, there was geography. Once the line left the more level country of the uplands, it followed Dry Run Creek down into the valley to Decorah. One of the train's first riders said it was a ride of "curves and bridges that would render one breathless to count."[12] Keeping the branch open meant contending with the area's weather extremes. In 1873 snow fell steadily from January 2 through January 4. Then on January 7 a relentless wind blew for thirty-six hours, erasing visibility and stacking snowdrifts twenty feet tall. Drifts stopped the passenger train from St. Paul outside Conover. The train sat stalled on the tracks with the wind howling, snow filling the air around it. Passengers crowded into a single car and kept a hot fire roaring in the stove, fearing that winds would lift the car out of its coupling and tip it over. They periodically shoveled snow that the wind drove through the cracks. It was twenty-four hours before a search party, provided with food, made its way—telegraph pole by telegraph pole—from Ridgeway. A freight got stalled outside of Cresco. It took between three hundred and five hundred men to dig the tracks clear, only to have more blizzard weather cover them again. The trench dug to clear the tracks between Conover and Cresco was in some places twenty-feet deep, averaging seven feet of snow.[13] In 1875 rain proved equally bad for a road that followed a creek bed. A flood took a heavy toll on the Decorah branch of the railroad. Sixteen out of the twenty-one bridges on the branch were washed away completely, and three of the five that remained intact were badly damaged.[14]

One of Decorah's inducements for the railroad was the town's huge capacity for waterpower, a power over which the area mills sometimes fought. In August 1879 the county sheriff supervised the lowering of Greer and Hunter Mill's dam on the upstream edge of Decorah's downtown after the Decorah Woolen Mill won a state supreme court case contesting the height of Greer and Hunter's impoundment. The factories in the town center had to learn to share their waterpower.[15] At the same time, the local paper argued that there was room for far more river development. The future of the town as a more extensive manufacturing center was, the editor argued, in "the wealth of water-power lying idle or gliding by the city. No stream in the State possesses such a fall, to the mile, and nowhere upon its entire course are those powers so massed together and so accessible, as in the five miles above, below, and in Decorah."[16]

Though people worked hard to bring the railroad to the Upper Iowa Valley, it generated equal parts of anger and goodwill once it arrived. The Chicago, Milwaukee and St. Paul, commonly called the Milwaukee Road, had a rail monopoly on Decorah's trade. This was a time when the attempts of Cornelius Vanderbilt and Jay Gould to build rail monopolies out of eastern cities were national news. The 1870s was the decade of the "Iowa Pool," an anticompetitive arrangement between rail companies operating in central Iowa, southeastern Iowa, and along the Mississippi.[17] Dudley Adams, an orchard man from Allamakee County, was national master of the Grange movement in 1873, when the Iowa branch of that populist farm organization directed much of its energy into government regulation of the rail network. Partly in response to the Grange, Iowa passed a railroad act in 1874 that sought to enforce equilibrium in the rates charged in competitive and noncompetitive rail markets.[18] Dudley Adams knew the importance of transportation to farmers. He was acting chairperson of the Waukon and Mississippi Railroad when that route was completed to Waukon in October 1877, totally financed by stockholders in Waukon and taxes in the two townships between Waukon and the Upper Iowa: Union Prairie and Makee. Waukon's railroad was wholly owned by the people of the county, unlike the one that reached Decorah.

In this environment, Decorah sought a second rail line. In 1869 a tax was voted in to support the extension of the Waukon and Mississippi railway from the east to Decorah, with the argument that the cost of eighteen cents per bushel then being charged to haul wheat would fall to twelve if competition were allowed its way. When the citizens of Frankville, through which the line would have run, refused to support the tax, the Baileys (Wesley Bailey had turned management of the paper over to his two sons in 1869) sawed away at them in their *Decorah Iowa Republican*: "These fellows remind one of the definition given of 'old fogies' and 'conservatives'—persons who hold on to the coat-tails of progress and cry 'Whoa!'" They pointed out that land values in Frankville Township had only risen half as fast as values in neighboring Military Township, where the train ran through the town of Ossian.[19] In response, the Waukon and Mississippi Railroad chose a more northerly route towards Decorah that followed Coon Creek to the Upper Iowa Valley. Even though some grading was done and bridge piers were built on the Upper Iowa River, the plan stopped when the Chicago, Milwaukee, and St. Paul bought the tracks on the Mississippi into which the Waukon route fed. The Chicago, Milwaukee, and St. Paul saw no need for a second route into a town it already served. Another attempt at getting a competing line to Decorah failed in 1881.

The railroad that successfully ran its line into Decorah from the east was under the directorship of the Burlington, Cedar Rapids, and Northern line and was constructed in agreement with the Rock Island line. When the second line reached Decorah in September 1884, the town declared a festival. Banners unfurled, bells rang, whistles sounded, and the Luther College band played marches and celebratory music. Wesley Bailey, the newspaperman who had supported every railroad scheme attempted for the town in the last twenty-four years, gave the main address to the assembled crowd. "We saw in the experience of other peoples," he explained, "that if one railroad was good, two were even better." He looked forward to "a quicker life, a richer activity, and a brighter position" for Decorah.[20]

As Wesley Bailey knew more than anyone in 1884, agricultural crisis made it essential that the region have ample rail service. By the 1870s the soil was exhausted from year after year of raising the same crop. A reliable cash crop, easily shipped, wheat had always found local, regional, national, and even international markets. During the Civil War, farmers turned to more mechanized forms of planting, cultivating, and harvesting their crops. They relied on more machinery and more horsepower to pull the machines. This required the kind of money that wheat could reliably return to them. In the *Decorah Iowa Republican*'s Thanksgiving issue of 1880, the editors used the metaphor of the earth as a bank, a metaphor that would continue to be used in soil conservation for the next 125 years: "No soil ever made, by the deposit of centuries, was rich enough to endure such a draft as has been asked of ours." They explained that "Nature has at last rebelled," because, in the bank of the soil, "vast deposits have been withdrawn year by year, until the balance is almost exhausted."[21] Samuel Wise raised a range of crops at his farm on Canoe Creek, and in his 1869–1870 diary mentions work with corn, oats, barley, hay, buckwheat, potatoes, sorghum, strawberries, pumpkins, and grapes. The only crop he ever mentions taking to town to sell, however, is wheat.

Other farmers were less balanced than Wise. Their endless acres of wheat resulted in soil depletion and a sudden epidemic of chinch bugs. Chinch bugs had their own niche in the prairie grasslands into which settlers pushed with their wagons. They didn't show up in noticeable numbers until plowing eradicated much of their old neighborhood and upset the balance that had kept them in check. The fields of lush green would, on a given day, show traces of crimson at the bases of the plants, a hatching of young bugs that looked like a shiny red dust. The plants would yellow as they were sucked dry and developed dark flecks: the black adult insects. Eventually, the entire field would wither to a whitish brown. In the dry year of 1865 chinch bugs gave a hint of what they could do, but then dissipated. In 1876 they thoroughly sapped the local wheat crop. By then, horror stories about insects had drifted back from settlements in western Iowa, Dakota, and Kansas. A farmer named Topliff, who had moved on to Kansas, wrote back to Decorah in 1875 asking for food and money, saying people around him were dying of hunger: "I spent all my money in improving my claim, not thinking the grasshoppers would destroy everything the first year. Where I should have had 1,000 bushels of corn, I did not have one bushel. There is no work to be had within two hundred miles of us."[22]

Chinch bugs were the Upper Iowa Valley's insect plague. Winter wheat, planted in the fall and harvested in early June, was left untouched. The problem was that in the long winters, with frequent January thaws followed by arctic temperature drops that could last through April, winter wheat often died. It was not a reliable alternative to spring wheat. There was little change for the next four summers. In 1879 the winter wheat harvest ranged from twenty to forty bushels per acre. Spring wheat produced no more than twenty bushels and sometimes went as low as five because of bug damage. Wheat crops also showed occasional signs of blight. Winneshiek County, which had become the fourth-greatest wheat-producing county in the nation, almost completely dropped wheat. R. F. B. Portman, a banker who moved to Decorah from England in the 1870s, wrote, "Winneshiek, the banner wheat county of the state, had to give up her crown."[23]

Careful observers knew that the bug infestation was partly their own doing. They knew that chinch bugs loved wheat and that they had planted field after field of a plant the insect favored. In the case of another infestation, the Colorado potato beetle, farmers knew that one of the crops they planted invited the infestation of an exotic new bug. When E. M. Hancock wrote his history of Allamakee County in 1882, he recalled, "The Colorado potato bug first appeared in this county, we believe, in the season of 1867. It is a native of the Far West."[24] The treatment for these destructive insects was manual removal. Samuel Wise's June 10 diary entry for 1869 said, "hauled one load of posts, killed potato bugs and worked at bee hives." For June 3 of the following year, the entry said, "killed potato bugs and hoed potatoes."[25] Hancock knew there was at least one biological control for these little insects. He noted in his history that "the rose-breasted grosbeak has increased in numbers wonderfully in the last fifteen years, since the advent of the potato-bug, of which it is inordinately fond."[26] Hancock showed a deep knowledge of natural history, and the bug infestations that had done so much damage in the years just prior to the writing of his history led him to conclude, "Species once common are becoming extinct, and others not native here are appearing year by year and taking the place of those that are disappearing." Besides noting the arrival of the potato bug, he recorded the increasing scarcity of, for example, the prairie chicken. He noted that rather than hunt woodpeckers, farmers should encourage their numbers for their control of tree-born insects. Hancock included a diatribe for all who cared to listen: "Not one in twenty of our boys knows what insects are useful to the farmer, nor what birds; and of the latter great numbers are annually slaughtered in wanton sport, which, had their lives been spared, would render valuable aid to the farmer and horticulturalist in ridding him of annoying and destructive insect pests."[27]

Though they did not know the exact biological cause of insect plagues, Hancock and others could clearly see the economic consequences. Flour mills and implement manufacturers, which had made money easily in the boom years, now lost business. For instance, John Ammon had set up a blacksmith's shop in Decorah in 1852. His business grew with the times. In 1879 his company folded with $200,000 in assets, $240,000 in debts (roughly $7 million in 2000 dollars), and no prospect for turning around its losses. Ammon, Scott, and Company's market for wagons, sleds, and farm equipment had been eaten away by grasshoppers further west. Its mill was sold to the previous owner, Henry Heivly, who ran it under new arrangements. Mills in the area began shifting their business from flour for export to flour for the local market, supplemented or completely replaced by the grinding of livestock feed. This shift from growing wheat for a national market to raising stock was indicated in an ad placed by implement dealer Henry Paine in an April 1880 Decorah newspaper: "Horses or other Good Livestock Wanted—in exchange for Cultivators, Mowers, Corn Planters, Reapers, Spring Wagons, Carriages, or other Farm Machinery." Partly because animals could be moved by rail, the market for livestock had become more promising than the grain market. The railroads also sealed the doom of some local manufacturers who would inevitably lose out to larger competitors. R. F. B. Portman, a Decorah banker, reflecting back on the 1870s, wrote, "In those days there were wagon and plow shops in nearly every town, and country cross-road blacksmiths generally made wagons and sleighs. The big organizations stopped all this. Minneapolis knocked the bottom out of the flour mills scattered all around us, the consolidated paper mills and the woolen mills did the same."[28]

≋ In the town that was home to the Riverside Creamery, the dam eventually produced electricity for a community that at its peak included two groceries, two taverns, a dance hall, a harness shop, a school, and a bank. Established on the river in 1857, the town grew north and south. The southern half of the town was in Iowa, the northern half in Minnesota. The Iowa half was Florenceville, the Minnesota half Granger. Into today's diminished Florenceville-Granger, Amish farmers drive teams of horses to pick up bags of feed supplement or large plastic tanks of fertilizer. Children come by buggy to the Amish schoolhouse. A tanker from Rochester hauls milk from the creamery to the cheese-processing factory fifty miles away. Applen has given me instructions about how to contact one of the farmers who brings ice-cooled milk to the creamery. My next visit will be to his farm.

≋ Shifting to livestock, late-nineteenth-century farmers in the Upper Iowa basin replaced cropped wheat fields with pasture. The *Decorah Iowa Republican* described the change under way in 1882: "Visitors . . . look in vain for the numerous wagons which formerly came loaded with wheat, and stood for hours awaiting the action of buyers. The wheat traffic is ended; but the era of condensed freights has come, and farmers when they come bring cattle and hogs, and receive dollars where they got dimes from wheat. Or else the cream and egg money lines their pockets with cash for what they buy."[29] "Condensed freight" was animal produce. Instead of only shipping large volumes of wheat or other grain, farmers could now, with the speed and convenience of the rails, ship animals fed on grain at home; they got higher prices for a smaller volume of produce, reducing shipping costs. One of the new forms of "condensed freight" hauled by rail to a waiting market was butter, and one of the persons who promoted this shift from grain to butter was William Beard, owner of the second-largest farm in Winneshiek County.

The first creamery in the state of Iowa opened in 1872 in Manchester, and its butter took first place in the judging at Philadelphia's Centennial Exposition in 1876.[30] Beard's sons watched the progress of the creamery business and converted their farm dairy operation, with its herd of two hundred cows, into a large, industrialized creamery. The Beard brothers announced this plan in January 1880 and William Beard, semi-retired and living in Decorah, announced his support. Beard attended the state dairy convention in Monticello, where the state's second creamery had opened in 1875; he returned to help convene the organizational meeting of the Winneshiek County Dairy and Stock Association in the spring of 1880. Wesley Bailey was elected secretary, Beard a district representative. In that same month, March 1880, the Beards advertised that the Ice Cave Creamery would commence operations in early April. The creamery would operate thirteen routes throughout the county, collecting cream directly from farmers. Farmers were asked to use a new patent, the Cherry Milk Pan, made by a Decorah firm, where cold spring water could circulate along the outside and through a central tube to cool the milk within. A glass window on the side of the can showed how many inches of the contents had separated, as cream, from the milk. Farmers would be paid, by the inch, for their cream. One inch of cream produced one pound of finished butter.

By the end of a year of operation, the Ice Cave Creamery was producing half a ton of butter each day.[31] By December 1880 the Ice Cave Creamery was operating from a large stone building just down the street from the Milwaukee Road depot. Butter was packed into fifty-pound tubs, loaded into iced boxcars, and shipped to Philadelphia. Buttermilk left over from churning was hauled a half mile to a farm where it was fed to three hundred hogs. By 1882 the Beards had opened two branch creameries: one south in Fort Atkinson on the Turkey River and the other in Hesper. A newspaper story from 1882 reported that Iowa was the number one creamery state in the union and that Ice Cave Creamery was its largest creamery.[32] When the Burlington, Cedar Rapids, and Northern (eventually to become the Rock Island line) came to Decorah in 1884, its track was immediately behind the Ice Cave Creamery building. The creamery's link to its eastern market was better than ever.

Dairying and stock raising were natural for the Driftless Area of the Upper Iowa. The Ice Cave Creamery's name advertised a cool-temperature resource: the cold-temperature cave just across the river from the creamery. With it came cold water, cold winters, and cool spring and fall temperatures. The Cherry Milk Pan, with its central channel for spring water, was designed to use the cool temperatures of spring water to good advantage. The first creamery to compete with Ice Cave was Smout's, which moved into the Klein brewery near the cold waters of Dunning's Spring. A state prohibition of alcohol closed the brewery, and the creamery business was a perfect replacement for premises already set up with cool storage vaults in the hillside and a ready supply of cool spring water. When the Beards built their expansion creamery in Hesper, they located where spring water would naturally enter the upper story of the building and flow by gravity into the cooling tanks and boiler. Eighteen creameries operated in Winneshiek County by 1894; a number located where cold-water springs could naturally feed their works. Where farms lacked springs, they relied on wells, where the water was pumped by wind power. A windmill manufacturing firm, the Decorah Windmill Company, started in town in 1887 to capitalize on this new market. The dairy industry harnessed both new and natural resources, reshaping the local farm economy in ways that promised long-term success. The power of the sun created the produce, the power of earth kept water at a cool temperature year-round, the power of wind pulled that water to the surface, and the firepower of steam moved the produce to market.

Making cream the main cash produce of local farms had two secondary effects in farming: stock breeding and a huge increase in permanent pasture. Good milk production required buying cattle bred for milking, and it required maintaining a program of careful breeding. The first registered cattle breed to make an appearance at county fairs was the Durham, but these were soon replaced by Milking Shorthorns, which produced more milk and found a higher price for breeding stock when farmers chose to sell. Farmers raised calves and hogs on the milk left behind when the cream was sold. The railroad made it easier to ship stock to distant markets. Ice Cave Creamery hogs, for example, were shipped by rail to Chicago. The second side effect, and for the river the more important one, was the increase of pasturage. The staple natural diet of milk cows is grass, supplemented by grain. Corn and hay were raised in rotation on cropland, supplemented with an occasional rotation of oats. Steeper or boggier land could be left permanently in pasture.

William Beard published several letters of advice for farmers in the *Decorah Iowa Republican*. These explained the system he had been developing over the years for his dairy herd: "Sow part of your lands to permanent pasture, thereby save plowing so much," he directed. "Sow timothy, clover, blue grass, in fact, the larger the variety of grasses the better.... As much timothy will grow on an acre with or without the added clover and blue grass."[33] In addition to promoting diversified pasture, he explained another innovation, the silage system where corn is cut green and fed, ears, husk, and stalk all together. Beard wrote in August 1881, "Some green sweet corn fed, stalks and all, will work wonders now . . . until September rains freshen the pasture."[34] When William Beard died in December 1882, his death was front-page news. The Baileys wrote in Beard's obituary that "the practical benefit" that the Ice Cave Creamery had "conferred upon the entire county is not easily estimated." Their tribute closed, "His works do follow him."[35]

Converting plowed wheat fields into permanent pasture meant that far less soil was washed from the hills into the river, with happy consequence for fish. When Decorah was considered as the site for a national fish hatchery in 1893, the Baileys summarized the environmental effect of the new agriculture: "The streams of Northeastern Iowa were all once natural trout streams, and our Trout Runs and Trout Rivers were named because of the fish that abounded when the white man drove the Indian out. When the sod was broken up, the favorable conditions were destroyed. Heavy rains washed the loose earth into them, and (with over-fishing) the result has been disastrous. But, since dairying has become the system of farming, all fields bordering on streams have been in a measure restored to the virgin condition."[36] Even before this time, in the decade when the region was shifting to dairy with its perennial grass crops, the state was attempting to address the steady loss of fish. Other hindrances stood in the way of regaining the "virgin condition" of Iowa streams, however.

In 1874 the Iowa legislature created and funded a fish commission "for furnishing the rivers and lakes with fish and fish spawn." The legislature also enacted a law that required all new dams to have fishways. It banned nets, seines, and traps in the catching of fish.[37] As the Upper Iowa was getting its first load of fish, Wesley Bailey complained about the way dams limited the movement of fish in the river. "It is a notorious fact that a few mill dams, such as that at McNutt's mill, exclude a class of large and valuable fish from the upper part of the river. Fifteen years ago, 10, 15 and even 20 pound fish were frequently captured in the Upper Iowa at Decorah. Today a pound-and-a-half fish is a 'big one,' solely because of these barriers."[38] The law required fish ladders as part of all new dams but allowed older dams to remain without them. Lacking a law to force McNutt to put in a fish ladder, interested Decorah citizens in 1880 paid to have one built at McNutt's Mill, but not before the spring migration of fish was again stopped there, allowing excited fishermen to remove them by the wagon full.[39] Seining and netting continued to go on more than line fishermen liked. In 1884, for example, a net was stretched across the mouth of the Upper Iowa by commercial fishermen, catching all fish that attempted to enter the river.[40] Impatient fishermen, like a field hand in 1909 who sought to supplement his slender income with the sale of fish to a local market, occasionally used the time-tested technique of dynamiting the deeper pools of the river and skimming dead fish by the basketful.[41]

True to the preference for familiar breeds, officials introduced Pacific salmon as their first stocking effort in the Upper Iowa. In the spring of 1875, fifteen thousand were placed in the river. In June the state stocked Atlantic salmon. The hope in stocking these exotics was similar to the plans being followed by Iowa stockbreeders, namely, importing proven breeds "to make the acres of Iowa water as valuable for food purposes as the best tilled acres of our best farms."[42] In subsequent years trout were stocked in the Upper Iowa and its Iowa and Minnesota tributaries. With the lessons of experience behind them, the fish commission eventually brought native fish, seined from sloughs and ponds on the Mississippi, by railroad tank cars for stocking in the upper stretches of the Upper Iowa.

The train also figured into the sporting adventure of the first person to dedicate a book to the Upper Iowa. Sumner Matteson was the son of a Decorah banker and real estate investor. After graduating from the University of Minnesota in 1888, where he had edited the first yearbook, Matteson spent two years as a clerk in his father's bank. Through a Decorah bookseller, Matteson printed the jaunty volume, *Ramblings on the Upper Iowa River: An Interesting Description of One of Nature's Paradises* (1890). Matteson's book recommends "drifting down the sinuous and scenic Iowa to the Mississippi, and returning by rail." He depicts his time in "nature's paradise" as a sporting adventure. "Afloat upon the crystal stream with rod and gun . . . the wild fowl rising to your fire on making sharp turns, and bass and pike rising to your fly as going trolling by." Canoeists today would still recognize the landscape Matteson describes in the book, though they might not describe it in the same language: "shooting the fussy ripple and rapid; gliding into the quiet waters of a long bend, through the deep wild wood—noting the play of the shadows of over-hanging trees, or abreast towering craggy peaks." Though Matteson later followed his bliss by selling bicycles and shooting photos in the American West, in 1890 he found it floating the Upper Iowa while shooting ducks and reeling in fish: "This is sport!—the acme of pleasure!—and that which makes life worth living—they say."[43] Thirty years later, Matteson would die pursuing more distant adventure; his lungs filled with fluid while he climbed Mount Popocatepetl, the highest active volcano in North America.

≋ One of my first ancestors to arrive in the river basin was Jeremiah Hochstetler, a man whose Amish background was unusual on the Iowa frontier. In my search for an icehouse full of Upper Iowa ice, Lauren Applen gives me the name of Jonas Hochstetler, one of the directors of the Granger Farmers Co-op Creamery. Hochstetler is a wiry man with a bushy dark beard and an intelligent twinkle in his light brown eyes. I start my visit with him by figuring out our relationship: a common ancestor who was the victim of an Indian raid in Berks County, Pennsylvania, in 1757. Hochstetler knows the name of each of his Hochstetler forefathers eight generations back, a mental record with which I cannot compete. Hochstetler moved from Wisconsin to the countryside four miles downriver from Granger in 1995. His was the ninth Old Order Amish family in his neighborhood, and he knew only one family here when he settled.

Hochstetler says he will show me how he uses well water and river ice to cool the cans in which he keeps his milk. Starting across the yard toward the prominent red barn, he explains the most important basic point: "We try to stay as simple as we can." As we walk past his white farmhouse with its ample open front porch, Hochstetler explains, somewhat bashfully, that he is not at that point milking cows. "I feel a little funny, because I'm on the creamery board. You see we had a little trouble with udder infections here on the farm, so I got rid of the cows last spring. Since then the price of milk has been so low, it hasn't seemed like a good idea to start up again."

Hochstetler stops to let me glance in the well house at the edge of the driveway to see the stationary Honda gas engine permitted by his church. Hochstetler uses the engine pump to fill the large stainless steel cistern tank he installed in the loft of his barn to provide a steady gravity feed of water to the rest of the farmstead. When the family milked cows, the engine pumped cool well water directly to the milk house. Now, however, the little motor sits quietly in the darkness, giving off a faint but pleasant smell of oil and grease.[44]

≋ My great grandmother, Delia Brandt, the grandchild of Jeremiah Hochstetler, rode the rails to improve her fortune in distant places. Her father died, falling drunk from a wagon, when she was twelve, and her mother remarried to a man who drank up more than he earned. With little prospect of her home life improving, Delia hired out as domestic help while still a girl. She began by helping Samuel and Catherine Wise with their growing family and ended up working in the home of E. E. Cooley, the lawyer who spoke at the public ceremony celebrating the 1869 arrival of the Milwaukee Road. Until she announced her resignation to the Cooleys, Delia felt ill-used and underpaid. The increase they offered her to stay was "$2.00 and a quarter [per week] and get a boy to bring wood and water and clean toilets,"[45] but her mind was set on the frontier.

Delia took the train west, where she homesteaded near Mitchell, in the Dakota Territory, in 1883. In the months when there was no fieldwork she hired out at a hotel, working from 5:00 A.M. to 11 P.M. In a letter back home to her friend, Catie (Mrs. Samuel) Wise, she said of Dakota, "I am sure it is better country for poor people than Iowa is." She did not, however, get rich. In her winter work, at one point, she made only $2.50 per week. She lamented to her friend, "I think it is all too bad that I have to be a woman for if I were a man I think I could do better than some men do."[46] She did the next best thing: took the train back to Iowa, married her childhood neighbor, David Musser, and returned with him to start a family on her Dakota farm. Other people went west as well. Samuel Wise's brother went out to the Dakota Territory at the same time as my great-grandmother. Like many in northeastern Iowa, he sold his land during the time of wheat failure and tried his luck elsewhere, in Artesian, Dakota Territory. In his fifth year there he wrote back to his brother that Dakota was "the Paradise of the World" save for its new political division into two future states, and its prohibition on intoxicating liquors.[47] In 1903 a horse-trading great-uncle of mine, Stephen Baker, took a trip to Dakota with friends by horseback and covered wagon, bringing along thirteen horses as walking capital. The novelty of such travel, by this point in the development of the railroads, provoked comment. "They reminded us of the old times when prairie schooners were an every day occurrence,"[48] the newspaper's neighborhood correspondent reminisced.

≈ Hochstetler shows me his barn. Stepping through the doorway of the lower level, I feel memories sweep over me that have been dormant for over forty years. My grandfather hand-milked his cows in a space with the same smell: animals, hay, and basement damp. Two darker draft horses and two copper-colored buggy horses stand with their heads in their mangers, keeping company with a Shetland pony for Hochstetler's kids. Freshly oiled halters hang on the posts at the end of each stall. A long alleyway stretches before me. The farther end, where the cows are normally milked, looks still and gray. Walking out of the barn, Hochstetler takes me to the fence at the edge of his fields. A grassy lane extends out from the barn to pastures beyond. In one, forty heifers cluster in the heat near a stock watering tank. In the absence of milk, these young female cattle will provide the main farm cash income. When milking, the family keeps around a dozen cows.

Hochstetler leads me back to the milk room, opening the creaky door. The room is clean but still. Along one wall of the room are wooden-lidded, concrete tanks to be filled with well water to keep cans cool. Hochstetler lifts a piece of machinery from its hook: a milk can cover with tubing and a paddle designed to extend down into the can. A stream of fresh water would shoot through the tubing, turning a small turbine in the lid that would move the paddle below to circulate the milk in the can around the tubes of cool water, bringing it from the body temperature of a cow to under fifty degrees in twelve minutes. This modern improvement on the Cherry Milk Pan helps natural forces do the work that on most twenty-first-century farms is done by electrically cooled bulk tanks.

≈ My great-grandparents returned from the Dakotas and bought a farm that made them neighbors to the next phase of development on the Upper Iowa River. On their wooded acreage, Delia and David Musser built their house, planted orchards, and established beehives. In the summer of 1908, workers began constructing a hydroelectric dam that would impound the Upper Iowa above the mouth of Coon Creek at the southern edge of the Musser farm. Workers on the dam stayed at the Musser farm, the nearest to the project, and again Delia brought in extra money by doing someone else's laundry and cooking. The Upper Iowa Power Company had constructed a dam upstream in 1907, at the site of the bridge piers built for the narrow-gauge Waukon and Mississippi Railroad that never completed its route to Decorah from Waukon. One week before that dam produced its first power, the foundations gave way, and the spillway and powerhouse crumpled under upsurging water from the new impoundment.

The young company pledged to rebuild but chose the downstream site, with a high rock bluff on one side and a rock bottom extending out. With turbines salvaged from the earlier plant, the replacement dam began generating electricity in March 1909. The demand for electricity was so great that the Upper Iowa Power Company replaced the original washed-out dam with a better engineered one in 1911. With the older Lower Dam and the newer Upper Dam in place, the power company petitioned for the right of way to extend power lines west along county roads. In 1913 *Popular Electricity* magazine praised the pair of power dams, stating that the Lower Dam, with its twenty-seven-foot impoundment and drop of water, was the second highest dam in Iowa, venturing that "the two plants together form probably the most complete small hydroelectric development in the Central States."[49] Decorah got electric streetlights, and the dams furnished power to the major towns in the Iowa counties through which the Upper Iowa flowed: Lansing, Waukon, Postville, Decorah, and Cresco. Though waterpower was still important, the electricity it generated could be transported over distance, liberating the engines of industry from the water's edge. Power from dams on the Upper Iowa River ran the works of an iron mine near Waukon, a Lansing button factory on the Mississippi River, and the clay works at Postville. With electricity, the source of power could become an abstraction, never intruding into the mind of the person who turned on a switch. The generation of electricity by the impoundment of river water was no abstraction to Delia and David Musser's family, however. On the new lake behind the dam, an excursion boat could be hired from a pair of brothers named Solem. The dam keeper, Julius Peterson, lived just below the Mussers. From their land the Mussers could walk to the powerhouse by a swinging bridge. The dam had no fish ladder and fish congregated above and below it, making it a popular place to drop in a line. Julius Peterson trapped muskrat in the lake. The Mussers' youngest child, David Jr., born after their return to Iowa, was ten when the dam was built. It became an obsession for him. He befriended Peterson and later ran this dam before being transferred to run another.

Nothing got people to pay attention to the river like a flood. A series of floods near the end of the nineteenth century made the people of Decorah uneasy. Uncannily, three of the worst floods in those years took place on June 23: in 1875, 1890, and 1902. Along the misnamed Dry Run in Decorah, eight houses and five barns were carried away or smashed in the 1875 flood. In 1890 the June 23 flood carried a half-ton water tank a half mile downstream and washed out a mile and a half of railroad track between Decorah and Ossian. Trout Run Mill was washed away. The newspaper commented that many of the town's board sidewalks were "rather demoralized from the effect of the water."[50] In each of these floods the worst damage in Decorah was done along Dry Run, the creek that cut diagonally across the town from southwest to northeast. The Dry Run did its worst damage in May 1902, when the creek swelled to five blocks in width along some of its Decorah path. John Garver stepped out to check on his chickens and was swept off his feet and drowned in the water that churned in a corner of his own backyard. A family who lived along the Milwaukee Road tracks, normally two blocks away from Dry Run, was trying to get to a tree in their yard when the mother slipped and dropped her three-year-old. The drowned body of the child washed down the tracks and was found at the depot a block away. The rest of the family got into the tree, save for the father, who survived by lashing himself to its trunk to resist the force of the current. In a flood to rival these, between July 19 and July 24, 1883, Decorah got 9.8 inches of rain, with 3.5 inches on the 21st and close to 4 inches on the 23rd. The normally dry wash due north of Decorah filled with enough water to lift stones—five feet square and eight inches thick—four feet up the ravine and twenty feet forward.[51]

Another flood affected the construction of one of the power dams on June 20, 1908. June 20 was a Saturday, the day people from the country came to town to do business. Among them was my grandfather, Nels Faldet, who eventually married Delia and David Musser's daughter, Grace. Nels had hauled produce to town with his brother's buckboard and team and was picking up supplies for the family's country store at Canoe, Iowa. It was a warm and sunny day. A tent was erected down by the river on the hitching grounds, and a piano had been hauled in for the band at an evening bowery dance. In the middle of the afternoon, people noticed the skies darkening to the north. Nels and other people from the country got their teams and started home. An oppressive heat set in and the sky grew black, as if night was about to set. Nels was hurrying his horses along the River Road, only half way home to Canoe, when it began to hail. He pulled into the barn of Nathan Drake, brother-in-law of Samuel Wise. From beneath the eaves of the barn he watched perhaps the worst storm in the region's history.

Nels was lucky. Another man, John Headington, got his team and surrey home and under the roof of his shed just in time to watch the wind smash the building down on all its contents. The hail, as large as baseballs and averaging the size, the newspaper reported, "of an English walnut," was brutal. The storm cut a path twenty miles wide along the whole Iowa length of the Upper Iowa. Buildings were shattered. In many buildings, balls of hail broke out every north-facing window, and many to the west. Bark was shredded from trees. Crops were leveled. Roofs were carried away. Windmills and telephone poles tipped to the ground. Horses, sheep, hogs, and cattle were killed by hail, crushed in the buildings where they took shelter, or swept away in torrents of water. In some places the hail piled up a yard deep. The river in Decorah rose two feet in fifteen minutes and remained in flood until noon the next day. In light of all this mayhem, one of the smaller casualties of this flood was that the temporary dam built to divert water from the dam construction project was destroyed. The following year, Nels Faldet's brother Bert was in the group of businessmen who petitioned Decorah's government to "protect a large part of the City from danger and damage from floods and high water along the valley of Dry Run."[52]

≈ Having showed me the water-cooled milking process, Hochstetler then shows me how the family uses ice. In a corner next to the cooling tanks sits a chest-type freezer, spray-painted black, its power cord removed. Inside, a block of ice could be set on the raised shelf. Three cooled milk cans could be set into the deeper end of the freezer to stay cool until the milk truck came. When we walk back outside, Hochstetler closes up the door as I blink in the bright sun. Thunder begins to rumble to the southwest. Near ninety degrees, the still heat encases us like skin. "We like the old ways best," Hochstetler explains. "That's why we don't use the electricity, the radio, the television. We don't use the electric bulk tanks either. Instead, at our co-op, we've stressed cleanliness, and to keep the milk just as cold as possible in the summer. That's why we take and put the milk in with ice from the Upper Iowa River now in the warm months." Just twenty-five feet from the milk house stands the ice shed. Hochstetler opens a door insulated with three layers of Styrofoam and steps inside. I follow him into the cool. The inner wall of the icehouse is also insulated and is also sealed by a tightly latched door. Hochstetler turns the latch and pulls the door open, gesturing for me to see what I've come to witness. From the floor to the ceiling, orderly one-foot blocks of ice gleam in the blackness. The blocks near the ceiling, closest to the heat of the roof, are melted into domes. As I lean forward to look into the darkness, cold pours around me in a steamy silent stream.

≈ Floods reminded residents of the Upper Iowa of Theodore Roosevelt's conservation agenda. The extensive flooding of 1902 inspired the editors of the *Decorah Republican* to suggest that better land use might eliminate floods. They pointed out that "settlement and improvement of a country tend to a quick release of excessive rainfall, the universal system of draining, tiling, and ditching incident to the reclamation of all wet lands insuring the rapid movement of the water to the streams and rivers, these augmenting the flood in the seagoing streams with a cumulative effect."[53] The hailstorm and flood of 1908, which washed out the coffer dam at the Lower Dam construction project, inspired local businessman Henry Paine to write an opinion piece the Baileys called "one of the most timely and valuable papers we have given our readers in years." Paine believed that letting steep hillsides and stream courses revert to woodland would lower high water and lessen low water. "What we must have in Iowa," Paine wrote, "is anything that will induce farmers to enlarge their groves. Planting rows of trees alongside every water course, covering our hillsides with trees and in so doing grow their own timber and fire wood." Paine lived on the crest of the river bluff on the upstream edge of Decorah. What he had seen in forty years of watching the waters shrink and flood below him showed in another wise observation: "With our streams surrounded by trees, this soil would be largely retained by the leaves and plants along the stream enriching the trees instead of being carried down to form more new land in the Delta of the Mississippi."[54]

Paine's insightful letter showed the growing realization that woodlands had importance beyond lumber and fuel.[55] Early trains ran on steam generated by burning wood. They also ran on a bed of wood: roughly 2,500 oak ties, or the produce of eight acres of woodland, in every mile of track. As much wood was used again eight years later when the ties needed replacement. The wood to keep the engine hot was just as apt to be local as the water taken in at the Decorah station to maintain a head of steam, or the river ice stored in the Rock Island rail yards to keep butter cool on its way to eastern markets. By the turn of the century, much of the harvesting work was done by steam-powered threshing engines, fed by seasonal help as well as the cooperative labor of a neighborhood's farmers. These engines also ran on wood. Much of the steeply sided land in the river basin was divided into woodlots, harvested sustainably, for such fuel. Other forest land, however, was cleared. Samuel Wise's diary shows how such practices worked in the later half of the nineteenth century. In 1869 and 1870 he was building his house. While he bought the finishing lumber on the river at Lansing, he used trees on his land for the house frame, as for fences and stakes. He burned wood to heat his house. In 1869 Wise spent all or part of fifty-nine days clearing forest, sawing logs, hauling logs and lumber, or working up firewood. For a day of land clearing, his journal read, "hauled stakes and rails and stumps and grubs." My grandmother, the daughter of David and Delia Musser, spent many days in the late 1890s doing similar work: tending to the team of horses that powered the grubbing machine, twisting stumps from cleared forest so the land could be cultivated for farming. The prairie and savanna landscape filled in with trees at the end of the era of fires. Now it was stripped to create cropland. President Roosevelt created the Forest Service in 1905 to help the federal government begin to address this problem across the country.

≋ Hochstetler walks with me back across the grass, which is turning brown in the late July heat, to show me his woodworking shop. Inside the large metal building, stacks of wood stand drying. The dresser of a bedroom set made from local cherrywood stands waiting to have its top attached. When I arrived at his farm earlier I heard the sander, an industrial-sized machine, humming from the depths of the shed. On one side of the building a diesel motor supplies power for the tools, on the other a large exhaust system pushes dust and sawdust into a container for removal. "We use all the wood," Hochstetler explains. "We burn all the scraps either in the stove here or in the house." An order's worth of seven or eight chests made of cherry and lined with aromatic cedar sits on the floor, completed except for the lids and the final finish. "I sell through stores, and through a man in Minneapolis who takes orders from the Internet," Hochstetler says. "I don't necessarily agree with the Internet. If it was used only for good, then it would be good. But it is used for everything. And a lot of that is not good." But Hochstetler depends on this technology. Furniture provides a necessary supplement to his farm income. Like the Granger co-op's milk, Hochstetler's chests are bought by a wide world of people whose daily lives are very different from his own.

≋ By the turn of the twentieth century, the frontier farmscape of sod and log buildings, timber rattlesnake fences, and scrub livestock was replaced by frame and brick houses, immense barns, wire fences, and fine-blooded stock. The atlas published for Winneshiek County in 1905 was partly paid for by ads that promoted such farms. Ads featured engraved illustrations of Short Horns, Angus, and Hereford cattle, Poland China Pigs, and Shropshire sheep with large, square bodies and short, tiny legs. The ads promote bulls named Hero, Baron Scotchman, Manfred, and Perfect I Am.[56] The farmscape that produced these animals was more thickly settled than it had been before or ever has been since. Between 1880 and 1905 the population peaked in the three Iowa counties through which the Upper Iowa flows. At that time, these counties had a combined population of more than fifty-seven thousand people. By 2000 their population had dwindled to under forty-six thousand. The two largest towns in those counties, Decorah and Waukon, were in 1900 one-half their current sizes. They were a smaller part of a countryside more evenly settled with small farms and villages. Farmers who didn't have a family as large as that of Samuel and Catherine Wise often hired for both the housework and the farmwork, as the Wises hired Delia Brandt when their children were still too young to be of much help. Others kept their farms small enough that they could do the work on their own.

Daily life on these farms was only indirectly affected by the train links to distant markets. In 1869 and 1870 Samuel Wise spent sixty-five days threshing for himself, his relatives, and his neighbors in a labor pool where only the difference was settled up with cash at the end of the season. Wise spent part of twenty-eight days tending bees and eleven days fishing. When he made a particularly good haul of fish on June 26, 1870, he spent part of the next day salting them for storage. He raised grapes and berries and pumpkins for Catherine's pies, preserves, canning, and baking. He was also well-known for his home-brewed beer, which he handed out generously to Norwegian neighbors who came by on their traditional rounds of Christmas fooling, dressing up in masquerade to travel by bobsled to farms where they would play tricks on the household, sing songs, and enjoy treats of Christmas baking and alcohol. Like Samuel Wise, Delia and David Musser also raised bees and cultivated orchards and vineyards. Honey, eggs, cream, hogs, and beef cattle could all be sold to make farm payments, buy equipment, and pay for the kerosene, cloth, sugar, coffee, and other goods that could not be produced on the farm. Much of the produce, however, was consumed on the farm: by horses and livestock and by the families and hired help who grew, harvested, and processed it. Though the trains increasingly allowed the import of fossil fuel, mainly in the form of coal, farms like the Wises' still mostly relied on sun, wind, and the powers of earth.

The river provided waterpower, fish, and ice but continued to exact a toll in return. The brother of Samuel Wise drowned in the river near the mill at Forreston in 1867. A dog found a baby floating near the mouth of Trout Run in 1885. The mother, Mary Larson, had been abandoned by Bert Eells, the baby's father, and had gone to throw herself and the baby in the river. Succeeding with the baby, she was unable to drown herself and was arrested. She was twenty-two, and the newspaper reporter who covered the case was moved to sympathize with her, observing, "There is nothing brutal or sensual in her appearance."[57] In May, three years later, the nephew of the sheriff who investigated the death of Mary Larson's daughter was washed off a bridge and into a torrent of water on Bear Creek. The fourteen-year-old boy had rushed to secure the family's cream cans in the milk house as waters rose in the ravine between the barn and the house. The water, knee-high over the bridge, knocked him down, and he swept forward one hundred feet in a sitting position, grabbing a fence when his father shouted for him to do so, but losing his grip and disappearing until the body washed ashore two miles away.[58] A Baptist minister, H. P. Langridge, excited by the broad expanse of water in the lake behind the power dam that had gone into operation in March 1909, became giddy at the thought of being the first person to swim across it. On a Saturday afternoon in late May, he changed into overalls and a thin shirt and, as his family and their party of Waukon friends watched, plunged in. "I can't make it," they heard him cry before his head disappeared beneath the water just over halfway across the lake. The power company drained the lake to recover his body.[59]

≋ After I shake hands with Hochstetler and walk toward my car, a bat zigzags through the sunlight before landing, curling into a tight dark ball in the dust of the driveway. It is late in the afternoon, and thunder rumbles in the distance, but what I most notice is the quiet. The black square buggy with a triangular, slow-moving vehicle sign sits, its shafts resting at a tilt, by the house. The diesel engine in the wood shop is silent. Though I asked for only a little of Hochstetler's time, he has taken a leisurely hour and a half to talk with me about the farm. As I turn my car onto the highway, I notice a sickle mower sitting solitary in the hayfield where it has laid flat a cutting of grass and alfalfa. Though humble by modern standards, Hochstetler's farm and livestock holdings are substantial in comparison with those of my relatives of a hundred years ago. But like the people of that time, his farm relies on the sun for crops, meat, and horsepower and the cooling power of underground water and river ice. Like them, too, he depends on a national market driven by fossil fuel to provide cash for what his labor and his farm produces.

≋ By the turn of the twentieth century, the phone and telegraph were serving Decorah. People like Samuel Wise, who had come to the area as a young man, were now elderly. They held Old Settlers gatherings to commemorate earlier days. World War I forced farmers to think of themselves as producing food for a nation. As during the Civil War, sugar was in short supply and the government encouraged Upper Iowa farmers to increase their sorghum acreage. Meat was viewed not simply as a commodity but as food for the troops, and by 1918 Winneshiek County was the fourth-largest stock-producing county in the state of Iowa. The U.S. Department of Agriculture encouraged farmers to add poultry to their farm's produce in the interest of supplying the nation with eggs and meat. The third generation of children born in the river basin had begun to enter the public schools. The landscape on the walk to and from home was more and more the one most people in the family considered to be their native place. Railroads, telegraph, and telephone connected them to the rest of the planet, but their quiet neighborhood in the Upper Iowa Valley was the place they knew as home.

Aiding the Land

1914 – 1945

Stewart Baker's family moved from Bluffton, in the northwest corner of Winneshiek County, to Madison Township, five miles west of Decorah, early in 1914. Borrowing horse teams and equipment from neighbors, they went by sleigh and bobsled across country, on a cold March first, driving their dozen cattle before them. Progress was slow. They fitted their pace to the cattle's speed and had to break through heavy drifts of snow. Stewart had rented his new farm in Madison Township for a cheap price. The soil of the place was exhausted, but he had a vision that he could rebuild the soil and one day buy the farm.

In the countryside before the automobile, people lived close to the land and the waters that drained it. Though the Bakers' new home was only five miles from Decorah, Stewart's wife Lula rarely left the farm. Stewart took care of business in town. On a wet April day in 1924, Stewart came to a neighbor to borrow the high-wheeled buggy with a top. He wanted to keep Lula dry while he navigated the deep mud on the slow trip to the hospital. The road was dirt. Even on good days, the trip by horse and wagon took an hour and a half. Virginia, the last child of six, was born in the recently finished hospital, the only child not to be born at home.

Eventually, the Bakers got an open-topped yellow 1928 Chevrolet, though for the safety of humanity it might have been better had Stewart stuck to horses. He was not very attentive to obstacles, animals, other vehicles, or the true track of a driveway. He drove fast and hated to waste gasoline by braking. Stewart and his teenaged son Steve took a trip north to LeRoy, Minnesota, where Stewart's father was living at the time. Stewart's father gave Steve an old, long-bored musket that had been lying around unused. On the trip home Steve and two other boys sat in the back seat of the open car. Though Stewart drove fast on the gravel road toward home, a Model T coupe pulled up behind them and passed. Stewart speeded up and did the same. Going faster, the other car passed them again. Stewart accelerated and passed a second time. When the Model T began to emerge from the cloud of dust to pass a third time, Steve decided it had gone far enough. He reached down to the floor, and swung the empty musket back around, leveling its sight at the other driver. The Model T disappeared behind them as Stewart sped on towards home. Speed expanded the world familiar to people, though some of that world would now pass by in a blur.

By the start of the Great Depression, there were twenty-five million cars in America, roughly one for every six people in the country. The gas that fueled Stewart Baker's yellow Chevrolet also fueled a bright bubble of speculation in Decorah when G. E. Fagg, a Texas oil drilling contractor, appeared in autumn 1921. The local paper announced that Fagg would soon "secure leases up and down the Upper Iowa River" for drilling rights to oil and gas. Local investors didn't want to be left out of the potential oil boom, so with Fagg they founded the Decorah Pioneer Oil and Gas Company. "It's all a gamble," Fagg told the community. "We don't want anybody to put in more than he can afford to lose."[1]

But people put in plenty. Backed by fifty thousand dollars of Roaring Twenties capital, raised by selling stocks, Fagg started drilling on the Bakke farm, just east of Decorah, above Trout Run. People started looking for signs of oil. For example, hoping he might walk away Winneshiek County's first tycoon, the miller at Springwater, on Canoe Creek, arrived at the science department of Luther College with a bottle of dark, gassy-smelling liquid that was bubbling up at his spring. In September 1922, with drilling capital running low, the news came out that there were "unmistakable" signs of oil at 2,700 feet in depth at the Bakke well. The *Decorah Journal* speculated that once oil was struck, Decorah would "spread and grow like the green boy tree."[2] Decorah Pioneer Oil and Gas was reorganized, this time with Paul Koren as president. Son of Vilhelm and Elisabeth Koren and pastor of the church his father had established on Trout Run, Koren had just organized the campaign to build Decorah's hospital. Now he helped raise the needed capital and bolster confidence in local oil investors. In April 1923, at a depth of 3,100 feet, Decorah Pioneer Oil and Gas began drilling around the clock, and the *Public Opinion* reported that several of the drillers on the rig had invested five hundred dollars each, the prospects looked so promising. The "black sand" the drillers were bailing out at that depth, however, did not turn into pay dirt. At 3,200 feet in depth, six hundred feet short of the maximum they had set for a test well, the drill bit broke off, and Koren announced in a July meeting to stockholders that Decorah Pioneer would suspend operations.[3] That was the end of the Upper Iowa's oil boom.

≈ Before she went to school, Virginia Baker spent her days at home, with mainly her mother for company. The farm was set at the bottom of a quarter-mile lane. A row of large cottonwoods grew between the farm lane and a creek. Across the creek was a steep gravel hill called the knoll that was fenced to be part of the bottomland pastures. Below the house at the end of the lane was the red barn, the milk house, a granary, a chicken house, a pig house, and a ceramic-block silo Stewart had built. In the absence of other friends, Virginia invented her own, a pair named Poodgie and Podgie. These two accompanied her as she waded in the creek or played with her dolls in the windbreak. One afternoon Lula saw Virginia sigh and drop dramatically into a chair on the porch. "My goodness, Ginny," Lula exclaimed, "how did you get so tired?" "Oh ma," Virginia explained, "I've had such a busy day. Poodgie and Podgie decided to move, and we had to move *everything*! We moved the knoll. We moved the creek. And it has worn me out!"

Streams flow through space and time, but they also flow through peoples' hearts and imaginations. Virginia, who would one day marry and become my mother, grew up with a creek in the meadow below her house as part of her daily company. Gas automobiles and gas tractors would reorient the lives of countryside residents like her. Speed would begin to loosen them from the intimacy with the land that comes from engaging with it at the walking speed of a horse or a pair of shoes. In this same period, however, the government began to take more serious notice of the need for a national system of conservation.

≈ Extreme conditions that faced the Upper Iowa River valley and the rest of the country during my mother's years as a teenager pushed the federal government to a new level of active involvement in the economy, public works, and conservation, aiding the farmer in part by aiding the land. The first extremity of circumstance was the onset of the Great Depression. American stockholders watched their investments shrink by almost 90 percent between late 1929 and the summer of 1932. For people living in the farm country along the Upper Iowa between 1929 and 1932, farm commodities and land prices fell by half. Anyone who owed money on land they had bought at premium prices had a hard time meeting expenses and making payments.

In the glory days of June 1929, the Winneshiek County State Bank announced the creation of "the Weiser-Algyer Investment Corporation to handle the growing investment, bond, and loan operations of the bank."

Like other banks, within the year it had difficulty coming up with cash to pay depositors unnerved by the stock market crash of October. When President Franklin D. Roosevelt declared a bank holiday upon taking office in 1933, the Winneshiek County State Bank closed permanently, as did another Decorah bank, the National Bank. Virginia's older sister, Florence, lost her first nest egg of independent savings when the banks closed. Even those farmers whose debts were low sometimes were unable to pay the taxes, levied mainly by the county, on their land. At a meeting of the Farmer's Union in the courtroom of the Winneshiek County courthouse in March 1932, the lowest depths of the Depression, sixty farmers discussed ways of reducing state and county government to lessen taxes. One proposed eliminating the county assessor's office. Another demanded "confiscation by the government of all fortunes in excess of a million dollars."[4] The secretary of that meeting, J. B. Borlaug, along with another Winneshiek county farmer, were among a delegation who went to Des Moines in August to plan the farm holiday that would withhold products from market in an attempt to drive up prices.

City and county governments reacted to the cries of desperation by creating a system of public work for scrip. In the spring of 1933, Winneshiek County bought twenty acres of wooded land and offered twenty cents per hour to men who would clear the land for firewood that the county could distribute to the needy. Over forty men responded immediately, working nine hours a day. Others worked on improving county roads. In payment they were given scrip dollars, printed by the county. To redeem scrip dollars, parties bought two-cent stamps from the county. With each transaction, the scrip dollar was affixed with a new stamp, signed and dated by the user. Scrip with all fifty stamps affixed was traded for U.S. currency at the courthouse. Scrip got people back to work, financed improvements in county services, and stimulated local business. Only local parties could use it. It stayed in circulation until March 1935. In another effort, the town of Decorah provided free garden plots and free seed to applicants in the summer of 1934 to keep needy families in vegetables.

Farm auctions became a common feature of weekly news. A typical auction bill advertised the spare simplicity of farm livelihoods, as Raymond Young's did, early in 1930: "6 Head horses, 6 Head Cattle, One Sow and Pigs, 25 Ancona Hens, Machinery, Harness, Hay, Etc."[5] As times worsened neighbors banded together in the bidding at sales. Some took part in the farm holiday, keeping their animals and crops back from the market, but these simply helped nonparticipating neighbors to slightly better prices that made participants' losses more extreme. One of President Roosevelt's responses was the federal government's first major intervention in farm production, the Agricultural Adjustment Act (AAA) that paid farmers to limit production, in Iowa, of corn and hogs. The AAA put farmers on an equal footing, able to choose to opt out of the markets and receive a subsidy for doing so. A number of area farmers sold hogs to the government in the summer of 1933. Federal shipments of pork came back to destitute families in October that same year. The government also paid to take one-fifth of the corn acreage out of production as a second way of raising corn and hog prices. Although markets slowly improved, many of the farmers who survived the Depression shrank back closer to the subsistence mode of farming that had characterized the countryside prior to the high prices that had come with the First World War. Stewart Baker, an active Methodist, came up with the idea of using farm produce to help out his church. In the fall of 1937 he started donating dressed roasting chickens for a benefit dinner that eventually served six hundred people each year. "Chickens finished on a feed of buttermilk make the tenderest servings," he claimed.

Another of the extremities challenging government in the 1930s was a dramatic turn in the climate that ruined farmers and farms. On a Sunday in mid-November 1933, the sky darkened at noon in Decorah. A gale wind filled the air with choking dust, driving it through cracks around doors and windows. Not until it began to snow that evening did the dust settle. There were three drought years in the 1930s that daily left a thin film of dust on the furniture. The holocaust that gripped dry-land farms of the Great Plains did not as profoundly affect farms around the Upper Iowa, but the dust in northeastern Iowa was a symptom of what was happening to farmland across America. Crops on the Great Plains shriveled and the dirt that had held them blew away. Some of it blew to eastern Iowa and beyond. This catastrophe made the government aware of how easily the soil that had fueled the country's long and steady increase in wealth could be erased by shortsighted farm policies. In conjunction with the Agricultural Adjustment Act, the federal government began the Soil Conservation Service to promote farming practices that would stop soil from washing off the cropped uplands into the river. At harvest time in 1932, just before Roosevelt was elected, the Winneshiek County farm agent called a meeting on the Lomen farm in the Trout Run watershed just south of Decorah to demonstrate how terracing, contour plowing, planting crops in strips, and rotating crops could help slow soil loss from over one hundred tons per acre to less than ten. An agricultural engineer from Iowa State showed the farmers in attendance how to lay out and construct terraces.

As the Depression worsened, the government further put into practice what Roosevelt called "the gospel of conservation."[6] The 1938 annual report of the Department of Agriculture acknowledged "soil as a basic agricultural resource,"[7] linking it to water. It trumpeted a national initiative to promote "educational work through soil demonstrations in selected watersheds throughout the country"[8] like the one that had been held on the Lomen farm in 1932. Federal soil conservation programs provided education as well as loans. As part of the federal work relief program, a Civilian Conservation Corps (CCC) camp, dedicated to soil conservation projects, was set up in Howard County. In November 1937 the camp moved to Decorah. CCC workers planted new acreages of trees on lands unsuitable for crop farming, dammed gullies, set up contour strips, and aided in terracing cropland. In the spring of 1939, the director of the Decorah camp told area business leaders that farm acres across Winneshiek County were eroded to the point of abandonment at twice the average rate for Iowa. "It would require fifty years or more to bring erosion under control in this country," he observed.[9] But the CCC work made a difference in keeping soil on the land and out of streams. In 1939 the state legislature of Iowa passed the act that organized the creation of soil conservation districts to better enable farmers to work together to protect their land and water with the help of federal programs.[10] Even the AAA had a conservation angle. Land in the Upper Iowa basin taken out of the corn and hog production cycle reverted to hay or meadows, perennial cover crops that would hold the soil in place through extremities of the Iowa and Minnesota climate.

Because stewardship made simple sense to him, Stewart Baker was a farmer who took to conservation without lessons from the extension service. A hard worker, he based his vision for the farm on a belief that if he treated the land well, it would repay his efforts. Stewart noticed that legumes such as alfalfa re-seeded and thrived in the fencerows of his Madison Township farm. The gravelly farm soil was high in the lime that such nitrogen-fixing crops need. He rotated his crops of corn, oats, and sweet clover and was one of the area's first farmers to try in his rotation alfalfa, a deep-rooted hay perennial crop that builds up soil nitrogen. Stewart pastured sweet clover for a year, plowed it under and planted alfalfa, hayed the alfalfa for three years, pastured it for a final year, and then plowed it under to plant corn or oats. He spread manure from his one hundred hogs and fifteen milk cows on his ground at a rate of about twenty acres per year. The result was one-third more corn per acre than when he began on the farm. This allowed him to cut back on corn acreage and increase his hay ground, meaning less soil plowed and less soil lost. Although soybeans became a popular crop, he avoided them because they kept the soil loose and vulnerable to erosion. In time, Stewart planted three hundred evergreens around the farm buildings as a windbreak and shelter for wildlife and started a small orchard on the hillside above the house. The unnamed creek that meandered through the property, eventually to join Twin Springs before entering the Upper Iowa, ran clearer than it had for seventy years. Though Stewart remained a simple man, his 160 acres became what the local paper called "one of the best farming successes in this section of Iowa."[11] His idea that aiding the farm would aid the farmer proved sound as well as satisfying. Five years after he moved to the rented farm, he was able to buy it.

The weather of the 1930s was marked by hot, dry summers. The year of greatest extremes, however, was 1936, which began when my mother was finishing seventh grade. Thirty-three of the thirty-five subzero days in January and February 1936 broke daily records for cold temperature in Decorah. In the span of twenty-four days, beginning on January 19, the high temperature was four degrees, registered on February 3. Otherwise, the weather stayed below zero. On January 24 the thermometer dipped to minus thirty-two. On Saturday, February 8, a blizzard blew in with winds at fifty miles per hour and four new inches of snow. The temperature that day and the next got down to minus seventeen. Trains could not get through for the first time in almost forty years. Roads were blocked. Decorah customers were rationed in their coal. Rural residents ran low on kerosene. When spring came, warm weather and lots of rain produced the earliest and lushest first hay crop anyone could remember. Weather that got up into the nineties in May meant that Virginia and her family put up hay that was ready a month early. But in late June the heat became a problem. For the third summer in the decade, drought set in.

In July and August 1936, the summer before Virginia's last year of country school, fifteen days still hold official record highs, including 111 degrees on July 14, the hottest official temperature ever recorded in Decorah. On that day the temperature range for the year hit 143 degrees, given the minus 32 recorded in January. To lighten the mood of its overheated Depresssion-era readers, the *Decorah Journal* inserted a box in the July 15 paper announcing, "Only 131 shopping days until Christmas!" On many days people unofficially reported temperatures, in the sun, ranging from 115 to 130. Pastures turned brown. Virginia and her siblings drove cattle up their farm lane to let them graze on ditch grass in the shade of the cottonwoods. The government eased its requirements on AAA lands to allow poorly established new grass to qualify for government payments, as well as failed fields replanted in grasses once the rains finally came. Fearing another Dust Bowl, the federal policy in Iowa was to encourage all possible acres to be seeded down in cover crops before winter.

〰 Unfortunately, the new answer to a familiar problem often has unforeseen and unwelcome consequences. Just as farmers were learning to better keep soil from washing away, a new chapter of water pollution began. Farmers had not regularly applied manure to fields to build up nitrogen as well as organic matter in the soil, but as they began to learn more about soil chemistry, fertilizing became more standard. In the 1920s farmers for the first time also applied pulverized lime and acid phosphate to their soil. The lime neutralized the acidity of soil and created the sweetness favored by new legumes, alfalfa and soybeans. Acid phosphate promoted root growth. The Winneshiek County extension agent wrote in the *Decorah Republican* in March 1921 that tests of lime and phosphorus would begin that planting season on farms around Decorah and Ossian.[12] Soil enriched with a general application of manure and phosphate fertilizer and sweetened with an application of lime produced dramatic yield increases. The county agent promoting the use of fertilizer in 1921 said that "on corn land the increase has been as high as 23 bushels per acre." That nearly doubled the amount of corn that was typically harvested in the days before hybridization. The problem was that a richer mix of nitrogen and phosphorus would now reach creeks, ponds, and the Upper Iowa River.

Ironically, the movement to chemical fertilizers was partly motivated by concern about pollution. Because Depression-era conservationists were most worried about soil loss, and because the government began to pay farmers to take cropland out of production, agricultural experts assumed they could boost production on each cropped acre to free up more land to be set aside with permanent ground cover. In the spring of 1937 the Tennessee Valley Authority (TVA) provided "superphosphate" fertilizer for tests on forty acres of Winneshiek County land, funded by provisions of the Agricultural Adjustment Act.[13] The goal was to show that even with fewer plowed acres, more corn could be produced. In 1932, the year before crop set-aside programs went in place, the nation had 113 million acres planted in corn. Corn acreage has not come near that ever since. With the success of these tests, farmers invested more in each acre of land they planted, even as the government paid them not to plant. The change in attitudes toward runoff between the wars was signaled when the county soil conservation officer lamented after a flood in 1945, "Winneshiek County lost hundreds of thousands of dollars worth of soil. It is not only the soil but the thousands and thousands of dollars worth of lime, fertilizer, manure, and labor invested in the top five inches of soil that the plow reaches that is being destroyed and carried down the river."[14] The loss was not just economic. The additives that enriched runoff soil now overfertilized streams.

In addition to promoting soil conservation, Roosevelt's government hired boys and men who lacked employment for public works projects that transformed the countryside. This process was furthered in the Decorah area by the election of a conservation-minded Democrat, Fred Biermann, to Congress in the same election that first put Roosevelt in the White House. Biermann served for six years. The Civilian Conservation Corps established a camp at the Winneshiek County Fairgrounds, housing men and boys in long wooden barracks.

In two of their bigger local projects, CCC workers created fish-rearing stations. In 1932 the Decorah Rod and Gun Club teamed up with the state game warden to bring in a fish expert to survey the prospects for better fishing. The expert, a professor from Michigan named Hubbs, recommended starting fish-rearing stations and stocking more mature trout. The club stocked such trout in Bear Creek and Trout Run in the fall of 1932 to grow over the winter before the fishing season in 1933. In 1933 Hubbs contributed to a twenty-five-year conservation plan for Iowa. This included recommendations that Decorah receive two rearing stations and that trout stream conditions be improved by erosion control, reducing pollution, providing cover and spawning grounds within streams, and planting shade trees along streams to help keep the waters cool. Hubbs understood the danger of soil erosion. "Erosion control is important in this area . . . to lessen the amount of sand and mud being washed into the streams, where it fills up the holes and levels off the bottom, smothering out the natural trout food," he wrote.[15] The report was well-timed. It presented a plan for public works just as the federal government was hiring public workers.

The state purchased Siewers Springs on Trout Run and the county gave Twin Springs to the state, both to be developed by the CCC as fish-rearing stations. The stations were designed by Paul Rice, a landscape architect hired by the CCC. Workers created a series of ponds at both sites, as well as a series of rectangular cement raceways at Twin Springs. The ponds at Siewers Spring were for raising trout and game fish. At Twin Springs a pond was designed for raising brown trout, and raceways were planned for raising rainbow trout. Each landscaping plan included areas of lawn, mature trees, and new drives. Like many of his contemporaries, Rice valued the importance of the natural landscape and native species. Oaks, white pines, ash, and native shrubs were planted. Walks, walls, stairs, and buildings were made out of native limestone, blending into the bluffscape of both sites. The Civilian Conservation Corps crushed rock for these projects as well as for improved gravel roads between the fish stations and other tourist attractions. The *Decorah Public Opinion* reported in September 1934, "We will soon have a dandy highway, well marked by the CC Camp . . . all a stranger has to do is to 'Follow the arrows.'"

By then, those in the Decorah area realized that auto tourism would provide a healthy boost to the local economy. An ad published in newspapers throughout the region in the summer of 1933 featured a map showing paved roads, the river, beauty and tourist spots, and public parks. "Drive to Decorah on Paved Roads and Relax Amid Nature's Beauty Spots," the advertisement read.[16] In keeping with the era's automobile fever, the Works Progress Administration (WPA) also improved roads in Winneshiek County, surfacing or resurfacing close to 250 miles in the "farm-to-market road improvement program."[17] WPA roads helped boost the automobile and truck travel that narrowed the time between town and the countryside, producers and their markets. Roosevelt's plan to put men back to work resulted in improvements to infrastructure and the environment that are still enjoyed seventy years later.

Had enough landowners been interested, another area could have been developed as parkland along the Upper Iowa. Bluffton-area farmers interested in selling some of their less productive land for cash banded together to offer the state over six hundred acres of land along the river from Bluffton to Coldwater Springs. The state was only ready to buy the land, however, if another four hundred acres could be secured to make a continuous state park. In the end, the additional landowners were not interested. Had the agreement been effected, a large state park, developed in the attractive CCC style, would occupy the entire length of one of the most scenic stretches of the Upper Iowa.

≋ My father, Mel Faldet, grew up on the banks of Canoe Creek. His parents, Nels and Grace, ran the Canoe country store. Before the rest of the countryside was electrified, they arranged for a power line to run directly from the Lower Dam to the neighborhood, including the store. From then on, the country neighbors could stop in to enjoy an evening lit by electricity and, more important, to eat Sugar Bowl ice cream, produced in Decorah, on the hottest nights of summer. Even after the installation of electricity, the house and store at Canoe had no indoor plumbing, and Grace pumped the water by hand from a cistern into her kitchen sink. Drinking water got carried up the back steps, pail by pail, from the well out back. The earliest picture of the Canoe Store, located on the banks of Canoe Creek, shows a horse and buckboard out front. In 1913 my grandfather, Nels Faldet, bought out his partner at the store. Two years later, on the day before his first son was born, he had the store building moved across the road and up the hill. The store was Nels's living, and he did not want it threatened by Canoe Creek floodwaters. At the new location he installed pumps for dispensing Standard Oil's Red Crown gasoline.

Nels Faldet and a number of the other farm neighbors got together after the Canoe Store had been moved across the road from the creek in 1915 and formed the Pleasant Cooperative Creamery, with Nels serving as its treasurer. They constructed the creamery building in 1916, just uphill from the original site of the store, with an icehouse nearer the creek. The men in the Pleasant Cooperative harvested the ice that cooled the butter from Canoe Creek or, more typically, from the lake above Lower Dam on the Upper Iowa. A record book distributed by the cooperative to its members had a picture of a large-eyed Jersey cow on its cover, and the motto, "Clean Cold Cream produces Clean Cold Cash." Wooden tubs of Pleasant Creamery butter were hauled to the Rock Island depot in Decorah for shipping to market in New York. Mel spent part of his youth hauling cream for Pleasant Cooperative up and down the steep hills of the farm country around his home. He lifted dripping cream cans from the cooling tank in the springhouse and drove them back to Canoe.

Throughout his days at Canoe, Mel joined those from the neighborhood who gathered at the bend in the creek just below the store to swim. His favorite recreation was catching large catfish from Canoe Creek. In 1930, when Mel was twelve, several thousand catfish and bluegills were stocked in Canoe Creek. Some catfish survived and reproduced in numbers that kept his fishing expeditions happy for the next twelve years, the fish growing older and bigger as he did. His early life connected intimately to the creek and to the river.

≋ Like the CCC, the WPA also helped improve the water quality of northeastern Iowa through a number of projects. With only $172 seed money from the State Conservation Commission, the WPA improved the quality of Bear Creek as a trout stream in 1937–1938. The WPA solidified banks; built aeration dams; and planted willows to provide shade, hold banks in place, and lessen runoff. Federal money also helped Decorah improve its water system with a new 850-foot well, new mains, improved sewer lines, and the labor to construct a sewage treatment plant. A news item in 1932 suggests the ineffectiveness of Decorah's sewage treatment before the federal government stepped in. The *Public Opinion* stated that "Otto Solberg brought Luther biologist Dr. W.L. Strunk a 5 1/2 lb. Northern Pike which he had picked up from the shallows of the river near the golf club grounds. The fish was obviously very sick. Dr. Strunk concluded it died from pollution: thought to be from the city sewage disposal plant."[18] Only about one-third of the town's sewage was filtered by the older plant constructed in 1915. The other two-thirds passed raw into the river. The settlement tanks of the new sewage treatment plant were designed to handle all the town's waste, taking over half the contaminants out of the town's water before reaching the river.

With the possibility of federal aid and a new focus on water quality, the town of Decorah began to reconsider its use of the river for swimming. As they had for generations, people swam around dams, in river bends, and in gravel pits. The dam above the West Decorah Bridge, which fed the mill-race to the center of town, created an impoundment where people docked boats. At his machine and metal shop on Water Street, H. F. Thompson built boats, often used on the water at the west edge of town. Teenagers swam above the dam as well as under the spillway. In the summer of 1932, Decorah paid to have a wading beach graded into the gravel pit on Emil Rosenthal's property below the Tavener Dam at the northwest edge of town. The prospect of government workers and federal money after Roosevelt was elected, however, made people begin to consider a place to swim that would be less dangerous. In the early 1930s the city was still pouring sewage directly into the Upper Iowa. Though they tended to swim on the upstream side of town, people were becoming conscious that river swimming was not hygienic.

One idea for more controlled swimming was to transform the area of wet pastures, a junkyard, livestock pens, and the city dump, collectively called "the hitching grounds" and lying between Water Street and the Upper Iowa River, into a riverside park, complete with a symmetrical swimming lake. In 1933, with Roosevelt's public works efforts under way, people formed plans for the lake. A. C. Bishop, editor of the *Decorah Pub-*

lic Opinion, most vigorously promoted the idea. The Chamber of Commerce named a committee to head up a bond issue on July 22, 1935. The leader of the initiative, clothing store owner Frank Germann, used the word "pool" in the petition that was drafted. Five days later a young man named Melvin Macal went swimming in the impoundment behind the mill dam just after lunch. Macal began to have cramps, and he drowned. The next week's *Decorah Journal*, the Democratic paper, reminded people that with a "sanitary swimming pool" children would escape infection and "the danger of drowning would be cut to the minimum."[19] By now Decorah had learned that the WPA would put unemployed laborers to work and pay for 45 percent of the cost of the project. The time seemed right. Within two weeks, seven hundred city residents had signed a petition calling for a bond issue to build a pool. The problem was that Bishop and supporters of the riverside park wanted the money to go for a swimming lake that could be made much larger, would require less maintenance, and could be used in winter months as a public skating pond. Those who wanted a pool questioned whether any expensive structure should be built along the river. A bond referendum passed with 71 percent of voters favoring it, but people continued to debate the location and type of the pool.

When work on WPA Project 1100 began in mid-July 1936, the project was a pool, located on high ground deeded to the city by Luther College. The pool was formally dedicated on July 8, 1938. With an art deco concrete building and driveway pillars of local limestone, the pool represented new as well as old. A newspaper ad depicting golfers, dancers, and swimmers encouraged people to spend their dollars in Decorah, reminding them to buy a swimming suit before they left town or to hang around and try out Decorah's new pool.[20] The sanitary swimming pool gave the rural town a new cachet of urban glamour that swimming in a river lacked.

≈≈ Country kids graduated from their township schools after eighth grade. They often stayed in town if they went on to attend Decorah High School. Mel finished high school the year before Virginia started. He stayed with his grandmother, Delia Musser. Virginia lived with a family that had moved in from Madison Township. With no rural busing and no way to manage the daily journey to town, Mel and Virginia could only go home on weekends. On Sunday they returned to town, bringing farm produce to help keep old-fashioned home cooking on the table during the week. High school made rural teenagers like my parents residents of a town they had previously visited irregularly.

≋ Decorah, the town my parents were getting to know in the 1930s, relied on hydroelectric power from the river for its electricity, but this came by power lines from miles away at the Upper Dam and the Lower Dam. The only Decorah business to continue to use waterpower on site was the gristmill at the center of town. Though a swimming lake in a park would have made a beautiful connection to the river, sentiment was moving in the opposite direction. People in Decorah were thinking of somehow putting their town in the valley above the danger of floods.

Floods in 1916 and 1919 made citizens resolve to do something about Dry Run Creek, which ran diagonally across the center of town. In 1919 engineers from Chicago did a preliminary survey. The firm suggested digging a tunnel through the "hog's back hill" west of town to carry Dry Run waters into the river before they reached Decorah. At a projected cost of $150,000, this seemed too expensive. In 1920 the city engineer produced a more complete set of surveys of Dry Run as part of a plan to deepen and straighten its channel to reduce flooding. The city backed away from the project once it found how expensive and provisional the solution would be. On Friday, March 31, 1933, Dry Run put three feet of water over the tracks at the Rock Island depot on the east edge of town and the river flooded so high that it stalled the large highway truck that had been ferrying stalled parties back and forth over the West Decorah Bridge.

Later that year personnel in the Army Corps of Engineers from St. Paul did a survey of Dry Run as part of a general proposal for flood control measures on the Upper Mississippi, agreeing that a diversion to empty the creek before it flowed through town was the best idea. Again, the diversion project was rejected because of cost, but with financing from the Federal Civil Works Board and supervision from the Army Corps of Engineers the town set over fifty men to work in November 1933, deepening and straightening Dry Run and strengthening its banks with rock.[21] In 1936 the city asked the WPA to help with further straightening, widening, and deepening the channel of Dry Run. Although large, these projects would not eliminate the threats of extreme inundations in the Dry Run basin raging in from the south and a river that frequently spread into the town from the other three directions. In September 1938 the Army Corps of Engineers again recommended cutting a path for Dry Run through a hill, but for the first time the engineers proposed a levee system to protect Decorah from the floodwaters of the river. The Corps proposed the project to Congress in 1940 and again at the end of April 1941 after revising its proposal to include even further levee protection to the town, a proposal estimated to cost close to half a million dollars. One month later the river helped make the breathtaking price seem a bargain when a flood around Decorah caused at least half a million dollars in damage.

The Decorah flood of 1941 was caused by an intense day of rain in a week of big rains. On the Monday, Tuesday, and Wednesday of Memorial Day week, 2.5 inches of rain fell. Then on Thursday, 7.7 inches fell. Torrents filled dry runs and creeks, taking out roads, road bridges, and power lines. Basements filled with water. The two railways coming into Decorah each lost a series of bridges and tracks and were closed for almost a month. Automotive traffic in and out was stopped for three days because of high water. Portions of several buildings along Dry Run washed away. Further down the river, at the Upper Dam, the entire first floor of a vacation home filled with water as the river flooded the valley from one hillside to another.

At the Lower Dam, the dam keeper's family members barely escaped with their lives. Interstate Power had just finished installing a new power-house, upstream from the original one. At a lower elevation, it diverted the flume directly between the ends of an oxbow. Between the old dam and the new powerhouse sat the dam keeper's house. Clifford Peterson had newly taken over the job of operating the powerhouse from his father, Julius. Rains downed electrical lines so that no power was going in or out from the dam. Clifford fell asleep sitting in the darkness on the couch with his young wife, Marie, reawakening around midnight. Deciding he should check on the dam as well as the new powerhouse before he went to bed for the night, he went out to his new car and turned on the headlights, which faced toward the dam and the old powerhouse. Several of the trees between the house and dam had disappeared. Walking forward to see what was wrong, Clifford came to a cascade of water that had begun to cut through the hill on the north side of the river and pour directly into the valley on the other side. Beneath the sod of the forest, the hill was sand. Water was eating its way towards him as he stood in the stark beams of his headlights.

Clifford rushed back to the house and woke up his wife and brother. His father Julius, who had operated the dam for thirty-three years, refused to believe they could be in any danger. The house sat on a rise fifteen feet above the upstream side of the dam and close to forty feet above the downstream side. Indian mounds one thousand years old rose in gentle circles between the house and the dam. Water had not come close to threatening the house in all the years of his work there. As Clifford argued with his father, the others began to move what they could into the yard, uphill from the dam. Marie Peterson carried their sleeping baby to the car and Clifford moved the car up the road. They carried out dishes and furniture, including a new bedroom set. Their only light was a kerosene lantern. Around 1:30 A.M. they heard groaning and cracking as water began to eat away the east side of the foundation. Julius, by then roused and active, resolved to make one last dash to the living room to rescue the lantern that still burned on the floor. Its light helped illuminate the crumpling of the house as it washed away.[22] Though the damage to Decorah was never again as extensive, the river crested at similar levels in 1942 and 1945. Flood conditions of the 1940s gave the Army Corps and district representatives in Washington ammunition for their efforts to win federal support for a flood control project the town had been shying away from for thirty-five years.

≋ Virginia Baker first saw Mel Faldet in her senior year of high school. He was cruising slowly down the pavement of Water Street, his left elbow out the open window of his new 1941 Plymouth sedan. The car was a blue bubble of steel, glass, and chrome on white sidewalls. Virginia thought Mel looked like a vision fresh from Hollywood. A school friend introduced them, and they began to date. They crooned melodiously to the hits of Bing Crosby that played on the car's radio. They went to movies in Decorah, and Mel took Virginia fishing on Canoe Creek. The war delayed their marriage, because my father enlisted late in 1941 and did not return until January 1946. In Fort Monmouth, New Jersey, just before Christmas in 1942, he wrote: "I was thinking of the days *ages* ago. Days in the blue Plymouth days. Days back home. Parties, shows, trips, picnics, hunting and fishing." Dates in the car, along with fishing days on Canoe Creek, were part of the world to which Mel ached to return. His work on warplanes, however, took him as far away as Guam before the war ended, while Virginia worked the switchboard in the local telephone office.

≋ Mel and Virginia began the gradual process of leaving the countryside as soon as they left their homes for high school. Mel's war service accelerated his separation. Although gasoline made for less work and easier travel, it emptied out the countryside of the Upper Iowa. Some left the countryside when they lost their farms to the brutal markets of the Great Depression. Others, however, left as a result of the adoption of the gas-powered tractor. The "traction engine" began as a heavy, expensive, and not very maneuverable machine. By the thirties it became useful, reliable, and affordable. By the end of World War II there was one tractor for approximately every two hundred acres of Iowa farmland. Tractors did not need oats or hay, never got tired, and could provide portable power for speeded-up machinery. Horses could disappear, hired men and women became less necessary, and children were less essential as extra hands. Farms had grown in size in the sell-off period of the Depression, and new cash demands for machinery and fuel pushed farmers to increase the acreage they farmed to meet their expenses.

Virginia's siblings each took up farming on their own places in Madison Township, one brother taking over the family farm that Stewart had rebuilt. The tractor and the automobile, however, had now made it less likely that people like my parents would continue their adult lives along the little creeks in the countryside where they had grown up. The portable power of fossil fuel liberated people from their restricted place in the countryside and tied them more completely to a global economy. Petroleum, fertilizers, and coal helped boost local productivity. Improved transportation allowed farm commodities to move more easily to market. Neighborhood and regional identity eroded in the wake of new rivers where the churning, mobile liquid was no longer water, but gasoline.

≈≈ When Virginia died in 1993 she was buried in the cemetery below the little frame church at Canoe where Mel had been baptized. The first Memorial Day after my father moved into the nursing home, I took him out to the cemetery at Canoe Ridge where he managed, with a metal walker, to get to the grave of his parents and then to the grave of my mother, the woman who, as a little girl, had helped her imaginary friends move the family farm's creek. Though he had carefully tended the soil and plantings for ten years, my father now leaned on the granite marker while I planted flowers and cleared weeds. Lichens had begun to grow on the shady side of the stone. Just over the fence, I could hear red angus cattle shifting as they grazed on new pasture.

On my father's second Memorial Day in the nursing home, we again drove to Canoe Ridge, but a series of miniature strokes had hollowed out his brain. He stayed in the car, no longer able to walk more than a few steps. It was a comfortable, breezy afternoon, with blue skies and scattered white thunderheads in the distance. I sent my ten-year-old daughter back to ask him how he was doing as I worked away at the weeds and flowers. "I'm doing fine," he told her. "It's a great day—a beautiful day!" By the marker to my mother's grave I dug with my trowel, loosening the clay soil my father had built up over the years, removing the weeds and the dead stalks of last year's flowers.

By the time I finished my work at the cemetery and loaded up the car, my father had grown tired, and he said nothing. I drove on past the church, past where the blacktop ended, and down the gravel hill to Canoe so dad could see his old neighborhood. As we drove past the old store, now converted to a house, I pointed it out. He said nothing. When I asked about the site of the old creamery, he made no response. We slowly crossed the bridge over Canoe Creek, turned in a farm drive, and returned toward the bridge again.

In truth, there is not much to see anymore in Canoe, Iowa, save for the creek, the hillsides, and the fields. The countryside center in which my father spent his childhood has disappeared. I hoped that seeing Canoe Creek again would bring back memories in my father's mind, of swimming in the deep bend next to his house, or walking out with my mother to catch catfish. He made no indication that the place meant anything. As we drove once again over the creek where he swam and fished as a boy, he looked blankly forward at the road ahead of the car, saying nothing.

The Juice

1946–1970

In the summers of 1948 and 1949, Fred Lubke sprayed his lawn with 2,4-D to kill dandelions. His youngest son Alan chased chickens, petted the barn cats, and played with his toys in the yard the days of the spraying and the following days. Alan developed acute lymphatic leukemia in February 1950. Fred and his wife Alice took their son to the local hospital in Decorah, then to the Mayo Clinic in Rochester, Minnesota, and then to University Hospitals in Iowa City, but he died seventeen days after first showing symptoms. He was four years old.

I interviewed my uncle Fred and my aunt Alice many years later, not long before their own deaths. Looking back, Fred said, "That spray—I'm sure that's what killed Alan." Alice explained that they used the herbicide because "they said—'this is easy.'" A weed control specialist from Ames spoke to a group of northeastern Iowa farmers in January 1950, the month before Alan died. The herbicide 2,4-D, the specialist said, was "the most outstanding weed control chemical to date," especially useful "to kill broad-leaved weeds in lawns."[1] In 1945, the year 2,4-D was patented as a herbicide, a University of Chicago botanist named Ezra Kraus swallowed a half a gram of pure 2,4-D each day for three weeks just to demonstrate the chemical's safety to a dubious public.[2] Over 1,500 commercial weed killers, many of them targeted for lawns, still include 2,4-D. Some of these weed killers are used on crops such as sugar cane. Though tests have shown an increased incidence of lymphocyte replication after exposure to 2,4-D, there is no scientifically confirmed link between the chemical and the onset of acute lymphatic leukemia or any other form of cancer. The link in my aunt's and uncle's minds between spraying those dandelions and losing their youngest son did not require scientific confirmation. They believed their carelessness had lost them the life of their child.[3]

In the period following World War II, technology offered to expand the horizon of human control over plants, over other living creatures, over rivers. For controlling plants, 2,4-D was powerful. Its use as a herbicide was developed in the chemical weapons division of the military during World War II, though it was not used in war until Vietnam.[4] The beauty of 2,4-D for farmers was its selectivity. It killed broadleaf plants without hurting grain and other grasses. It worked on the greenest of plants. Weed control offered by 2,4-D and other herbicides became a point of pride for farmers and homeowners. Heraclitus said "to extinguish [hubris] is more needed than to extinguish a fire." Fred Lubke's pride in his weed-free lawn was extinguished alongside the life of his young son. Control and technology kindled an unlikely desire in the population at large. The more highly engineered and urban the landscape of America became, the more fiercely people hungered to see the traces of that engineered world disappear when they stepped up to the banks of the Upper Iowa River. What people pushed away with one hand, they felt impelled to reach for with the other.

≈≈ John Lubke, Fred and Alice's surviving son, works the family farm, in addition to the farm down the road he and his wife Joan bought in the early 1970s. An elected representative on the Winneshiek County Soil Conservation Board, John is also a member of Practical Farmers of Iowa, an organization with a commitment to farming that is "profitable, ecologically sound and community-enhancing." On some acres John produces certified organic crops. On other acres he uses herbicide. When John began partnering with his father in the running of the farm back in the early 1960s, he advocated that they go back to using the chemicals to which Fred had developed an aversion after Alan's death. Originally, the reason was because it was easy and what everyone was doing. Today, some of John's reasons for chemical use connect to soil conservation. Cultivation necessary for organic farming loosens the soil, and on steeper slopes John worries about soil loss where he has had to weed with a cultivator instead of chemicals.

On a fall day in 2003 I join John as he gets ready to harvest soybeans. Having started to convert some of his parents' farm and his own farm to organic acreage, he plans to convert both farms completely the next year. This means that as a soil steward, he would restrict his bean acreage to the flatter fields. This may also pay off financially. "You can do better with corn, anyway," he rationalizes, saying that "$4 per bushel, 100 bushels per acre is $400 per acre of organic corn. With beans you'd be lucky to get a return of $300." John's harvest of herbicide-treated beans might be the last for years to come on the place his parents made their home.[5]

≋ Although Fred used 2,4-D to make his lawn prettier, farmers mainly turned to herbicide to cut their financial losses from weeds in their tilled fields. Tillage and the importation of plants from around the world brought at least one new weed for every crop. Resident weeds like ragweed, foxtail barley, and knotweed were joined by imported quack grass, bull thistle, burdock, knapweed, bindweed, horsetail, lamb's quarters, velvetleaf, and mustard. Weeds grow quickly and lavishly in the ground opened and disturbed for crops. Shading out or stealing the moisture from crops, they lower yields. The seeds they release impair the quality of grain and mean more weed problems in years ahead. Fred took down a pig shed one winter, removing a concrete platform that had been in place at least forty years. That spring the uncovered ground grew thick with pigweed from seed that had been buried four decades. Stewart Baker, Alice's father, cultivated weeds until the corn was too high, then walked the fields or sent his children to do so. In her childhood, Alice and her siblings each covered four rows in a single pass, carrying a hoe to eliminate weeds. In the Depression my mother, Alice's sister, got paid a penny a plant for each mustard weed pulled on the family farm. Though it required manual labor, Stewart Baker was death on weeds.

In the mid-1950s the farm supplier who did the most business with my grandfather Stewart advertised Atlacide, a brand of sodium chlorate, a general weed-killer that required spot application for weeds, since it could kill any green plant it touched. In 1958 atrazine was marketed for the first time, a herbicide that could be sprayed over an entire field of corn and, like 2,4-D, would single out weeds, eliminating the need for cultivating. Herbicides, as Alice said, were "easy," and atrazine made weed killing so easy in corn that farmers expanded their fields beyond what their grandparents could ever have dreamed.

Larger fields, however, were a raging advertisement to insect pests with a preference for corn, the promise of unlimited food stretching to the horizon. In 1942 the European corn borer arrived in Iowa, joining the northern corn rootworm, the cutworm, and other insects that had long shared their taste for corn with Iowa farmers. The arrival of the corn borer moth was perfectly timed to invite the use of some of the increasingly popular new insecticides. The 1940s had brought a new wave of chemical pest controls, the leader among them DDT.

In May 1947, as the residents of Decorah were tilling the soil of their gardens, the local paper published a photo of a woman standing in a small cloud as she worked in an immaculate garden, surrounded by a white picket fence. The headline above it read, "For Garden Without Pests, Dust Early with D.D.T." The caption beneath the photo read, "Cover the plants with a cloud of dust which leaves a light coating over all leaves, on both sides."[6] The woman in the picture stands in a cloud of poison. A week later the paper announced that the entire town of Decorah would be sprayed with DDT to eliminate flies for the coming summer. The campaign specially targeted restaurants, groceries, taverns, and businesses that produced food: the pop factory, the ice cream factory, and local dairies. Other businesses had their screen doors and windows coated with DDT. Boy Scouts went door-to-door, handing out literature that explained the benefit of DDT in controlling insects.[7] Each time customers opened the door of a business in Decorah through the hot days of the summer of 1947, they jarred loose a microscopic cloud of pesticide. Enough citizens asked questions that the local extension agent made inquiries. He came back from the state entomologist with reassurance. "DDT is practically harmless to you or your children," he announced. "Nor will it harm your livestock. Only ordinary care is needed in its application."[8]

A Decorah newspaper ad for insecticides in 1950 read "DDT ... $1.95 in thirty gallon drums. WE HAVE TOXAPHENE (For Cut Worms in Corn). We Sell Spray Equipment."[9] Toxaphene is a particularly toxic mix of over six hundred chemicals. Though it killed cutworm, it also posed a high risk to the respiratory, nervous, and excretory system of the incautious amateur applicator who purchased the spray equipment with which to spread his pesticide. Toxaphene, like DDT, tends to linger in the environment and in bodies of animals exposed to it. For years farmers had cut down on insects through crop rotation, through strip cropping, and through the timing of their plowing or planting. Now they increasingly relied on chemicals to control the insects that damaged their crops.

≋ Insecticide poison left its mark in my immediate family. Although my father worked in town, my parents wanted an acreage on which they could continue farming. In 1951 they bought twenty acres of open land just outside Decorah on which they could raise livestock and keep a big garden. The first livestock they purchased was a flock of sheep. My grandfather Stewart, an experienced sheep raiser, offered to help them get started. He took it upon himself to take care of the worms that annually worked their way into the digestive tracts of ewes. One year in the 1950s, however, he pulled the wrong bottle from the shelf in his shed. The bottle he thought was meant for the sheep was a garden insecticide. What he mixed in the soda bottle that he used to dose sheep was Paris Green or copper ace-toarsenite, an arsenic poison used to kill potato bugs.

Virginia helped her father herd her sheep into a pen where he gave them each a dose of the concoction he had mixed, forcing the bottle into their mouth, tipping back their head, and releasing them to rejoin the flock. Each ewe flicked her shoulders to regain her composure as she trotted away. Stewart didn't realize his mistake until he returned home and saw the proper bottle sitting on the shelf. He rushed back to administer a purgative to flush out the poison, but for many of the ewes it was too late. Throughout the afternoon sheep wobbled on their legs and fell, breathing unsteadily, or drooped drunkenly against the trunks in the grove of box elders below the barn. Their entrails were gripped with spasms of vomiting and diarrhea. Some went into convulsions and died, a silent wooly heap to be dragged away. By evening some had begun to recover, but a number of my parents' little flock were dead.

The death of her sheep was a story my mother often told me when I was a child. I had not been there to witness it, so she felt impelled to re-live that day of high drama in her young adult life where she had to watch something horrible, with little she could do. More than pitying the sheep, however, she pitied her ageing father. He generously had come to help her but had instead given her new farm a serious blow by killing her ewes. In guilt, he made up for my mother's loss with some of his own new lambs.

Looking back on the story today, however, my attention goes to the bottle of Paris Green that dealt out death to the flock. It rested on the shelf to be mixed with water and poured over my grandfather's garden, coating plant leaves and the soil with a metallic compound equally lethal to potato bugs, sheep, or people. Paris Green was, by the 1950s, an antiquated insecticide. It was probably sitting there unused and unremembered because, by then, Stewart had moved on to DDT and toxaphene.

≋ Controlling the Upper Iowa was a project for engineers. The Army Corps of Engineers first completed work downstream on the Mississippi, the series of twenty-nine locks and dams done during the 1930s to ensure a nine-foot channel for barge traffic. The deepened channel improved the transport of grain up and down the Mississippi. Controlling the river as a corridor for commerce was the Army Corps's main interest in the Mississippi. Since the Upper Iowa was too shallow for commercial transportation, the Army Corps's main interest in it was flood control. In 1949 Congress authorized the Army Corps $858,000 to straighten and dredge the final six miles at the mouth of the Upper Iowa. Since 1920, farmers on the final stretch of the river had been working for relief from flooding.[10] When the locks and dams created a pool in the Mississippi between Lansing, Iowa, and Genoa, Wisconsin, the flood danger worsened. The mouth of the Upper Iowa filled with debris. People who wanted to fish the river were unable to enter from the Mississippi. Upper Iowa floods in the 1940s caused considerable damage to farms and houses along the lower stretch of the river: nearly a quarter million dollars' worth of damage in 1941 alone. The 1949 appropriation granted these farmers relief in the form of a half dozen miles of deepened and straightened channel.

In the wake of the flood devastation of 1941, the flood project Decorah had dreamed about since 1920 was approved by Congress. In 1948 work began. Railroad tracks and a highway had to be moved. In April the timber crew cleared the Hog's Back Hill. Roverud Construction began the work of scraping, blasting, and hauling away the ridge between Dry Run and the river reaches west of Decorah. The first water of Dry Run flowed down its new concrete diversion channel to the river in September 1950. From then on, what remained of the Dry Run Creek running through Decorah originated from springs or wells in and around the city limits. For the first time in a hundred years, the town was safe from the raging of its central creek.

To make the town safe from the raging of the Upper Iowa River that now contained the diverted creek waters, the Corps first bought up the floodplain properties in Decorah and paid the Bernatz Mill owners to give up their waterpower and convert to diesel. In October 1950 a storm sewer was installed in the old millrace and its channel was filled. As the project for moving the river was being developed in 1946, Representative Fred Biermann suggested that the new levee should be paved to serve as a scenic riverside drive. Biermann had represented the district in Washington, D.C., when federal aid was first sought for the flood control project, and he had been serving as Decorah's park commissioner since 1922, but his idea was rejected.

Instead of serving as a new link to the river, the dike became a visual barrier. People on Water Street watched as heavy equipment gouged out a new channel on the far side of the valley. The old river bend that turned towards the town center was dammed, and the new channel was opened. From the western edge of Decorah to its eastern edge, a dike was constructed that would carry water, at full flood, past the town at a height that was well above the first story of residences in the shadow of the levee. Even before the diversion and dikes were built, the city had improved its wastewater treatment plant. In 1946 the city replaced the passive WPA system with a mechanized trickling filter system. Large arms now circled over gravel beds, dripping water that would be cleaned by the bacteria in the filter gravel. Though Decorah had put a wall between itself and the Upper Iowa, the town had also taken a further step in reducing the pollution it dumped in the river.

≈≈ Fred Lubke had grown up on the old Addicken Brewery property at the mouth of Twin Springs, the stretch of the river into which the new Dry Run diversion emptied. He remembered the river floods: "From our place, right across the bottoms, it would be one great big sea of water." And he also remembered their aftermath: "That was a mess. After a flood it would take a week to go through the fields and pick up the trash. There'd be parts of fences and old trees." The good side of it was that the river deposited silt in the corn bottoms. "Father said he could raise more corn on those twelve acres than he could on the whole rest of the farm," Fred recalled. "He had rye on there one year, and there was no end of it. It got about nine feet tall, and they had a terrible time trying to harvest it." He remembered the spectacle of Dry Run floods in his childhood as well: climbing over the top of the Hog's Back Hill behind their house to watch livestock and pieces of farm buildings being swept down into Decorah.

Besides dating, Fred and Alice had courted through the rural mail and over the telephone party line. They married just after Christmas in 1939. Because Alice was a rural schoolteacher, she was bound by contract to stay single. They kept their marriage a secret until near the spring conclusion of the school year in 1940. That summer they moved in together. Occupying half of the house of Fred's grandmother, they started farming. "We had a telephone, and that was the extent of our expenses. We burned wood. We didn't buy electricity. We didn't buy gas," Alice said. Stewart Baker gave them a sow and some piglets as well as a draft horse. Fred's grandmother sold them cattle on a time arrangement, and Fred's father loaned them farm equipment. Fred bought two more draft horses. Since other farmers were buying tractors, "You could buy that horse-drawn equipment pretty cheap. I bought a plow for a couple of bucks." Having gotten their start at Fred's grandmother's, they took out a mortgage in 1944 and bought their 160 acres in Madison Township for just under ninety dollars per acre.

The farm that Fred and Alice bought in Madison Township in 1944 is in the uplands ten miles west of Decorah. It sits on a small ridge that feeds, on one side, the headwaters of the Turkey. The water that drained from the roof on the other side of Fred and Alice's house in a thundershower was among the first waters to form the Dry Run Creek that Fred had watched raging in his childhood. Besides getting help on the new place from their families, their new neighbors also aided them. On the new farm they raised hogs and milked, by hand, fifteen to twenty dairy cows. To start with, they carried pails of milk to the house, using a hand-powered separator to remove the cream, and carried the milk back to the barn to feed the calves and hogs. They stored the cream in a tank in the cool of the basement until it could be picked up, twice a week, by the creamery.

Fred and Alice kept their cream in the house because they had an electric pump to fill the water tank there. In the early 1940s, the power grid was extended to their part of the country. Part of the federal program to remake the countryside in the 1930s was to offer loans for rural electrification. In Decorah, as in most places in the country, private enterprise had provided electricity to the town center, where the dense population made the market profitable. The Upper Iowa Power Company, later purchased by Interstate Power, supplied electricity there as well as for Waukon and Cresco, the largest towns in Allamakee and Howard counties. Smaller companies used hydroelectric power to provide other small towns along the Upper Iowa. The countryside, however, remained dark until government loans made electrification possible.

Although opposed by private power companies, electrification came to the countryside of northeastern Iowa throughout the decade of the 1940s, with a long pause in construction during the years of the war. In 1936 interested citizens held meetings in Burr Oak and Decorah. Farmers in Howard County had already begun to organize, and townships in Winneshiek joined them to form the Howard-Winneshiek County Rural Electric Cooperative. By 1940, farmers from parts of Chickasaw County had joined with them to form what eventually was called the Hawkeye Tri-County Electric Co-op REA (Rural Electrical Administration). When the Co-op was formed at the beginning of the decade, only a tenth of the farms in the three affected counties had electrical power. By 1946, half of those farms had electrical service. By 1950, close to 90 percent of the farms in the area served by Hawkeye Tri-County were electrified.

In the meantime, Interstate Power was crying foul against its new rural sister company. During World War II, Interstate Power ran ads announcing that it and other companies were "supplying plenty of electricity for war work and the Home Front, too . . . and besides that . . . balancing a big plate of taxes."[11] As the Rural Electrification Administration geared up to expand again after the war, one of Interstate Power's newspaper ads argued that "when government goes into business and competes with its own citizens, the American tradition of fair play is set aside."[12]

One of Fred and Alice's neighbors recalled the arrival of the REA. "Boy, that was a happy day. Yes it was," he reminisced. "Everybody got a deep freeze. Everybody got a radio. Everyone put in water systems. Everything was booming after the electricity came."[13] Stewart Baker, Alice's father, was excited about the prospect of rural electrification. He joined the board of directors of the co-operative in 1948, when the company's assets passed a million dollars for the first time. In the exuberance of the moment, 1,500 members showed up for the spring 1948 annual Tri-County REA meeting. Stewart was so committed to the work of the REA that he served as treasurer until he died, eighteen years later. His nine fellow members of the board served as the honorary pallbearers at his funeral. The REA paper, sent to all subscribers, reported at his death, "We shall always remember Stewart as a sincere friend and loyal director." Stewart's loyalty came from the conviction that electrical power was a good thing for the farm families along the Upper Iowa.

The grid slowly transformed the countryside. The REA was formed by people who signed contracts to pay a fixed amount each month for years to come to buy a base amount of energy. Families electrified in small steps, starting with electric lights. These made it easier to do chores and milking in the evening and encouraged farm families to stay up later at night. REA customers replaced their battery-powered radios and telephones with ones that drew alternating current. In 1947 the Winneshiek County extension home economist began holding "selection of electrical equipment" sessions to teach farm wives about the use and potential of appliances such as freezers, hand mixers, and vacuum cleaners. A power company adviser assured farm wives that "freezing is one of the simplest and easiest methods of preserving foods."[14] Instead of canning up fruits, vegetables, and meat in pale blue pint and quart jars to store on basement shelves, farm wives were given extension service advice on the use of plastic packages and freezer wraps.

In the barn, too, electricity made changes. By the 1950s, milking machines were emptying the udders of waiting Holsteins. In the 1960s it became common to empty the canisters of milk into stainless steel, refrigerated bulk tanks instead of individual water-cooled cans. By the 1970s, farmers were installing pipeline systems that eliminated the need for anyone manually to carry milk until it was placed on the grocery refrigerator shelf. Electric barn fans and heaters meant that the temperature could be controlled easily in spaces where livestock was penned. The size of buildings became larger. Electric augers and elevators meant that feeding large numbers of livestock became more automated. More animals could be kept in one place with less human labor. By the year 1970, the average dairy herd in Winneshiek County was twenty-four cows, and the average dairy farm around two hundred acres.[15] The number of county farms in the dairy business had dropped by one-third since the mid-1950s, but the level of production remained the same. Herds and farms were getting bigger, partly because electrification made it possible.

Alice and Fred kept conservative pace with these changes. They subscribed to the REA, hooking their farm up to the lines. Within a few years of buying the farm, they milked with Surge vacuum-powered buckets and moved the separator to the barn. Fred and his father built a milk house where an electric pump pulled up well water into a protected concrete tank in which the milk cans were stored, the overflow running outside to fill a watering tank for cattle. Reliable geothermal coolness of well water was pumped with the steady, reliable power of new electricity. The creamery began to buy both their milk and cream and to pick it up every day. In the mid-1960s Fred bought a used bulk tank, upgrading their milk rating from grade B to grade A, losing the free cooling power of water in exchange for electrical refrigeration.

Fred replaced his horsepower with gasoline power. The Madison Township farm was bisected by the Milwaukee Road railway. When Fred's team bolted out of control for the third time at the sound of a fast train roaring out of the draw or an engineer blowing his whistle, Fred traded his horses for a Massey Harris tractor. Alice's brothers and brother-in-law helped with their equipment, a corn picker and a bailer, for harvesting with the new machine. Neighbors provided a thresher for the oats. "We had corn, basically, and hay and oats," Fred said. "And that's about the size of it. Alfalfa hay was the big crop to pay off the mortgage. You see that's because alfalfa hay properly cured, cut at the right time, is a complete food for a cow." Fred and Alice paid off the farm mortgage in four years. In the excellent farm markets that followed the Second World War they sold cattle, milk, hogs, and any extra corn they raised.

≋ Taking me with him in his four-wheel-drive pickup to check his cows and calves, Fred and Alice's son John looks back on those days. "I remember Dad selling ear corn for $2.50 a bushel back then," he recalls. When I ask what a bushel of shelled conventional corn would be today, forty years later, John pulls a cellular phone out of his pocket and dials the co-op. "What's your in-price of corn today?" he asks. I hear the tinny voice on the other end of the receiver—"$2.03 per bushel of shelled corn," John repeats, putting away his phone. "A bushel of shelled corn weighs fifty-six pounds, a bushel of corn on the cob is, I believe, thirty-six. It's been a long time since anyone dealt with ear corn." The $2.50 Fred was paid in, say, 1963 would be over $14.00 in 2003 money. The $2.03 John would be paid for the heavier bushel of conventional corn would have translated into 35 cents forty years ago. John graduated from high school in 1959 and, in those prosperous days of farming, went on working the farm with Fred. "I always wanted to farm. Mother encouraged me to go to college. I could have, but I wanted to farm," John explains. "I enjoy what I'm doing, even though it seems like it's more of a challenge all of the time."

≋ Originally, small hydroelectric dams like those on the river below Decorah, at Lime Springs, and at Granger, Minnesota, supplied electricity in the region. These, however, were eclipsed by electricity from coal-burning plants located along the Mississippi. The deepened Mississippi channel allowed coal to be brought upriver by barges, and the deep impoundments above dams served as cooling reservoirs. In 1946 Interstate Power considered building a coal-powered generating plant in Decorah, but the Upper Iowa offered too low a volume of water to serve for cooling. Instead, they built a fifteen-thousand-kilowatt plant at Lansing.[16]

In the 1950s Interstate Power decommissioned both the Upper and Lower Dams it had operated on the river for over forty years. Interstate gave the land at the dams, as well as land in Decorah, to the state for forest reserves. In the 1970s nuclear plants were added to the electrical grid in Welch, Minnesota, and Palo, Iowa. Like coal-fired plants, nuclear facilities relied on water for steam and cooling and sat on the banks of rivers, just as the gristmills and sawmills of the nineteenth century had. Instead of the force of falling water, tons of burning coal and white-hot nuclear reactions now generated the power that brightened living rooms, cooled milk, or heated toasters for northeast Iowa households.

New electrical power had environmental and physical costs that happy subscribers had not foreseen. One was air, polluted by sulfur and heavy metal, pouring from the smokestacks of generating plants. Another was the disposal of nuclear wastes. A third problem came from the electrical machinery itself. One night a storm damaged the transformer that had faithfully converted the line voltage of the REA lines to the electrical current that Fred and Alice used throughout their farm. An REA lineman replaced the transformer with a new one, cutting the old canister loose and letting it drop to the ground. It hit the earth with a low thud and burst open, spilling liquid on the grass at the base of the pole. After the lineman left, Fred was bothered by the mess in his roadside ditch. He picked up the greasy transformer and put it in his junk pile. He cut down the grass that had been spattered with the oily chemical and carried it away, wiping off his hands and feet with a rag.

Years later he found out that the wet substance he had cleaned up was PCB, Polychlorinated Biphenyl, an emulsion used in electrical equipment. PCB is a very stable and persistent chemical in the environment. It is also an organic compound that is readily absorbed by plants and animals. Congress outlawed the further production of PCB in 1977 because it was scientifically linked to cancer, immune and endocrine system sickness, reproductive problems, and neurological damage. It can also cause skin problems. As Fred aged, he showed persistent symptoms of acute dermatitis. When the weather grew colder, his lower legs itched and burned. For months he suffered from a general rash and weepy sores. Chronic acute dermatitis is one of the possible results of PCB exposure. Fred blamed his annual months of suffering on the liquid spilled from the transformer that brought power to his farm.

Though Fred grew up witnessing how much soil the river washed from upland fields and deposited in his father's bottomlands, he came around slowly to the value of soil conservation—an idea that, by the 1940s, had become a gospel. From the pulpit where Vilhelm Koren and his son Paul had preached sermons in Norwegian on the subjects of predestination and salvation by grace in earlier generations, the Reverend Oscar Engebretson preached conservation as God's message for Lutherans. Engebretson, pastor at Washington Prairie Lutheran between Trout Run and Trout River, organized a rural church life seminar at Luther College in 1946. The keynote speaker told the assembled representatives from little churches around the countryside, "It is just as wrong to steal from the soil as it is to steal from your neighbor."[17] The government also saw the similarity between soil and money. Each could be lost, stolen, saved, and exchanged for other forms of wealth. The most important soil conservation legislation of the 1950s was the Soil Bank Act of 1956. Land taken out of production was "banked" soil, kept back as a reserve when other soil became exhausted by the demands placed upon it, or until, as actually happened around 1970, the international market for grain again made the farming of marginal acres profitable.

In 1951, the year after his son Alan died and seven years after he first worked the Madison Township farm, Fred still plowed his fields straight back and forth, the way farmers had been doing along the river for one hundred years. Then, one night, rain came down in torrents. Fred took John out to the field with him the next morning to survey the damage. Seeing the gullies and fans of displaced soil, Fred confessed that he felt guilty about the waste and destruction that he had helped create. That fall he had two contour strips laid out with the help of the Soil Conservation Service, a practice he eventually extended to other fields. John got his best early lesson in soil conservation a few years later when he watched a neighbor plow a steep slope and plant it, with no contouring, in corn. Within three years the upper field was down to bare rock, and during that time the road below had been covered, after each heavy rain, with soil washing its way toward Dry Run Creek. John, a teenager setting his sights on becoming a farmer, understood that in a very short time, productive acres could be bankrupted permanently.

≋ In 1962 the Decorah Public Library added a controversial new book to its shelves, Rachel Carson's *Silent Spring*. Local readers of *The New Yorker* already knew what Carson had to say. Carson, a biologist, understood the living world as the product of a long and complex process of evolution that engineering attempted to deny. "Nature," she wrote, "has introduced great variety into the landscape, but man has displayed a passion for simplifying it. Thus, he undoes the built-in checks and balances by which nature holds the species within bonds."[18] The large fields of corn or soybeans that consumed the smaller fields and fencerows of a previous era of farming along the Upper Iowa were a standing example of the simplification about which Carson complained.

Carson lamented the idea, increasingly present in the minds of rural and urban people, that their success was dependent on a war against nature. It was a "chemical war," Carson wrote, that "is never won, and all life is caught in its violent crossfire."[19] Carson explained, with brilliant clarity, the life of the soil and the complex interrelations between soil, plants, and animals. Her book signaled a shift in attention from the soil to the waters that pass through the soil. Carson's book highlighted that water is the bearer of loads in the physical environment. In that environment,

Carson warned, chemicals "pass mysteriously by underground streams until they emerge and, through the alchemy of air and sunlight, combine into new forms that kill vegetation, sicken cattle, and work unknown harm on those who drink from once pure wells."[20] Slowly, Carson's ideas gained a following in Decorah as elsewhere around the nation.

When Carson forecast springs without birdsong, few people listened, but when the springs that fed their own drinking supply became contaminated, people took note. The public outcry against pollution increased throughout the decade of the 1960s. The district conservationist for Winneshiek County wrote in 1968, "It is no secret that we are facing an environmental crisis."[21] He pointed to chemicals and pesticides, animal waste, and silt that mixed with drinking water or the waters in area streams. What he called an environmental crisis found its expression, as Carson had highlighted, in water problems. The state of Iowa put new regulations in place, requiring commercial applicators of chemicals to pass a test on material safety. A heavy rain in July 1969 killed several thousand trout in the fish-rearing ponds on Trout Run. The local superintendent placed part of the blame on chemical fertilizers.[22]

The increasing evidence for the toll pesticides were taking on wildlife had also become national news. The Iowa House moved to ban DDT in the spring of 1970. Decorah schools participated in the celebration of the first Earth Day on April 22, 1970. The lead-up to these activities inspired a local boy, Myron Otteson, to call attention to the large amount of motor oil piped into the waters of Dry Run by Decorah garages, an embarrassing wake-up call for the city fathers. In an ill-timed initiative, the Winneshiek County weed commissioner announced, that same week, the kickoff of a campaign whose unfortunate slogan was, "Let's Go. Kill Weeds Now." As part of the campaign, the county stepped up its spraying of herbicide in roadside ditches. One of the many who objected was a woman who said she was "sickened" at the county's destruction of "wild roses, gentians, wild asters, Queen Ann's lace, wild sumac, shooting stars, and native ferns," a list that echoed similar ones in Rachel Carson's book.[23] Just weeks before the campaign, the federal government barred the use of the brush-killer 2,4,5-T on agricultural land and areas near homes or streams.

In the "Let's Go. Kill Weeds Now" campaign the county announced it would be using 2,4,5-T, whose effects had become notorious as part of the Agent Orange used to defoliate large sections of Vietnam. This, too, outraged citizens. By June the Iowa Highway Commission stepped in to ban the roadside use of the chemical throughout the state. In August 1970 the U.S. Department of Agriculture banned DDT for almost all agricultural and domestic uses. The conservation movement had become an environmental movement, no longer focused on forests and soil but reaching out to all the elements of the living world and more attentive to the lethal effects of engineered products in the environment, the latter now including water and the air. In announcing the creation of the Environmental Protection Agency in July 1970, President Richard Nixon stated that it had "become increasingly clear that we need to know more about the total environment—land, water, and air" and that the time had come to protect, develop, and enhance the "total environment."[24] More important for rivers, in 1972 surface waters were given protection under the Federal Water Pollution Control Act, which created new standards, new means of enforcement, new federal authority, and new mandates to the states.

Around the time that environmentalism was influencing public opinion about chemicals in the environment, a movement began to protect the Upper Iowa River from further development. In a world that felt increasingly engineered, politicians found backing to protect some of the areas of wildness that remained. The Upper Iowa emerged as one of those areas. In October 1968 Congress passed the Wild and Scenic Rivers Act. The intent was to complement the lock and dam systems built, by then, into rivers like the Mississippi, with a series of free-flowing streams of outstanding "scenic, recreational, geologic, fish and wildlife, historic, [or] cultural values."[25] Through the work of the area's Democratic representative in Washington, John Culver, the Upper Iowa was quickly added to the list of sixty-four rivers to be considered for protection. Because of the integrity of the river and its uniqueness in Iowa, it survived the first screening to become one of twenty-seven rivers in the nation studied in detail by the Bureau of Outdoor Recreation. In addition, Culver was granted a request that the study be speeded up so that it would be completed by October 1970 rather than by 1973.

Within two months a citizen's group, Northeast Iowa Committee for Outdoor Resources Preservation, had formed to promote the success of the wild and scenic rivers proposal for the Upper Iowa. In the appeal that went out, inviting residents to the initial public meeting for NEICORP, the press release asked, "If a flat South Dakota can have its Black Hills, why can't flat Iowa develop something almost as enticing in the scenic wonderland of Northeast Iowa?"[26] The protected public corridor of the river would bring in tourist dollars by offering an escape for jaded city dwellers. Conservationist William Mills, writing later that year, observed that in a state known for putting corn and pork on America's table, the Upper Iowa might be viewed as offering "food for the soul."[27]

≋ The Upper Iowa River provided both food for my table and food for my soul when I was young. My father and I often turned spadefuls of composted sheep manure in the shade of the windbreak cedars to fill a can with pink earthworms, or we seined minnows from a creek. With our bait and tackle we went to the river, fishing at the Lower Dam or downstream. Through the fine spray that filled the air immediately below the falls at the dam we tossed in our minnows, hoping for crappies or white bass. I was never so tense with concentration as when my eye followed the white line that disappeared into the darkness of the agitated water, my finger pulled tight to feel the first signs of a bite. One of my earliest memories is of leaning so far over the river to observe a stringer full of fish that the earth caved away beneath me. I was fished out by an uncle.

There was no brilliance that glimmered like the side of a white bass, twisting suspended beneath the bend of my pole. There was no red as potent and dark as the gills through which I threaded the point of the stringer. After catching redhorse suckers in the spring, I watched my father cut open the belly, stripping out roe for his breakfast fry-up and throwing the rest of the fish to the ground to be seized and eaten by the barnyard cats. When I ate the pan-fried fish my mother cooked, the taste was the same as the smell of the misty air at the river's edge. The flesh was shiny and pale, but flavored with butter and a crisp coating of browned flour. Kitchen flavors mixed with the memory of the riverbank.

At the age of twelve, fishing was my wildest passion. When I walked the soft paths to the river I disturbed the aroma of spearmint, horsemint, or the woody scent of broken nettle. Crickets chirped in the grass. In late summer cicadas buzzed in the trees overhead. Toward darkness frogs sang at the edge of the stream, and mist rose from the cool water as bats flitted. Families that lived along the stretch of river we fished all knew my father from his childhood, so we never asked permission to walk up the riverbank or jab a forked stick in the mud on which to rest a second pole. I grew up thinking of river access as a birthright. Besides harvesting fish, I drank in deep impressions of a world that was familiar but always surprising. By the time I graduated from high school in 1975, though, my passion had all but disappeared. I was leery of eating the flesh of animals that had grown up in what was, in one way, nothing more than the storm sewer for a countryside rich with menacing chemicals.

〰〰 The constituency for river preservation had at its core a new group of outdoor recreationists: canoeists. Beginning in the late 1950s, people floated the river in aluminum canoes. Light and needing no draught for a propeller, they could carry one or two people down almost the entire length of the river. Navigable for six months of the year, the Upper Iowa now qualified as a public waterway. With the passing of the age of water-power, there were few dams to impede boats. Because of improved sewage treatment, the river was cleaner below Decorah than it had been in decades. Few people were harvesting trees for firewood, and the hills were thickly forested. The corridor of the river looked wilder than it had in years. The goal envisioned by the federal government was to protect this scenic beauty and develop it for further recreational use in hiking, horseback riding, angling, hunting, and, most of all, canoeing.

Canoeists, though, had already begun to anger landowners by cutting or damaging the up-to-a-dozen fences across the river between Kendall-ville and Decorah. They trespassed on private property to picnic, have parties, or camp, leaving their litter and excrement behind them. NEICORP, which grew to include two hundred people, believed that making the river corridor public property would eliminate the issue of trespass and that a better developed system of camping places and access points would promote more orderly river use. The water of the river was already a public resource; the creation of a protected corridor would make the adjacent land public as well.

As the Wild and Scenic River study went forward, the prospect of the protected corridor began to get more attention. In July 1970 Iowa put into effect its own Scenic Rivers Act. That same month the Republican Party of Winneshiek County sent its proposals for the state party platform, including, "We urge immediate action by the state government to protect the Upper Iowa River and Coldwater caves from pollution, exploitation and damage."[28] But the political will of people along the river to preserve it was less united than politicians had originally guessed. Public hearings, required as part of the process, were left until the very end of the study. In August 1970, just before the October deadline, hearings were set for the county seats of Howard, Winneshiek, and Allamakee counties. Federal officials who came to propose their plan and get a public response to it had talked to experts and other officials. They had not yet talked to any of the hundreds of landowners up and down the river, who came to the hearings prepared to dislike what they heard.

One of the misconceptions that led to apprehensiveness and anger before the public hearings had to do with the possibility of classifying the Upper Iowa as a "wild" river. To qualify for this designation, development around the river would have to be rolled backward, taking bottomlands out of agricultural production, removing bridges and roads, and limiting river corridor access to foot trails. Reacting to public apprehension about this, the Decorah newspaper, which had so far been enthusiastic in supporting the proposal, editorialized the week before the meeting: "The Upper Iowa . . . is not really a wild river. . . . The Upper Iowa deserves preservation as it is."[29] State and federal officials who came to hold the hearing agreed; no part of the river was suitable for the designation "wild." They were ready to propose classified status for eighty miles of the river, from near the Mississippi to the point where it left Minnesota. The least developed stretches above and below Decorah would be classified "scenic." The stretch in the center, from Bluffton to the Lower Dam, would be classified "recreational." In each of these designated miles of the river, roughly seventy-five acres would be purchased, with easements being used to protect another ninety-four acres from further development.

The plan was to purchase a strip of riverbank on each side of the Upper Iowa and steep bluffs visible from the water. Agricultural bottomlands would be kept agricultural, and farmed hillsides visible from the river would be used to produce harvestable timber through conservation easements. The plan would designate eight areas already owned by public entities or used as canoe access points and campgrounds as suitable for developed recreational facilities. Several other areas would be developed as primitive canoe landings, and two hundred miles of trails would be created along the river.

Recreationists and preservationists came ready to support this concept: a corridor of parkland with no equal in the Midwest. When the hearing was held in the science hall at Luther College on a warm August night in 1970, the room was over capacity, with three hundred people. Close to one hundred of those people were landowners. After the state and federal officials presented their plan, Congressman Culver made an appeal for conservationists, recreational users, and farmers to work together to make the proposal become a reality. Members of the Isaac Walton League, the Decorah Parks Board, and NEICORP spoke to defend the idea.

Landowners attacked it. Most of the landowners present had created their own group, the Upper Iowa River Preservation Association (UIRPA), to preserve the river as it was: a largely undeveloped stream flowing through private lands. The chair of UIRPA, John Malanaphy, stated his anger that landowners had so far gone unconsulted. The attorney who represented UIRPA warned people that if the federal government took over thirteen thousand acres out of private hands for the eighty-mile corridor, it would raise taxes on other property. Others characterized the government plan as a "land grab." The chair of the Allamakee County chapter of the National Farmers Organization said that if the plan were to be implemented, landowners along the river would be little better than "Indians," with the government telling them, "Here is your reservation, boys."[30]

The meeting simmered for three heated hours. When it was over, the landowners' UIRPA group, unappeased, put out a call for more members and began circulating petitions. Their attorney advised them, "If we can stop them at the Federal level, and then at the state level, then we can come up with a plan of our own for the preservation of the Upper Iowa. We have to stop them first before we can talk to them."[31] If the federal and state government didn't want to talk to landowners until it had its plans developed, then landowners wouldn't talk to the government until it had no alternative but to consider their plan.

〰 John Lubke's experience as a landowner provides a clue to the resistance the Wild and Scenic River Plan received once it came to local public hearings. Fred and Alice's farm was bisected by the tracks of the Milwaukee Road. When the railroad abandoned those tracks in the late 1980s, Fred and John assumed that the right-of-way would revert back to them. The original agreement, signed by the railroad, said that in the event that the line was not built, the right-of-way would go back to the owner of the farm. Instead, however, the track was purchased by the County Conservation Commission for use as a biking trail. To get from one field to another, John would have to make a very long and time-consuming loop out to the public road on his tractor, or he could drive across the gravel biking trail. When John crossed the path with his tractor in the sight of a conservation officer, he was charged with criminal trespass. The county dropped the case only a few days short of its coming to a jury trial. Though John was sympathetic with the need for public access, he didn't see why it needed to interfere with his private livelihood.

In February 1971 the Department of the Interior filed the report of its study, recommending the plan they had originally proposed at the public hearings but putting implementation entirely in the hands of the state. Governor Robert Ray asked that the federal government pay 75 percent of the cost of acquiring lands, instead of the planned 50 percent. Secretary of the Interior Rogers Morton said 75 percent was out of the question. The Upper Iowa had been designated a scenic river by the state and the nation, but to develop the full plan would require the purchase of over thirteen thousand acres of land, half funded by state taxpayers, in a climate where the idea was unpopular with landowners. The river had gotten the special attention it deserved, but the attention had not much helped move it closer to a higher level of preservation. The Iowa Conservation Commission began buying a few whole farms through which the river ran when they came up for sale, but the Upper Iowa remained preserved in the way the landowners wished, by remaining a river meandering largely through private property: property mostly devoted to farming.

≋ John and his wife Joan took over the active farming of his parents' property in the 1970s, while Fred and Alice continued in the house that had been their home for thirty years. Alice kept her henhouse and eggs and put in a yearly garden. Fred maintained the fence lines, the ditches, the yard, and the buildings. As Fred's dermatitis worsened, they replaced the forced air furnace with electric radiant heat, and Alice worked by trial and error to take anything from his diet that made the rash flare on his lower leg. After Fred died, John stopped in on his daily rounds to check on his mother. When she passed away, the farm passed on to John, their only living child.

On the fall day when I join John to see how he puts up beans, he has two bits of good news. His daughter-in-law has given birth to a new grandchild, and his son Jon is likely to soon get a job developing the county's satellite information and to take up residence in the family home that Alice's death has left empty. As John gets ready to harvest the beans from his parents' farm, he explains his work. "I farm my place, the folks' place, Morris Bergan's place, some of Uncle Stevie's place, and some of Uncle Robbie's place. The way I figure it, I'm on my own working farms that used to support four farmers and their families. And they made a good living doing it." I join him in the cab of the combine. A sticker on the window says, "Please be careful. We love you. Your family." John does most of his work alone, and farming is one of the most hazardous professions in America.

It's unusual for John to have someone else sharing the cab of the combine. He rides eight feet above the sickle bar that moves quickly back and forth at the leading edge of the machine, which pours a narrow cascade of soybeans into a bin and fans a shower of straw and husks across the ground it has just cleared. The earth beneath the soybean plants is rusty orange, mixed with small gravel. "It's been so dry this year," John shouts above the roar of the machine, "these plants are maybe three times shorter than normal. The moisture in these beans has been testing out at about 10.6%. It would be better if it were up around 13." Mixed into the red soil are the broken stalks of corn, the remants of last year's crop. "This field was no-till: soybeans planted over corn stubble I had passed over with a soil finisher. That's why I needed to use herbicide on these beans." The beans pour out in a hissing stream, light and fleshy-colored, slowly filling the bin. "I've had this rig a while now," John says. "It cuts a fifteen-foot swath. The new machines, those big ones, they are twenty or even thirty feet wide. There's one feature I like about this one, though, that those new ones don't have." "What's that?" I yell. John looks at me with a meaningful pause and then replies: "It's paid for!"

The machine hums forward at a steady three miles per hour, slowly working its way in round-cornered rectangles from the edge of Fred and Alice's old bean field toward the center. John points out the bicycle trail where the train once scared his father's horses. "For the good of the country, it would be better if it was still a railroad," John says, shaking his head. "Steel on steel is the most efficient way to move grain, way better than beating up the roads."

When I need to go home, John stops at one corner of the field and I climb down to walk back to my car. The combine moves off again, and I drive slowly across the field and into the farmyard, past the lawn Fred used to spray for dandelions. John has taken down several of the outbuildings. The barn, where John milked cows for over thirty years, now sits empty. As I pull out of the driveway and start down the road, I look back to see the combine. The big machine looks tiny, like a spider in the large, dry landscape, making slow successive circles on the last day of harvest for what may be the last herbicide-treated crop of soybeans on this farm for years to come.

On the Place by the River
They Raise Children

1971–2004

In 1973 Paul and Pat Johnson decided to pull up stakes from their lives in Michigan to look for property in the Driftless. What drew them was an environmental wish list: diversity of habitat, good soil, four distinct seasons, no large urban area, clean air, plenty of sunshine, and good water. They drove dusty gravel to the end of the road northeast of Decorah where they saw a white farmhouse, a red barn, and a valley that overlooked a grove of tall pines on the far side of the Upper Iowa, the waters of which ran hidden through a channel of trees. The place spoke to them. Though neither had any ties to the area or prospects for work, they could see on that farm a future for themselves and their three children: Eric, Andy, and Annika. Asked later what it was he raised on the farm they purchased, Paul answered: "children."

By moving to the country and buying Oneota Slopes Farm, the Johnsons went against the flow of an exodus. When steel plows first broke ground on the prairie sections of the Upper Iowa, over half the population of America lived on farms. By 2000, less than 2 percent of the country lived on an active farm; few people buying milk, butter, or ground beef in a supermarket knew how these foods were produced on the land. Pat had grown up in the Chicago suburbs, and Paul's father was a pastor, but they wanted to join the shrinking minority of people who farm for a living. Pat secured a job in the county schools to help provide income and benefits. Because they had a dairy barn and lots of slope to their fields, Paul decided they should try milking, raising animals that would prosper from fields of permanent pasture and hay that would keep the soil in place. They planted the steepest farmed slopes with evergreens for Christmas trees. By the fall of 1976 they had purchased a small herd of Jersey cows and were selling milk to the local cooperative. They planted a garden of vegetables, berries, fruit, and grapes and filled the henhouse with chickens. The Johnson children knew where their food came from: all of it.

As Paul and Pat knew, the choices made by farmers have great bearing on the health of the Upper Iowa. The economy in which farmers operate is largely indifferent to the ecology of rivers. While the government supports conservation, it is also often at odds with it. Farmers like the Johnsons who follow their conservation-minded dreams have to hope consumers and politicians will support them. That means pioneering new ways of farming, new farm markets, and new constituencies to stay in tune with the river basin environment and keep their farms sustainable.

≈≈ When I slow to a stop at the Johnson farm, it is a winter day in 2003. As we sit at their sunny, circular table, Paul drinks his morning coffee, and Pat moves between the table and work at the sink. Looking back at thirty years on the farm, they credit their initial success to help they received from neighbors. "It was good timing. We feel fortunate that we could take up traditional farming at the tail end of the time when it was still working," Pat says. Although new to the neighborhood and farming, they quickly felt the hospitality of farmers around them. "We weren't here but a month when we got a call that the neighbors were having a housewarming for us," Pat recalls. "And that continued, that we'd drop in a lot at the neighbors and talk over farming, or raising kids." Paul affirms, "No matter what your question, the neighbors would give you an answer or come by to help. We shared equipment and work, and we had workdays, five of us farm families. We built our barn. We put up a hog shed at one place, and put up firewood at another." But this has changed profoundly. "A couple of years ago, my seeder broke down, and I didn't even know who to call," Paul laments. "I don't have a neighbor anywhere who has a grain drill any more."

The Johnsons' experience was partly a matter of timing. They started out in a decade where markets made farming more profitable than it had been for over half a century. In 1970 the last extension of the Soil Bank program was allowed to expire. World grain markets made it too expensive for the federal government to pay farmers enough to keep land out of production. Steep, less fertile, and boggy lands that had been kept in grass under the Food and Agricultural Act of 1965 were put into cropland. The land the Johnsons had purchased more than doubled in value by 1980 as farmers sought to increase their landholdings and their profits. By 1980, Pat and Paul were thinking about expanding their operation. They had gotten their start by buying cheap equipment: the small tractor, bailer, plow, and other equipment that other farmers sold to buy something bigger. Between Pat's job off the farm and conservative spending, they paid off their original hundred acres in five years. But they weren't confident that they could maintain such profits in the years ahead. "We watched neighbors get a new pickup, while we drove the old one. I was feeling down in the dumps about it," Paul remembers. "I felt like I was an unsuccessful farmer."

In that year, however, the market reversed. "We watched some of those people go out of the farming business because they were overextended," Pat says. Demand for grain dropped, and so did prices. Land values crashed on acreages that had been bought in an expensive market at interest rates that topped at over 18 percent. By the 1980s, bankers who had encouraged farmers to take out loans were foreclosing on those same farmers' land. In those years it was good that the Johnsons did not to have to worry about a mortgage. Instead, their sons Eric and Andy bought into the farming operation. Through involvement in 4-H, Eric purchased some of the cows, managing the expenses and the profits. Andy came to own half of the Christmas tree operation. Moving to the farm overlooking the Upper Iowa was a way of realizing a dream for the Johnsons. What began as the survey of a series of maps evolved into a daily routine of chores, stewardship, and community life that has extended into the next generation of their family. Though the Johnsons' move was grounded on a critical and rational survey of information, their success is equally infused with old-fashioned values that include respect for land and water.

Hoping to make a difference on a higher level, in 1984 Paul ran as a Democrat for the Iowa House of Representatives. He won and was reelected twice, serving until 1990. Although the district usually leaned Republican, Paul's involvement in dairying helped win farm votes. He also proved a compelling spokesman for conservation. The good water that was part of the Johnsons' wish list when they moved to Iowa was less easy to find in the wells and watercourses of Paul's new constituency. It was an environmental issue that made Paul the voice of the people, regardless of political party. Polluted drinking water concerned everyone.[1]

One of the projects Paul Johnson took on in Des Moines was drafting and passing Iowa's 1987 Groundwater Protection Act. The bill attempted to clean up the underground sources from which Iowans drew their drinking water. Only a few farms in the 1980s got by with the wells dug for them in the nineteenth century. Many were on their third well, each drilled to a deeper level and each more protected from the contaminated surface of the soil through casings, caps, and thicker layers of stone. By the time Paul went to Des Moines, a grassroots movement was targeting water safety, aiming to get human and animal wastes, pesticides, and fertilizer runoff out of rural wells. A local group, Winneshiek County Citizens for Clean Groundwater, pressured the county Board of Supervisors to tighten the requirements governing rural wells. In the spring of 1987 the supervisors passed new water regulations requiring rural residents to apply and pay for a permit to drill a well, the county sanitarian to inspect the well before its first use, and obliging drillers to submit records to help establish a better picture of the area's subsurface. In addition, the county required permits for the construction of rural sewage drainage fields and inspection of the field before it is filled in. Paul's legislation helped defend rural wells while also seeking an alternative to the chemical farming that contaminated them. The act taxed pesticide manufacturers, pesticide dealers, and fertilizer sales. The resulting revenue paid for water testing, a center that would study the Iowa health effects of environmental toxins, and the Leopold Center for Sustainable Agriculture. Such efforts reduced contamination in groundwater and increased monitoring of surface waters like the Upper Iowa and the streams that feed it. "Good water" didn't just refer to the farm well; it also referred to the water flowing past, on its way to the Gulf of Mexico.

A toxic spill of the sort targeted by the Groundwater Protection Act threatened Decorah's drinking water in 1992. A dry cleaning business a block west of the pumping station spilled perchloroethylene, a carcinogenic cleaning agent that can pass through concrete and is heavier than water. The contaminant fanned out to the city wells to the east, shutting down the first one it touched and registering at lower and lower levels in all the wells downstream. The incident showed how quickly and pervasively a surface contaminant can enter the underground water supply.

The city was also cleaning up its contributions to the Upper Iowa. It completed its current sewage treatment plant, two miles downstream from the city center, in 1985. The plant was finished in time to comply with standards for point-source pollution from city treatment plants that went into place with the 1977 amendments to the federal Clean Water Act. The new plant, which replaced the system constructed twenty years earlier, returned water to the river that was as clean as the river water. The system was engineered to eliminate the overflow that sometimes happened at the previous plant in rainstorms or during periods of peak use. Federal law ensured that the solids produced by the plant were plowed into the soil to prevent the chance of runoff.

The Clean Water Act did much to stop pollution from identifiable sources like dry cleaners, industries, and sewage treatment plants. It was less prescriptive about the more generalized pollution sources typical to traditional farming. But in the intervening decades, farming, especially livestock farming, became more like other industry in its size and focus. Small herds or flocks of animals used to roam over large open pastures. Today large numbers of animals are typically squeezed into one tight building. The farm has become a factory. Some have welcomed the removal of animals from river and creek bottoms and erodable hillsides. However, confinements also present new environmental problems, especially in the raising of hogs. Confinement operations draw together pigs by the thousands and wash their wastes into large holding pits. Among the gases produced by these cesspools are hydrogen sulfide, ammonia, and methane. In the open pit beneath or beside a facility housing 1,200, or 2,400, or 4,800 hogs, gases are plentiful and permanent. Anyone living within two or three miles of the operation knows it. They may be unable to get away from the smell without leaving home. As a result, they may suffer from headaches and depression, their eyes and nose might be irritated, and they might have symptoms of asthma or diarrhea. The pits represent a water pollution threat as significant as that posed by the sewage of a medium-sized town.

For the Lepperts, a conservation-minded family that has farmed in the French Creek watershed for over a century, factory hog farming became a living nightmare in the late 1990s. Their farm was directly across the road from a 3,300-hog operation that opened in 1998. That year the Lepperts, other concerned neighbors, and the Sierra Club of Iowa filed a lawsuit against Murphy Farms, the corporation operating the hog confinement.[2] Among the Lepperts' supporters were the Hawkeye Fly Fishing Association and the National Federation of Fly Fishers. The confinement buildings, the storage facility, and the fields into which manure would be plowed all rested on top of a trout-fishing paradise.

Three federal agencies, the state, and watershed landowners worked together to help French Creek sustain one of the best populations of brown trout in Iowa. French Creek fish also supplied viable brown trout to other Iowa streams. By 1999 brook trout native to the Upper Iowa basin were reintroduced to French Creek. Much of the watershed was owned by the DNR, to be preserved for prime trout habitat. The Lepperts, fly fishers, and conservationists were in coalition against the corporate farm that posed a threat to this stream. The advocates of factory farming say that such operations focus livestock in secure, highly engineered locations and keep hog prices competitive in national and global markets. Critics like the Lepperts see confinements as threats to water quality, threats to air quality, threats to country life, and threats to traditional farming.

Confinement production began with poultry farms and extended to hogs, animals suited to a diet of grain that can be trucked in from anywhere. Much of the confinement industry is therefore owned and developed by feed and grain companies, part of an industrialized agricultural system geared to a healthy profit margin for corporate giants like Cargill and Monsanto. More recently confinement has extended to dairy cattle, animals that thrive best on a diet that includes grass, hay, or the chopped green stalks of corn.

The best example of a dairy in the Johnsons' neighborhood that has grown to keep pace with the market is Foresight Farms, a corporation made up, in part, of two great-great-grandsons of Samuel Wise Sr., who bought his Winneshiek County farm in 1854. In 2004 this operation includes 740 milk cows, 600 replacement heifers, close to 200 beef cows, and 2,000 acres of cropland. In addition to the family owners, it steadily employs sixteen workers, with an additional four in peak season. Since each milk cow daily eats about eighty pounds of food, the farm needs to provide close to eleven thousand tons per year for the dairy herd alone. The dairy cows at Foresight Farms are not always confined. In the months before they calf, when the cows are not being milked, they are put out on pasture. Once they calf and are placed in the dairy, four rows of cows, each roughly 150 animals long, flank alleyways large enough to accommodate the tractor that hauls in feed. The animals also use these alleys to walk to the milking parlor three times every twenty-four hours. Each cow's milk production is boosted with rbST, a hormone shot every fourteen days. After four years of confinement dairying, with milkings three times a day, the cow's production falls off, so she is culled.

Involving three generations of two families, Foresight Farms is the face of family farming, reconfigured through incorporation to meet contemporary economic demands. Though confinement dairying has its critics, nearly half the land of Foresight Farms is in perennial root cover, and the operation produces both milk and beef and keeps a large number of people employed in agribusiness. The semi-trailer of milk shipped each day to Des Moines gets accolades from its buyer. Farming by the numbers is efficient.[3]

≋ Carefully monitoring the numbers, consolidating management, and increasing operations is also the way the Upper Iowa River is taken care of at the turn of the millennium. In 1998 Jim Fredericks, of the area Resource Conservation and Development Agency, wrote a grant to the River Network for assistance in efforts on the Upper Iowa. With the help of that grant, he hired Lora Friest to conduct water quality monitoring and coordinate conservation work in what was named the Upper Iowa River Watershed Project. Friest grew up on a farm in northeastern Iowa and brought a good background to her task. Stopping by my house to talk, she reveals that to work in Iowa is an act of reconnecting with her past. "I moved out to Montana in the early eighties. People like me were moving there for the clean water, clean air and the abundant natural areas," she explains. "But in moving there, we were putting a strain on those resources." Watching this happen, Friest realized that in leaving behind the developed agricultural landscape of her Iowa home, she was contributing to a problem. "It occurred to me that, at some point, people would have to recognize that there would be no more unspoiled places to move. We would need to sit down where we are and figure out how to reverse what we have done: clean up our streams and rivers, learn how to have healthy working landscapes." Friest decided to return to her roots. When she got the job directing the Upper Iowa River Watershed Project, she set about doing the kind of development she could live with: helping farmers, businesspeople, city planners, and conservationists realize their dreams in ways that would incorporate good stewardship of the Upper Iowa watershed.

Friest's background in science and management makes her believe in the fundamental importance of good statistics. Her first act as watershed coordinator was to hire someone who knew how to use satellite mapping in a way that would give her a statistical profile of the whole watershed. Using satellite mapping allowed the Upper Iowa River Watershed Project staff to draw information from various subwatersheds, six counties, two states, and several federal agencies to put together a picture of the whole river. Their philosophy has been to work first on the worst sources of soil loss, nitrates, and fecal coliform. Working across a watershed the size of the Upper Iowa was a new experiment, but it paid off. "We were looking at 640,000 acres. And that is an effort that had not been tried before," Friest explains. "But now the Iowa DNR uses it as a model for what is being done elsewhere. They realized we did some things right." Friest also convinced the Iowa Geological Survey to do a more conclusive study of how groundwater is affected by runoff in the karst formations in and around Decorah. To address increasing nitrate levels, her office promoted prairie and wetland restoration where nitrate pollution is the highest, as well as reforestation of the steepest, most highly erodible hillsides. Returning habitats that once filtered out nutrients cleans up the water that reaches the river. The vegetation also retains water on the land. Because of the widespread practice of laying drainage tile to move water off the land, out of the soil, and into the river, Friest says, "we don't have the infiltration we once had and we're losing our groundwater recharge. Wells are drying up."

In 1999, as Friest got started as watershed coordinator, she helped start the Upper Iowa River Watershed Alliance, an organization of nonprofits, businesses, and individuals who recognize they have a common interest in promoting river health. Friest and subsequent coordinators have helped people living in the watershed see that they would need to work together to improve water quality. They provide good science and information to people who feel an investment in conservation. As Friest says, "You have to marry conservation with economics, the need to derive a family income from the land."[4]

≋ Making conservation pay is the philosophy of Dan and Bonnie Beard, whose farm straddles Canoe Creek three miles from the Johnsons. Their way of staying in farming has been to turn to an approach that will pay them a premium price for a product that takes a level of deliberation and care which limits the size of their farm. They run an organic dairy that relies on an approach called "managed intensive grazing." Dan's great-great-grandfather, William Beard, began practical farming experiments when he moved to the county in the 1850s. William Beard and his sons promoted the first large-scale dairy in the county in the 1880s. One hundred years later, Dan Beard left school ready to milk cows and try out some experiments of his own. Growing up in a dairy family, Dan knew he wanted to farm, but his approach over the years has shifted from conventional dairying to intensive grazing to organic farming. Organic milk pays a premium price, but the primary reason for Dan and Bonnie to shift to organic farming was idealistic. By 2002 they had stopped using any chemicals on the land or antibiotics for their cattle. "It was the way we wanted to farm," Dan philosophizes—"environmentally."

I visit the Beards on a summer afternoon when the heat index is pushing one hundred degrees. The white house and weathered red outbuildings sit below the road on a farmstead overgrown with trees. Dan walks across the driveway from the dairy parlor to meet me, wiping off his hands on his denim shorts. He has a hesitant way of talking, but he is a man of enthusiasm. "Basically," Dan explains, "managed intensive grazing is harvesting solar energy. The product is milk. It's cheaper for the cows to harvest the grass than for us to do it for them." The Beards have divided their farm into sixty separate grass paddocks. Their herd of 119 milk cows is put into a fresh paddock after each milking. To bring in the cows from their afternoon paddock, Dan has me join him on the bench seat of their Kawasaki four-wheeler, a vehicle that looks like a mud-spattered, industrial-strength golf cart. We start downhill through the farmyard toward the creek bottoms. Scattered trees become a forest as the hill steepens on either side of the dusty lane. "A lot of this land," Dan says, "is not tillable, but it is still really productive as pasture." The grazing philosophy that Dan and Bonnie have put in practice was developed in the 1950s by André Voisin, a French scientist. He realized that plants and animals developed interdependent relations. The hooves of cattle loosen and aerate the soil. The cattle's grazing stimulates growth. Cattle excrement fertilizes regrowth. In moderation, these animal activities help grass and clover. For their part, cattle thrive on grass and clover at their prime. Left free to roam, cows follow their noses, seeking out plants that are filled with energy and nutrition. Left penned in the same pasture, they overgraze the best plants until they are forced to eat less desirable plants. Neither the pasture nor the animals are well served. Managed intensive grazing holds cows back from pastures until the grass is again at this prime, usually eleven to fourteen days after it was last grazed. Though grazing is as old as civilization, Voisin's approach is a modern refinement, facilitated by the ease of creating new paddocks with electric fencing.

As we turn a bend near the base of the woods, a view of the lush bottomland opens up: a cow herd the color of deer, mixed with a few animals of black, white, and roan, stands—heads down—in a green field through which Canoe Creek meanders. We jostle slowly to the far end of the enclosure; then Dan angles the Kawasaki around. Already the cattle are drawing together into a single herd, ambling slowly toward the lane down which we have come. They hesitate as they cross the creek, slow to leave the water that flows cool around their legs.

When we return to the yard, two boys wait in the shade of the barn, playing with a farm cat and her kittens in the grass. Bonnie Beard, in rubber overshoes, jeans, and a green polo shirt walks from the house to clean the pipelines to the bulk tanks. The boys walk over to help as Dan shows me the milking parlor. At the front of the room is a series of whiteboards, neatly covered with columns of names and numbers. The names on the board range from the exotic—"Spilde, Music, Scary, Sonnet, Tattoo"—to the mundane—"Sadie, Maxine, Jenna." The natural food of a cow is grass, and on their grass diet the Beards' cows live long, productive lives. When Bonnie comes into the parlor and picks up on our conversation, she tells me about one cow who had her last calf at the age of fifteen. "We didn't milk her that year. She seemed to want to just raise that last calf, and so that's what we let her do. She lived to be sixteen." Bonnie's voice betrays her strong bond of attachment to the animals in her care. "Soleil, one of the cows here, was in a herd we bought ten years ago. She's got to be at least twelve." The life the Beards' cows lead is long compared to a confinement herd. The Beards quit milking in December to give the herd a rest through the harshest part of the winter until they calf in the spring, but through the rest of the year they milk each animal twice a day. Bonnie says that the whole herd will get some corn, some minerals, and some dried kelp after milking. "But we like to think the best reward," she says, "is to turn them back into grass that is nice and lush. Grass is as good a feed as a cow can eat."

Most dairy farms rely heavily on grain because it is rich in nutrients that produce milk. Relying mainly on grass, the Beards' cows give less milk per animal than the herd at Foresight Farms. But the margin of profit per animal is good; the labor is more devoted to cows than crops. Since the farm is also organic, the Beards have no outlay for chemical fertilizers and pesticides. Equally important, the milk and beef the Beards produce is organic, fetching a higher price. Ironically, since they pride themselves in a low outlay of fuel and anything coming from petroleum, Dan and Bonnie's milk is often shipped to the coasts. "The demand is out East and out West," Dan explains, "but most of the producers are like us, here in the middle of the country." The company to which they sell their milk has a red barn in green fields on its label. On the milk cartons a farmer waves in greeting as a Holstein turns her head to look in your direction. The label pretty well reflects the feeling of Dan and Bonnie's family operation. The consumer has to believe in the value of organic and small-scale farming to purchase a half-gallon of the Beards' milk; it may be twice the cost of its commercial equivalent. Because of cost and the slim understanding of what "organic" means, organic produce is a small part of the American market. But it is also the fastest-growing part of the agricultural economy, increasing at a rate of 20 percent per year. Though their approach is out of step with most of American agriculture, the Beards are trying a new version of old-fashioned farming for which a growing number of consumers pays a premium. These consumers buy the milk in part because they share Dan and Bonnie's desire to return to a solar-based farming system that sends less pollution into rural streams, and in part because they believe that the produce of this system makes better food.[5]

≋ While the Beards moved into organic farming and others who stayed in dairying got bigger, Pat and Paul Johnson have quit dairy farming and expanded their tree farm. When Paul served in the Iowa House, they were able to keep dairying. But when Bill Clinton took office, he named Paul the chief of the Soil Conservation Service. To move to Washington, the Johnsons sold their dairy herd. Though they returned to Iowa in 1997 after four years, in 2001 Paul accepted appointment as director of the Iowa DNR, a job that put him in Des Moines full time and made it, again, impossible to dairy. However, he resigned his post after two years in protest against the way the department was undercut in funding, staffing, and enforcement. Though Paul Johnson has spent a lot of time in government, he has a limited tolerance for bureaucracy.

Johnson dislikes the slant in government policy toward cheap commodities and steady profit for the biggest agri-industrial corporations at the expense of small farmers and conservation. In response to the crisis of the 1980s that put so many of the Johnsons' original farm neighbors into businesses other than farming, the government in 1985 reinstated a set-aside program. Recognizing that the great plow-up in the booming agricultural markets of the 1970s allowed billions of extra tons of soil to be lost every year, Congress passed the Food Security Act. Under one title of the 1985 act, the Conservation Reserve Program was created. It helped pay farmers to plant grass or trees on their most environmentally sensitive land and to keep that land out of row crop production for ten to fifteen years. Congress also, however, set up a subsidy program to guarantee that farmers producing key commodities would meet their costs. For two decades farmers have either been paid by the government to keep marginal land protected or paid by the government to plow it up yearly for corn and beans. Even if farmers choose to put their marginal land in reserve, they often have to plow it for crops for several years to make it eligible for set-aside subsidies. The result has been, in some cases, the plowing of lands never before tilled—ostensibly in the name of conservation.

The commodity subsidy program has kept farmers alive, but in a system of flattened grain prices, subsidies help force farms to get bigger. Iowa October corn sold for $2.54 per bushel in the good markets of 1975, $2.11 in the farm crisis market of 1985, and $2.05 in the subsidized market of 2003.[6] Had that 1975 corn price kept up with inflation, a bushel would have cost farmers close to $9.00 in 2003.[7] Farmers keep up with rising costs by increasing their acreages, their yields, and their subsidies. Their increased production gluts markets and depresses grain prices, hurting small farmers around the world who can't compete with the low price of American grain. Johnson is excited about the benefits of conservation programs but angered by programs that produce surplus commodities at the expense of the soil. The state of Iowa now subsidizes an ethanol industry based on surplus corn. Conventional corn demands petrochemical fuel, fertilizer, and chemicals to produce. Political spin sells ethanol as a "green" fuel. If it were produced from a perennial low-input crop like switchgrass or hemp, that would be true. But based on corn, ethanol does little to reduce the nation's dependency on petroleum and exacts a high cost from the soil and water of farm states like Iowa and Minnesota and every place downstream.

Johnson's answer is to replace commodity subsidies with what he calls "conservation commodities." "Every farm should have subsidies for helping produce bluebirds as well as corn," he says. "If we don't do that, life on earth is in trouble." Instead of bigger farms, Johnson would like to see smaller ones. He wants more people living in the countryside, more closely connected to agricultural practice and agricultural policy. This, he believes, will bring needed change in politics and the marketplace. He is proud of some of the programs put in place under his direction of the Soil Conservation Service, but he would like to see resource conservation go further. "It's time we take the lead and show how it can be done. Reward the small farmer, reward them handsomely, for producing conservation benefits." The Johnsons would like to see more farmers back on the land around them, farmers who would be paid for building up soil and clearing up water rather than for producing small mountains of petroleum-based surplus corn.

≋ In the interests of conservation, state legislators, in 1990, designated the sixty-four-mile stretch of the Upper Iowa River below Kendallville, Iowa, to be a Protected Water Area (PWA). The PWA program was enacted in 1984 to protect scenic and natural rivers, lakes, and adjoining spaces from development that would diminish their recreational appeal or environmental quality. As when the river was proposed to be part of the national Wild and Scenic River system, landowners turned up to criticize the plan when a meeting was held in Decorah to discuss public reaction to the published proposal. Leaders of the opposition reactivated the Upper Iowa River Protection Association to resist government encroachment on their rights to property. The goal of PWA designation was to protect the "natural and scenic characteristics of the area." This meant promoting and enforcing resource management principles that would limit erosion and pollution. The plan also called for the purchase of farmland and easements that would preserve the visual corridor of the river. The rules have yet to be written that would allow this to have much meaning, in part because UIRPA took the DNR to court over the legality of the new program, and the state's successful defense was that it had not made purchases or enforced rules in the way UIRPA argued to be illegal. As when the river was designated a scenic and recreational stream in the 1970s, in the absence of a clear authority, and nervousness about encroaching on land rights, the DNR has stuck to the practice of occasionally buying up whole farms in prime conservation areas.

≋ One winter week after talking to Paul and Pat Johnson, I come back to talk to their son Andy, their partner in growing and selling Christmas trees. On the porch is a wooden box labeled "Christmas Tree Money." Paul is away with one of Andy's daughters, while another girl helps Pat bake anise-flavored Christmas cookies. Andy pulls on his coat and boots and takes me for a walk around the tree farm. As our boots crunch in the snow, he talks about the soil as much as the trees. Stopping at the top of a ravine filled with trees, he says, "This tree farm is planted in gullied cropland. This is a head-cutting gully in sandy soil. If my folks hadn't stopped it, it would be up the hill by now." As Andy speaks, wisps of steam form in the crisp, still air. After college, he worked in the Peace Corps helping Guatemalan peasants practice sustainable agriculture. In graduate school he reconnected with the home farm; the thesis he wrote for his master's degree was a study in the resource conservation of the Upper Iowa River. The tree farm gets him back to Decorah from his current home in Georgia three times a year: for planting in April, for shearing at the end of June, and for harvest just before Christmas. Raising trees fits Andy's values as a conservationist. His family mainly raises pines, which compete well with the grasses and weeds that grow up around them in the summer. Mowing around the trees occasionally, they avoid herbicides. Because of the competition from the plants around them, the trees sometimes don't make it, and they mature more slowly, but trees and the grassland around them hold the sandy hillside soil in place and create a good habitat for animals. "There are owls out here all the time," Andy says. He contrasts this with industrialized tree farming. On Christmas tree plantations in Georgia, where Andy lives, the ground is plowed and the trees are planted, sheared, and harvested by heavy machinery. In the warm climate the trees grow to harvestable size quickly. Rows are kept weed free with herbicide, and the monoculture of trees is sprayed with fungicide and insecticide. After one crop of trees is harvested, the ground is plowed again for the new crop. Through a promotional campaign, Andy has been developing the market for Johnson trees at Twin Cities' food co-ops, where people are willing to pay extra for a chemical-free, fresh-cut tree, grown sustainably on a small midwestern farm.

Like Dan and Bonnie Beard, Andy Johnson hopes the future will bring more educated consumers who will pay for conservation, which he defines in part as "adapting to your landscape, working with biodiversity." Conservation consciousness in consumers began with concern about the health benefits of organic food, he explains, not "about the health of the land or the health of farmers." That has changed. He is happy to see the trend of highlighting the source of food and buying local produce. The next phase, he hopes, will be certification that is attentive to the scale of production. "If you want people on the land growing things, then consumers need to be able to choose to buy from small farmers." Andy's comments echo his parents' original intuition about farms staying small. One day he hopes to make his full-time home on this small farm. As we walk up to the door of the house, I hear the sounds of his daughter and his mother working in the kitchen and realize that Andy is trying to farm in a way that will make Oneota Slopes attractive to the next generation, with soil, like the farm family that works it, staying in place. Paul and Pat's plan of, first and foremost, raising children on their farm is working.[8]

≋ Driving away from the Johnsons', I circle back the long way to town, along the road that follows the river across from their farm. The river in December runs often out of sight, buried in snow. In my childhood, my father often drove this River Road back to town after church, pointing out homesteads that had disappeared, or the sharp curve above a bend that had swallowed somebody's car on a Saturday night, or the dense windbreak that dignified a well-kept farmstead. Wedged in the front seat between my father in his Sunday suit and my grandmother and her cane, what I saw were clumps of cedar and lilacs, empty of buildings, stretches of undisturbed river water, and lines of evergreens.

Those childhood drives along the road I am now traveling took place on a day given over to rest. Sunday was a day set aside, when the whole family could afford to take the long way home. "Sabbath" and "sabbatical" refer to times set aside. The ancient Hebrews applied the same principle to agriculture as to the days of the week, giving land a sabbatical every seventh year. They knew that land needs rest and regeneration, a year now and then to grow nothing but grass. The farms I have recently visited all grow grass and trees to help balance out the other uses they make of the land in exacting economic markets. That balance is good. A sabbatical that allows room for the land and the water to recharge is important if people are going to have a long and happy future in the Upper Iowa basin, leaving a healthy environment to their children and grandchildren. When Paul Johnson says that land along the river needs to produce bluebirds if life on earth is going to have a future, it is his way of saying that the cure for large-scale environmental problems begins with recharging natural systems one field, one farm, one creek at a time.

This is a book of stories, little stories that contribute to one big story. If there is a single point behind them, it is that the river has always been made up, in part, of the basin through which it has flowed. In the ten thousand or so years of human habitation along the river, people have been part of the stream that feeds the river. But that stream also includes bluebirds, as well as rock ravines, big bluestem grasses, and field corn. The health of the river, the Mississippi into which it feeds, and the ocean into which the water runs is best guaranteed by keeping the incredible mosaic of biological communities that feed the river intact and healthy. Though it is hard to see it at the time, taking care of the land and water is a way of taking care of ourselves and, ultimately, of our children's children. A second point in that big story is that the ethical commitment to land and water needs to be maintained across those generations, as Andy Johnson's parents passed it on to him. The world, as Heraclitus knew, is in flux. Though some challenges remain the same, human changes bring new environmental problems, as knotty and complex as the ones that came before them. And the larger environment of which we are a microscopic part has cycles beyond our control, playing out over millennia. Working wisely with those cycles, keeping the measure of our success several generations beyond us, is key to our survival here.

As my car rumbles over the snow-packed gravel back to Decorah, headlights pointed upriver, I realize that my study of the Upper Iowa has taught me lessons that allow me to do something not all that different from what my father did on those country drives home from church forty years ago. I now can imagine with my mind's eye what I cannot see in fact: the trace elements of nitrate in the clear water under the ice; the elk that once grazed the savanna now cleared for smooth, snow-covered fields; the deeper impoundment of water that once generated power for the city's lights and created the fields of ice that kept its butter cooled through summer; and the sense it makes to include trees in the mix of plantings tended on a farm. My family name is borrowed from a shift in the land surface, or the way water flows across it. *Faldet* means, in Norwegian, "the fall." The man who passed that name down to me lived on a steeply pitched farm of that name bisected by a noisy brook. The name I have passed on to my wife and daughters refers to the fall of water across a particular succession of slopes in Norway. The river and I run in different, sometimes independent, directions. But having studied the river carefully, I now know we run and fall also as one, in a deep, fixed course of elements brought together in a single stream.

Notes

THE SMELL OF RAIN

1 Foster, "The Ioway," 2.

2 Albert Ettinger, quoted in Beeman, "No Clear Solutions."

3 Iowa Department of Natural Resources (DNR), Watershed Monitoring, 6–7.

4 Leopold, "Round River" and "Land Ethic."

THE TWO NAMES OF THE RIVER

1 K. Knudson, interview and canoe trip.

2 G. Knudson, *Guide to the Upper Iowa River*, 38.

3 The first city to the north of Decorah—Rochester, Minnesota—has found that this same Decorah edge pushes its groundwater out into the "green filter" of hillside forest floors and in so doing removes 80 percent of their nitrate pollution. Hillside development threatens to degrade most of that filter by 2045 unless the city enacts currently considered zoning changes.

4 Northwest Ordinance, Article 4.

5 Long, "Voyage in a Six-oared Skiff," 12.

6 In 2008 waters exceeded the record 1941 flood level when they crested at 33,800 cubic feet per second at Decorah on June 9. The levee system held the river, though water on the populated side of the dike caused flooding as it rose, unable to flow into the river.

7 The chapter is written from the perspective of a fall 2003 canoe trip. In March 2005 the Environmental Protection Agency (EPA) issued the Clean Air Mercury Rule that, together with the Clean Air Interstate Rule, is intended to reduce mercury emissions from power plants.

8 Alexander, *History*, 288.

9 "The C[itizens'] A[ssociation]: Action of the Executive Committee Thursday Evening," *Decorah Iowa Republican*, March 31, 1881.

10 "Hydraulic Quarrying," *Decorah Republican*, July 31, 1884.

11 Hall and Whitney, *Report on the Geological Survey*, 460.

12 Alexander, *History*, 402–3.

13 Roverud, interview.

14 K. Knudson, *Multiple Use Preservation*, 9.

15 Ibid., 8.

16 McMullen, "Water Quality," 55–56, 59, and Andrew Pablo Johnson, "River Runs," 69.

17 Iowa Department of Natural Resources, *Upper Iowa River Protected Water Management Plan*, 11.

18 Ibid., *Water Quality in Iowa During 2002 and 2003*, 197.

19 Eckblad, interview.

BIG RIVER IN THE DRIFTLESS

1 See Hall and Whitney, *Report on the Geological Survey*, vol. 1. In the *Report*, Whitney mostly avoided the topic of drift, unlike his assistant, A. H. Worthen, who discussed the drift formation of every county on which he reported. Whitney explained the soil of the prairie surface by saying, "the whole region now occupied by the prairies of the northwest was once an immense lake" (25). Near the end of his report he writes, "superficial detritus, commonly called drift and alluvium, over the surface, forms one of the most important subjects for investigation falling within the scope of the geological survey." But instead of an explanation, he says this will be "an important topic for consideration in a future report" (323). Whitney's ultimate general rejection of widespread glacial action in North America and Europe was his monograph, *Climatic Changes* (1882), where he attributed the geological changes in recent earth history not to a cold, icy climate that had warmed but to a warm, wet climate that had cooled and dried.

2 McGee, *Pleistocene History*, 200.

3 Schultz, *Glaciers*.

4 Kalishek, interview.

5 The Driftless Area National Wildlife refuge, an area of 775 acres scattered across four Iowa counties, includes parcels in several watersheds. The main mission of the refuge is to protect northern monkshood plants and the Iowa Pleistocene snail.

6 Pusateri, et al., "Habitat."

7 Roosa, "Profile."

8 "Old Settlers' Re-Union," *Decorah Republican,* August 29, 1895.

9 "The Decorah Ice Cave: It Is Rapidly Making Decorah Known All Over the World," ibid., October 5, 1911.

10 Information on Decorah's ice business from Rosell, interview, and Boice, interview.

ROOTS AND FIRE

1 Richard Kittelson, interview.

2 Kittleson and Dideriksen, *Soil Survey.* A new county soil survey came out on CD ROM in 2006.

3 A. Johnson, "And a River Runs," 57–58. Nathan Parker, describing Winneshiek County in his 1855 handbook, *Iowa As It Is*, said "The county is well timbered,

about one-fourth of it is heavily timbered, one-third is prairie, and the balance is burr-oak openings" (180–81).

4 Kittleson and Diderikson, *Soil Survey,* 190.

5 The Iowa average in the bumper year of 2002 was 165 bushels of corn per acre. An acre of steep land on Trout Run is likely to produce between 100 and 150 bushels. A bushel of corn, dry enough to market, weighs 54 pounds.

6 Kittelson promoted this program for both the 2003 and the 2006 Conservation Reserve Program sign-ups, supported by extra funds from the Farm Bureau. In the end, five Trout Run landowners signed up 62.4 acres, less than one-tenth of Kittelson's goal.

7 Theler and Boszhardt, *Twelve Millennia,* 71, with further information on the Trout River site from Colin Betts of Luther College and his student, Reed Fitton.

8 Ibid., 80.

9 Benn et al., *Data Recovery Excavations,* 60.

10 Theler and Boszhardt, *Twelve Millennia,* 88.

11 For a study of the paleoclimate of the ecotone based on data collected on the Upper Iowa, see Baker et al., "Holocene Paleoenvironments."

12 Thompson, interview.

13 Hall and Whitney, *Report on the Geological Survey,* vol. 1, 14.

14 "From the note-book of the Itinerating Editor," *Decorah Gazette,* March 10, 1859.

15 Seastedt, "Soil Systems and Nutrient Cycles," 164.

16 Beltrami, *Pilgrimage in America,* 176–77.

17 Marquette, "Mississippi Voyage," 237.

18 La Potherie, quoted in Wedel, "Peering at the Ioway," 39.

19 La Potherie, "History of the Savage Peoples," vol. 1, 366.

20 Ibid., 367.

21 McHugh, *Time of the Buffalo,* 69–70.

22 Fletcher, "History and Government," vol. 4, 237.

23 Lynch, Tomscha, and Schulte, "Historic Vegetation Composition."

24 Kurz, *Journal,* 331, diary entry for April 26, 1852.

25 Jackson, *New Roots,* 114–36.

THE OLD ONES

1 Dinsmore, *A Country So Full,* 92.

2 Ibid., 92.

3 Radin, *Winnebago Tribe,* 65.

4 McGee, "Notes," 959.

5 Ibid., 961.

6 Radin, *Winnebago Tribe*, 65.

7 Meggers, *Prehistoric America*, 113–15. See also Gibson, *Poverty Point*.

8 Alana and Pete Fee, interview.

9 Orr, "Iowa Archaeological Reports," vol. 7, 55A.

10 Ibid., vol. 4, 141.

11 Keyes, "Federal Project 1047," 334.

12 Keyes, "In a Day's Work," 339–47.

13 Dorsey, "Social Organization," 339–40.

14 Orr, "Iowa Archaeological Reports," vol. 8, 50.

15 Field, "Diet of the Prehistoric Indians," 9.

16 Mallam, *Iowa Effigy Mound Manifestation*, 35.

17 Ibid., 38.

18 Foster, "Ioway and the Landscape," 2.

19 McKusick, *Grant Oneota Village*, 8–9.

20 Wedel, "Oneota Sites," 12.

21 McKusick, *Grant Oneota Village,* 39–41.

22 Ibid., 66–67.

23 See Baerreis, "Commentary," 146.

24 Dorsey, "Social Organization," 336–38.

25 Orr, "Iowa Archaeological Reports," vol. 6, 105.

26 McKusick, "Art that Predates Columbus," 12.

UNKNOWN WORLD

1 McKusick, *Grant Oneota Village*, 57.

2 Perrot, "Memoir," vol. 1, 159.

3 Wedel, "Peering at the Ioway," 15.

4 Ibid., 31.

5 Ibid., 32.

6 La Salle, *French Regime*, 110.

7 La Potherie, "History of the Savage Peoples," 369.

8 Park, *World of the Bison*, 40.

9 Skinner "Societies of the Iowa," 710.

10 Kambesis, interview.

11 La Potherie, "History of the Savage Peoples," 368.

12 Ibid., 369.

13 Ibid.

14 Ibid., 370.

15 Sandoz, *Beaver Men*, 69.

16 Hennepin, *Father Louis Hennepin's Description*, 169.

17 Indian trapping and hunting methods are discussed by Sandoz in *Beaver Men*, 131–32.

18 Sandoz, *Beaver Men*, 49.

19 "Beaver Fur Hat."

20 See Burke, "Chemin des Voyageurs," 60–92.

21 For the French composition of early Prairie du Chien, see Ekberg, *French Roots*, 102–8.

22 Blaine, *Ioway Indians*, 56.

23 Ibid., 54.

24 Carver, *Journals of Jonathon Carver*, 157.

25 Scanlan, *Prairie du Chien*, 64.

26 Cruzat, "Message," 504–5.

27 Pike, *Journals of Zebulon Montgomery Pike*, vol. 1, 25.

28 Ibid., vol. 1, 26.

29 Ibid., vol. 1, 27.

30 On the map of his journey, Pike drew in the Dakota village on the south bank of the Upper Iowa. Ibid., vol. 1, plate 13.

31 Blaine, *Ioway Indians*, 94.

32 Ibid., 95.

33 Cruikshank, "Robert Dickson," 140.

34 Long, "Voyage in a Six-oared Skiff," 12, 50.

35 Ibid., 13.

36 Forsyth, "Fort Snelling," 150.

37 Meyer, *History of the Santee Sioux*, 44.

38 Lace, interview.

39 Blaine, *Ioway Indians*, 146.

40 Ibid.

41 Ibid., 146–47.

42 Rayman, "Confrontation at the Fever River."

43 Atwater, *Remarks Made on a Tour*, 148.

44 Ibid., 33.

45 Marston, in Blair, *Indian Tribes*, vol. 2, 151.

46 Hagan, *Sac and Fox*, 115.

47 Van der Zee, "Neutral Ground," 324.

48 Forsyth, "Fort Snelling," 152.

49 Mancall, *Deadly Medicine*, 164–67.

50 Unrau, *White Man's*, 12–24. See also Hagan, *Sac and Fox*, 206–7.

51 "Dakota and the Black Hawk War," 312. Reprinted conversation of June 22, 1832, between General Street and Dakota chiefs, first printed in *Illinois Galenian*, July 11, 1832.

52 Faragher, *Daniel Boone*, 271.

53 Van der Zee, "Neutral Ground," 315–16.

54 Abernethy, "Early Iowa Indian Treaties," 256.

55 Ibid., 258.

56 Ibid.

57 Ibid., 371.

58 Young, "United States Mounted Ranger," 454–55.

59 Abernethy, "Early Iowa Indian Treaties," 378.

60 Young, "United States Mounted Ranger," 456.

61 Hagan, *Sac and Fox*, 198.

62 Denniston et al., "Evidence for Increased Cool."

63 Van der Zee, "Neutral Ground," 321.

WE HAVE NEVER SOLD ANY COUNTRY

1 Seymour to Fletcher, October 23, 1845, National Archives, 234:863, 1058–60.

2 Anton Grignon, quoted in Hexom, *Indian History*, n.p.

3 Paquette, "Wisconsin Winnebagos," 421.

4 Lurie, "Winnebago," 699; Smith, *Ho-Chunk Tribal History*, 52–53.

5 In April 1843, soldiers at Fort Crawford were ordered to destroy all canoes belonging to the Winnebago found on the east side of the Mississippi, another move intended to keep the Winnebago on the west side, National Archives, 234:863, 44.

6 Sullivan, "Annexation," 5.

7 Letter from Henry Rice to Thwaites, October 14, 1887, in Paquette, "Wisconsin Winnebagoes," 407.

8 Letter dictated by Whirling Thunder to H. M. Rice, March 4, 1842, National Archives, 234:862, 170.

9 Turkey River Sub Agency Report, July 24, 1843, National Archives, 234:862, 589. Sixty years later, when Abraham Jacobson wrote his "Reminiscences of Pioneer Norwegians," he recalled that "Ole Halvorsen Valle . . . was employed in breaking up pieces of bottom land on the Upper Iowa river. One of the largest fields thus prepared for the Indians to plant their corn was situated just below the outlet of Trout Run." If the first plowing Valle did was on Trout Run, it is possible that Kara-mani-ga was making his village there in 1843. The area plowed for Winneshiek (Coming Thunder) in 1843 may have been on the bottoms near the outlet of Trout River. See Jacobson, "Springfield Township," 214.

10 National Archives, 234:862, 382–84.

11 Lowry letter to Chambers, May 31, 1844, National Archives, 234:863, 382–84. In July and August 1844, a map made by Company B of the First Dragoons shows Yellow Thunder living near the mouth of Trout Run and Little Decorah having a village further down the Upper Iowa. Neither Waukon Haga nor Walking Turtle are listed on the map, even though Lowry had ordered fields made for them on the river.

12 Jonathon Fletcher, report to James Clark, Superintendent of Indian Affairs, Iowa Territory, August 15, 1846, Reque Collection.

13 John Thomas, September 30, 1842, report to David Lowry about the agency farm, National Archives, 234:862, 95–98.

14 The changing view of the frontier in the 1840s is discussed well in White, "Power of Whiteness."

15 Fletcher report, August 15, 1846, Reque Collection.

16 Fletcher, "Origin and History," 234.

17 Lowry, "Moral Questions," 535.

18 Smith, *Ho-Chunk Tribal History*, 53.

19 Letter from Fletcher to Clark, January 10, 1846, Fort Atkinson Research Files, Joel Post, MS 173, b.1, f.40, State Historical Society of Iowa, Iowa City.

20 Robb, "Journalist," 215. See also the Murdock account in "The Winnebagoes," *Decorah Republican*, December 24, 1896.

21, Hexom, *Indian History*, n.p.

22 Paquette, "Wisconsin Winnebagos," 422.

23 Fletcher, "Origin and History," 233.

24 Fletcher report, August 15, 1846, Reque Collection.

25 Treaty agreement, reprinted in Hovde, "Study of the Development," 22.

26 Lowry, "Moral Questions," 530.

27 Ibid., 529.

28 Waukon Haga Decorah, quoted in Hancock, "History of Allamakee," 368.

29 "Report on Pupils Attending Winnebago School, May 1844," National Archives, 234:863, 394–95.

30 Margaret Porter, quoted in Newhall, *Glimpse of Iowa*, 37–39.

31 "Specimen of Writing, September 1842," National Archives, 234:862, 77, and Paquette, "Wisconsin Winnebagos," 406.

32 September 1842 school report, National Archives, 234:862, 77–79.

33 Lowry, "Moral Questions," 526.

34 House, interview.

35 Lowry, "Moral Questions," 527.

36 "Inventory of goods seized by Lieut. Hamilton on Red Cedar River," submitted by David Lowry on December 13, 1843, National Archives, 234: 863, 148–49.

37 Sibley, "Reminiscences," 265.

38 Fort Atkinson State Preserve display, Fort Atkinson, Iowa.

39 List of Goods, National Archives, 234:862, 81.

40 Sparks, *History of Winneshiek*, 8–10.

41 Lowry defense, National Archives, 243: 862, 385–87.

42 Waukon Decorah speech to John Chambers, July 1843, National Archives, 234: 862, 554.

43 As an example, in the third quarter of 1844, Thomas Provencal and George Fisher had been licensed to trade for Dousman's outfit on the Upper Iowa. See Statement of Licenses by James McGregor, U.S. Sub Indian Agent, Third Quarter of 1844, National Archives, 234:863, 519.

44 Capt. Morgan letter, January 23, 1847, Reque Collection.

45 "Death of Henry Rice," *Decorah Republican*, January 18, 1894.

46 Fletcher, 1845 "Report of Licenses Granted," National Archives, 234:864, 113.

47 Dearborn letter to Chambers, January 4, 1845, ibid., 234:810.

48 "Narrative of Spoon Decorah," *Wisconsin Historical Collections*, vol. 13, 455.

49 Lowry 1842 census, National Archives, 243:862, 118.

50 Whirling Thunder to David Lowry, February 14, 1842, Reque Collection, folder RG15, Luther College Archives, Decorah, Iowa.

51 John Chambers, July 17, 1843, speech to Winnebago, National Archives, 234:862, 522.

52 Whirling Thunder statement to Henry Dodge, June 20, 1845, Reque Collection.

53 Smith, *Folklore*, 13.

54 Smith, public appearance.

55 An origin story related by Chief Little Hill to Jonathan Fletcher is in "Origin and History," 228–30.

56 The survey took place in June and July 1835. "Journal of Marches," 369.

57 Waukon Haga speech at July 17, 1843 treaty session, National Archives, 234:862, 526.

58 Waukon Haga speech at July 18, 1843 treaty session, ibid., 234:862, 537.

59 Robb, letter of July 1, 1848, in "Journalist," 215.

60 Mark Diedrich, ed., *Winnebago Oratory*, 82.

61 Reed, "Narrative," 17.

62 Robb, "Journalist," 215.

THE GREAT IMPROVEMENT

1 Koren, *Diary*, 104.

2 Land Survey, surveyor's section line field notes, Township 97 north, Range 8, secretary of state, State Historical Society of Iowa, Des Moines.

3 Gue, *History of Iowa*, 258.

4 Davis, phone conversation.

5 Cheeseman, interview.

6 "Forty-Four Years Ago: Pen Pictures of Iowa and Winneshiek County in 1856," *Decorah Republican*, February 1, 1900.

7 Koren, *Diary*, 208.

8 Ibid., 232.

9 Alexander, *History of Winneshiek*, 631.

10 Adams quoted in Sparks, *History of Winneshiek*, 94–95.

11 "Old Settlers' Re-union, Two Hundred and Fifty Unite in the Meeting and Have a Very Good Time," *Decorah Republican*, August 29, 1895.

12 "Immigrants," *Decorah Iowa Republican*, May 24, 1866.

13 Beard letter, November 16, 1852, in "Beard Branch," 32.

14 "The Flood," *Decorah Iowa Republic*, March 23, 1865.

15 From the account of Jane Cray Gates, "Reminiscences of Pioneer Days," in Davis and Buresh, *Lime Springs*, 12–13.

16 Robinson, interview.

17 Beard letter, November 1, 1852, in "Beard Branch," 31.

18 Koren, *Diary*, 97.

19 Ibid., 223.

20 Ibid., 173.

21 Ibid., 196.

22 Ibid.

23 Ibid., 343.

24 Barnes, letter.

25 Koren, *Diary*, 263.

26 Bogue, *From Prairie*, 70.

27 Advertisement, *Decorah Gazette*, March 10, 1859.

28 Beard, "Observations and Records," April 15, 1851; record for 1854, in "Beard Branch," 24–25.

29 Ibid., 25.

30 "Grinding," *Decorah Iowa Republic*, February 4, 1864.

31 Sparks, *History of Winneshiek*, 96.

32 "Grapes," *Decorah Iowa Republic*, September 22, 1864.

33 "Fruit Trees and Shrubbery!" ibid., May 4, 1860.

34 Koren. *Diary*, 242.

35 Orr, "Iowa Archaeological Reports," vol. 9, 1–4.

36 Ross, *Iowa Agriculture*, 58.

37 Fredenburgh, quoted in Bailey, *Past and Present*, vol. 1, 245.

38 Koren, *Diary*, 170.

39 Street, "Letter to *Friends Review*," 455.

40 Beard letter, November 1, 1852, in "Beard Branch," 31.

41 From *Iowa as It Is in 1856*, reprinted in *Decorah Republican*, February 1, 1900.

42 "Planing Machine," *Decorah Iowa Republic*, July 24, 1862.

43 Alexander, *History of Winneshiek*, 261.

44 "Gleanings: From the Note-Book of the Itinerating Editor," *Decorah Gazette*, March 10, 1859.

45 J. & G. S. Ammon advertisement, *Decorah Iowa Republic*, September 19, 1861.

46 "Judge Williams' Excavator," ibid., May 25, 1865.

47 McGee, *Pleistocene History*, 359.

48 "Notes of Talks with Mr. George P. Bellows," in Orr, "Iowa Archaeological Reports," vol. 9, 1.

49 Beard letter, December 19, 1852, in "Beard Branch," 33.

50 "Old Settlers' Re-union, Two Hundred and Fifty Unite in the Meeting and Have a Very Good Time," *Decorah Republican*, August 29, 1895.

51 Freeling Van Leuven, quoted in David and Buresh, *Lime Springs*, 8; Hans Peterson Luvbraaten account in Clarence M. Peterson, "Saga of the House of Luvbraate, *Decorah Public Opinion*, January 28, 1942. See also Dinsmore, *Country So Full*, 26–27.

52 Koren, *Diary*, 256.

53 Ibid., 82.

54 Ibid., 137.

55 Ibid., 230.

56 Ibid.

57 Garland, *Son of the Middle*, 77.

58 Koren, *Diary*, 272. Prairie chickens have since disappeared from all but a handful of locations in Iowa and from the entire Upper Iowa River basin.

59 Ibid., 228.

60 Street, "Letter to *Friends Review*," 455.

61 "Piscatorial," *Decorah Iowa Republic*, July 24, 1862.

62 Bent, *Tales of Travel*, 68.

63 "Favors," *Decorah Iowa Republic*, May 11, 1860, and "Pickerel Fishing," ibid., April 27, 1860.

64 "A Nice One," ibid.

65 "Proceedings of the Board of Supervisors," ibid., January 12, 1865. Animals called "wildcats" in public records of the day were almost certainly bobcats, but cougars were present at first settlement and, possibly, lynx.

66 Hancock, "History of Allamakee," 344.

67 Bent, *Tales of Travel*, 108.

68 Neill, *History of Fillmore*, 412.

69 Koren, *Diary*, 106.

70 "Grow Wool! — Raise Sheep!" *Decorah Iowa Republic*, August 10, 1860.

71 Horn, *English Colony*, 58.

72 Koren, *Diary*, 167–68.

73 Ibid., 234.

74 Beard letter, November 1, 1852, in "Beard Branch," 31.

75 "Mishap," *Decorah Iowa Republic*, February 23, 1865.

76 "Lynched!" ibid., May 11, 1860. See also *History of Howard County*, 4.

77 Advertisement, *Decorah Iowa Republic*, February 26, 1863.

78 "Make You a Home," ibid., May 11, 1860.

79 "Out of Town," ibid.

80 "Rose Harbor Holstein Farm," undated news clipping, reprinted in "Beard Branch," 39.

STEAM, WIND, AND THE POWERS OF EARTH

1 Wise, "Roots Grow Strong," 217.

2 "Northern Iowa R.R." *Decorah Iowa Republic*, June 20, 1861.

3 Broehl, *Cargill: Trading*, 3–22.

4 Booth, quoted in Davis and Buresh, *Lime Springs*, 54.

5 *History of Howard*, 11.

6 Sires and Fitzpatrick, *First 100 Years*.

7 Hancock, "History of Allamakee," 353.

8 "Railroad Celebration," speech by E. E. Cooley, in *Decorah Iowa Republican*, October 1, 1867.

9 Bent, *Tales of Travel*, 53.

10 Wise, "Roots Grow Strong," 225.

11 Applen, interview.

12 "Winneshiek County Fair: A Stranger's View of It." *Decorah Iowa Republican*, October 1, 1869.

13 "The Blockade Raised." ibid., January 24, 1873.

14 Ibid., July 2, 1875.

15 "A Water-Power War," ibid., August 28, 1879.

16 "The Future of Decorah," ibid., August 21, 1879.

17 See Grodinsky, *Iowa Pool*.

18 Ross, *Iowa Agriculture*, 98–103.

19 "Anti-RR Meeting at Frankville," *Decorah Iowa Republican*, July 21, 1879, "Don't Want It!" ibid., August 14, 1879; "The Difference," ibid., August 7, 1879.

20 "Last Rail Laid this Afernoon Amid General Rejoicing," speech by Wesley Bailey, in *Decorah Republican,* October 23, 1884.

21 "Thanksgiving—What of the Future?" *Decorah Iowa Republican,* November 25, 1880.

22 *Decorah Iowa Republican,* March 19, 1875.

23 Portman, *Decorah's English Colony.*

24 Hancock, "History of Allamakee," 346.

25 Wise, "Roots Grow Strong," 223, 230.

26 Hancock, "History of Allamakee," 345.

27 Ibid., 343.

28 Portman, *Decorah's English Colony,* n.p.

29 "A Business Outlook," *Decorah Iowa Republican,* October 5, 1882.

30 Ross, *Iowa Agriculture,* 80.

31 "Ice Cave Creamery," *Decorah Iowa Republican,* March 31, 1881.

32 "Largest Creamery in World," *Decorah Republican,* September 28, 1882.

33 William Beard, "Corn for Green Fodder—Grasses," *Decorah Iowa Republican,* April 21, 1881.

34 William Beard, "To Farmers Engaged in Dairying," ibid., August 18, 1881.

35 *Decorah Republican,* December 7, 1882.

36 Ibid., December 7, 1893.

37 Alexander, *History of Winneshiek,* 81.

38 "Fish Culture," *Decorah Iowa Republican,* March 19, 1875.

39 "Fish and Fishing," *Decorah Republican,* May 20, 1880.

40 "Fishy, but True," *Decorah Republican,* February 12, 1885.

41 "He Dynamited Fish," ibid., May 20, 1909.

42 "Fish Culture—What the State Is Doing about It," *Decorah Iowa Republican,* June 25, 1875. The salmon experiment failed, in part, because of dams that stopped the fish from migrating.

43 Matteson, *Ramblings,* n.p.

44 Hochstetler, interview.

45 Wise, "Roots Grow Strong," 342.

46 Letter from Delia Brandt to Catie Wise from Creekside Stock Farm, Dakota Territory, July 1883.

47 Wise, "Roots Grow Strong," 76.

48 Northern Canoe correspondent, *Decorah Republican,* May 2, 1903.

49 Florence N. Clark, "Putting the Small River to Work," reprinted in ibid., June 19, 1913.

50 "An Anniversary Flood," ibid., June 26, 1890.

51 "The Heavens Opened," ibid., July 26, 1883.

52 "Petition for Flood Control."

53 "Flood Lessons," *Decorah Republican*, June 25, 1903.

54 Paine, "The Electric Power Dam: The Conservation of Flood Water—The Influence of Forestry—A Double Profit to All," ibid., December 24, 1908.

55 To give a sample of the use of wood for fuel, Hancock reports that in 1875 the businesses of Allamakee County consumed 3.5 million cubic feet, in "History of Allamakee," 353.

56 *Standard Historical Atlas.*

57 "Is It Murder?" *Decorah Republican*, October 22, 1885; "The Inquest," ibid., October 29, 1885; "The Infanticide," ibid., December 10, 1885.

58 "Only a Little Short of a Hurricane—Magne Langland Drowned in Highland Township," ibid., May 10, 1888.

59 "Drowned at Power Dam," ibid., May 27, 1909.

AIDING THE LAND

1 "Believe Oil and Gas about Decorah," *Decorah Journal*, September 28, 1921.

2 The *Journal* probably meant "bay," a tree the psalmist claims to grow with a speed unrivaled by other living things. "Claim Oil Shows at 2700 Feet," ibid., September 27, 1922.

3 "Oil Drilling Stopped," *Decorah Public Opinion*, July 19, 1923.

4 "Farmers Union Has Convention," *Decorah Public Opinion and Republican*, March 17, 1932.

5 Ibid., January 2, 1930.

6 Fox, *John Muir*, 183–84.

7 *Soils and Men*, 200.

8 Ibid., 12.

9 "A Day at Work and Play in Decorah CC Camp Is Topic of Camp Leaders," *Decorah Journal*, April 20, 1939.

10 Ross, *Iowa Agriculture*, 181.

11 "Sound Soil Building Program Results in Better Farm Home," *Decorah Public Opinion and Republican*, April 5, 1934.

12 "Commercial Fertilizers Becoming Popular in Iowa," *Decorah Republican*, March 31, 1921.

13 "Fertilizer Use Demonstration in This County: TVA Will Supply Superphosphates for Experiments," *Decorah Journal*, February 18, 1937.

14 "Top Soil Losses Run Thousands through Area," ibid., July 2, 1941.

15 "Possibilities of Improvement of Our Fishing," *Decorah Public Opinion and Republican*, August 3, 1933.

16 *Decorah Journal*, July 26, 1933.

17 "$323,136 Spent on WPA Works in Winneshiek," ibid., January 19, 1939.

18 "Pollution Kills Fish," *Decorah Public Opinion and Republican,* April 21, 1932.

19 "Swimming Pool for Decorah?" *Decorah Journal,* July 31, 1935.

20 "Vacation: All Work and No Play Is Poor Business," ibid., July 8, 1937.

21 "51 Men Start Work Dry Run Improvement: Creek Bed to Be made Both Wider and Straighter," *Decorah Public Opinion and Republican,* November 30, 1933.

22 Peterson, interview.

THE JUICE

1 "Farmers Hear of Weed, Borer Plans," *Decorah Journal,* January 31, 1950.

2 Kraus died in retirement in Oregon in 1959, aged fifty-nine, fourteen years after his demonstration of eating herbicide. For an account of his eating 2,4-D see Burnside, "History of 2,4-D."

3 Alice and Fred Lubke, interview.

4 Burnside, "History of 2,4-D."

5 John Lubke, interview.

6 "For Garden without Pests Dust Early with D.D.T.," *Decorah Journal,* May 15, 1947.

7 "Spraying in Early June: Chamber Hears Plans for All-Out Drive On Pests Here," ibid., May 22, 1947.

8 "DDT Called Harmless to Man," ibid., July 10, 1947.

9 Ibid., May 30, 1950.

10 "Straightening the Upper Iowa," ibid., March 18, 1920.

11 "Butch is on a Balanced Diet," advertisement in ibid., April 29, 1943.

12 "Hey, Ref—Aren't You Out of Bounds?" advertisement in ibid., February 14, 1946.

13 Morris Bergan, interview.

14 "Electricity on the Farm," *Decorah Journal,* July 10, 1947.

15 Statement by extension director John Rodecap in "Dairy Farming Still Vital to Area," ibid., June 4, 1970.

16 "Interstate Plans New Power Plant at Lansing to Serve Decorah Area," ibid., April 11, 1946.

17 "Sin Seen in Soil Thefts: Lutherans at Seminar Hear Call to Reponsibility," ibid., March 14, 1946.

18 Carson, *Silent Spring,* 10.

19 Ibid., 8.

20 Ibid., 6.

21 "Pesticides, Animal Wastes, Silt Contribute Pollution Problem," *Decorah Public Opinion,* November 18, 1968.

22 "Trout Die As Oxygen Depleted," *Decorah Journal,* July 3, 1969.

23 "Reader Slaps at Weed Campaign," *Decorah Public Opinion*, May 5, 1970.

24 Nixon, "Reorganization Plan."

25 *Upper Iowa Wild and Scenic River Study*, 1.

26 "NE Iowa Another 'Black Hills'?" *Decorah Public Opinion,* January 27, 1969.

27 "Upper Iowa River Offers Food for the Soul As Well As the Body." *Decorah Journal*, November 27, 1969.

28 "Republicans Support Cave, River Plans," ibid., July 16, 1970.

29 "Upper Iowa Unique Scenic River," ibid., August 20, 1970.

30 "Scenic River Opposition Packs Decorah Hearing," ibid., August 27, 1970.

31 "Landowners Seek More Help in Scenic Rivers Fight," ibid., September 3, 1970.

ON THE PLACE BY THE RIVER THEY RAISE CHILDREN

1 Patricia and Paul Johnson, interview.

2 Veysey, "French Creek Defense Project."

3 Wise, interview.

4 Lora Friest, interview.

5 Beard family, interview.

6 United States Department of Agriculture, National Agricultural Statistics Service, *Agricultural Prices Summary*.

7 Since my 2003 interview with the Johnsons, the sharp rise in oil prices has also raised corn prices (to over $5 per bushel in February 2007) due to increased production costs and higher market prices for ethanol.

8 Andrew Johnson, interview. Since our interview, Johnson and his family have moved back to Oneota Slopes.

Bibliography

Abernethy, Colonel Alonzo. "Early Iowa Indian Treaties and Boundaries." *Annals of Iowa* 11, no. 4 (1914): 240–59, and 11, no. 5 (1914): 358–81.

Alexander, W. E. *History of Winneshiek and Allamakee Counties: Iowa.* Sioux City, IA: Western Publishing, 1882.

Allen, J. David. *Stream Ecology: Structure and Function of Running Waters.* New York: Chapman and Hall, 1995.

Applen, Lauren. Interview by author. Granger, Minnesota, March 24, 2004.

Atwater, Caleb. *Remarks Made on a Tour to Prairie du Chien Thence to Washington City in 1829.* 1831. Reprint, New York: Arno Press, 1975.

Baerreis, David A. "Commentary." In McKusick, *The Grant Oneota Village,* 146–47.

Bailey, Edwin C. *Past and Present of Winneshiek County Iowa: A Record of Settlement, Organization, Progress, and Achievement.* 2 vols. Chicago: S. J. Clarke, 1913.

Baker, R. G., E. A. Bettis III, R. F. Denniston, L. A. González, L. E. Strickland, and J. R. Krieg. "Holocene Paleoenvironments in Southeastern Minnesota— Chasing the Prairie-Forest Ecotone." *Palaeogeography, Palaeoclimatology, and Palaeoecology* 177 (2002): 103–122.

Barnes, M. M. Letter, November 12 and November 16, 1854. Typed copy in Winneshiek County Historical Archives, Decorah, Iowa.

"Beard Branch: A Family History and Its Descendants," by Laura Beard. Decorah Genealogy Library, Decorah, Iowa.

Beard family. Interview by author. Decorah, Iowa, July 22, 2004.

"Beaver Fur Hat." White Oak Society. http://www.whiteoak.org/learning/furhat.htm (accessed December 3, 2003).

Beeman, Perry. "No Clear Solutions to State's Tainted Water." *Des Moines Register,* February 12, 2006.

Beltrami, Giacomo Constantino. *A Pilgrimage in America: Leading to the Discovery of the Sources of the Mississippi and Bloody River; with a Description of the Whole Course of the Former, and of the Ohio.* 2 vols. 1828. Reprint, vol. 2, Chicago: Quadrangle Books, 1962.

Benn, David, E. A. Bettis, III, Gina Powell, Neal Lopinot, and Derek Lee. *Data Recovery Excavations at Middle Archaic Site 13db493 Dubuque Township Dubuque County, Iowa.* Cresco, IA: Bear Creek Archeology, 2002.

Bent, George Payne. *Tales of Travel Life and Love: An Autobiography.* Los Angeles: Times-Mirror Press, 1924.

Bergan, Morris. Interview by author. Ridgeway, Iowa, October 2003.

Blaine, Martha Royce. *The Ioway Indians*. Norman: University of Oklahoma Press, 1979.

Blair, Emma Helen, ed. and trans. *The Indian Tribes of the Upper Mississippi Valley and Region of the Great Lakes as Described by Nicolas Perrot, French Commandant in the Northwest; Bacqueville de la Potherie, French Royal Commissioner to Canada; Morrell Marston, American Army Officer; and Thomas Forsyth, United States Agent at Fort Armstrong*. 2 vols. Cleveland, OH: Arthur H. Clark, 1911.

Bogue, Allan G. *From Prairie to Corn Belt: Farming on the Illinois and Iowa Prairies in the Nineteenth Century*. Chicago: University of Chicago Press, 1963.

Boice, Dean. Interview by author. Decorah, Iowa, September 1996.

Brandt, Delia. Unpublished correspondence to family of Samuel Wise. Personal collection of author.

Broehl, Wayne G., Jr. *Cargill: Trading the World's Grain*. Hanover, NH: University Press of New England, 1992.

Burke, William J. *The Upper Mississippi Valley: How The Landscape Shaped Our Heritage*. Waukon, IA: Mississippi Valley Press, 2000.

Burnside, Orvin C. "The History of 2,4-D and Its Impact on Development of the Discipline of Weed Science in the United States." *Biologic and Economic Assessment of Benefits from Use of Phenoxy Herbicides in the United States* (Special National Agricultural Pesticide Impact Assessment Program Report, Number 1-PA-96). http://www.24d.org/abstracts/chapter2.pdf (accessed August 26, 2006).

Carson, Rachel. *Silent Spring*. Boston: Houghton Mifflin, 1962.

Carver, Jonathon. *The Journals of Jonathon Carver and Related Documents 1766–1770*, ed. John Parker. St. Paul, MN: Minnesota Historical Society Press, 1976.

Cheeseman, April. Interview by author. Old Town, Iowa, August 22, 2004.

Cruikshank, Ernest Alexander. "Robert Dickson, The Indian Trader." *Wisconsin Historical Collections* 12 (1892): 132–53.

Cruzat, Don Francisco. "Message to the Sauks and Foxes, 1781." *Collections of the State Historical Society of Wisconsin* 3 (1857): 504–5.

"Dakota and the Black Hawk War." *Wisconsin Historical Collections* 5 (1868): 310–14.

Davis, Anna May. Phone conversation with author. March 2004.

Davis, Anna May, and Jane Buresh. *Lime Springs: Then and Now, The Story of the First 114 Years of Our Town*. Lime Springs, IA: Lime Springs Centennial Committee, 1968.

Decorah Gazette (1858–1860). Microfilm. Preus Library, Luther College, Decorah, Iowa.

Decorah Iowa Republic (1860–1866), *Decorah Iowa Republican* (1866–1882), *Decorah Republican* (1882–1928). Microfilm. Preus Library, Luther College, Decorah, Iowa.

Decorah Journal (1900–present). Microfilm. Preus Library, Luther College, Decorah, Iowa.

Decorah Public Opinion (1895–1928, 1942–present). Microfilm. Preus Library, Decorah, Iowa.

Decorah Public Opinion and Republican (1929–1942). Microfilm. Preus Library, Decorah, Iowa.

Denniston, Rhawn F., Luis A. González, Yemane Asmerom, Richard G. Baker, Mark K. Reagan, and E. Arthur Bettis III. "Evidence for Increased Cool Season Moisture during Middle Holocene." *Geology* 27, no. 9 (1999): 815–18.

Diedrich, Mark, ed. *Winnebago Oratory: Great Moments in the Recorded Speech of the Hochungra, 1742–1887.* Rochester, MN: Coyote Books, 1991.

Dinsmore, James L. *A Country So Full of Game: The Story of Wildlife in Iowa.* Iowa City: University of Iowa Press, 1994.

Dorsey, J. Owen. "The Social Organization of the Siouan Tribes." *Journal of American Folk-Lore* 4, no. 12 (1891): 331–42.

Driftless Area National Wildlife Refuge. U.S. Fish and Wildlife Service. http://www.fws.gov/midwest/driftless/.

Eckblad, James. Interview by author. Decorah, Iowa, June 16, 1996.

Ekberg, Carl J. *French Roots in the Illinois Country: The Mississippi Frontier in Colonial Times.* Urbana: University of Illinois Press, 1998.

Faragher, John Mack. *Daniel Boone: The Life and Legend of an American Pioneer.* New York: Holt, 1992.

Fee, Alana and Pete. Interview by author. New Albin, Iowa, October 28, 2003.

Field, H. P., "The Diet of the Prehistoric Indians of Northeast Iowa." *Journal of the Iowa Archeological Society* 1 no. 2: 8–13.

Fletcher, Jonathan. "Origin and History of the Winnebagoes, Their Traditions of the Creation of the World and of Man, Biographical Sketches of their Living Chiefs, Incidents of the Black-Hawk War, Tribal Rank, Geographical Notices, Wild Animals, Fabulous Monsters, Knowledge of Astronomy, Arithmetic, and Medicine." In *History of the Indian Tribes of the Unites States*, ed. Henry R. Schoolcraft. Vol. 4. Philadelphia: Lippincott, Grambo, 1857.

Forsyth, Major Thomas. "Fort Snelling: Colonel Leavenworth's Expedition to Establish It, in 1819." *Minnesota Historical Collections* 3 (1880): 139–67.

Fort Atkinson Research Files. State Historical Society of Iowa, Iowa City.

Fort Atkinson State Preserve display. Fort Atkinson, Iowa.

Foster, Lance Michael. "The Ioway and the Landscape of Southeast Iowa." *Journal of the Iowa Archeological Society* 43 (1996): 1–6.

Fox, Stephen R. *John Muir and His Legacy: The American Conservation Movement.* Boston: Little, Brown, 1981.

Friest, Lora. Interview by author. Decorah, Iowa, September 16, 2003.

Garland, Hamlin. *A Son of the Middle Border.* New York: Macmillan, 1923.

Gibson, Jon L. *Poverty Point: A Terminal Archaic Culture of the Lower Mississippi Valley.* 2nd ed. Department of Culture, Recreation, and Tourism. Louisiana Archaeological Survey and Antiquities Commission, 1996. http://www.crt.state.la.us/crt/ocd/arch/poverpoi/mapopo.htm (accessed March 2004).

Grodinsky, Julius. *The Iowa Pool: A Study in Railroad Competition, 1870–84.* Chicago: University of Chicago Press, 1950.

Gue, Benjamin Franklin. *History of Iowa from the Earliest Time.* 4 vols. New York: Century History Company, 1903.

Hagan, William Thomas. *The Sac and Fox Indians.* Norman: University of Oklahoma Press, 1958.

Hall, James, and J. D. Whitney. *Report on the Geological Survey of the State of Iowa: Embracing the Results of Investigations Made during Portions of the Years 1855, 56, & 57.* 2 vols. Des Moines, IA: C. Van Benthuysen, 1858.

Hancock, E. M. "History of Allamakee County." In *History of Winneshiek and Allamakee Counties, Iowa,* by W. E. Alexander. Sioux City, IA: Western Publishing, 1882.

Hennepin, Louis. *Father Louis Hennepin's Description of Louisiana; Newly Discovered to the Southwest of New France by Order of the King,* trans. Marion E. Cross. Minneapolis: Minnesota Society of the Colonial Dames of America/University of Minnesota Press, 1938.

Heraclitus. *Heraclitus: the Complete Philosophical Fragments,* trans. William Harris. http://www.middlebury.edu/~harris/Philosophy/Heraclitus.html (accessed August 1, 2006).

Hexom, Charles Philip. *Indian History of Winneshiek County.* Decorah, IA: A.K. Bailey and Son, 1913.

History of Howard County, Iowa. Cresco, IA: Howard County Historical Society, 1989.

Hochstetler, Jonas. Interview by author. Harmony, Minnesota, July 25, 2006.

Horn, Henry Harcourt. *An English Colony in Iowa.* Boston: Christopher Publishing, 1931.

House, Samantha. Interview by author. Black River Falls, Wisconsin, July 2001.

Hovde, David. "Study of the Development and Maintenance of Legends Concerning the Neutral Ground Period in Northeast Iowa." MA thesis, Wichita State University, 1975.

Iowa Department of Natural Resources. *Upper Iowa River Protected Water Management Plan.* N.p., January 1990.

———. *Water Quality in Iowa during 2002 and 2003: Assessment Results.* http://programs.iowadnr.gov/adbnet/index.aspx.

———. Watershed Monitoring and Assessment Section. In *Category Five of Iowa's 2006 Integrated Report: The Section 303(d) List of Impaired Waters.* October 2007. http://wqm.igsb.uiowa.edu/WQA/303d/2006/Iowa_06-final-IR-Cat-5-303d-List.pdf.

Iowa Trout Fishing Guide. Des Moines, IA: Department of Natural Resources, 1994.

Jackson, Wes. *New Roots for Agriculture.* San Francisco: Friends of the Earth, 1980.

Jacobson, Abraham. "Springfield Township: Remembrances of Pioneer Norwegians." In Bailey, *Past and Present,* vol. 1.

Johnson, Andrew Pablo. "And a River Runs through It: Landscape Conservation on the Upper Iowa Watershed." MA thesis, University of Michigan, 1993.

———. Interview by author. Decorah, Iowa, December 21, 2003.

Johnson, Patricia and Paul. Interview by author. Decorah, Iowa, December 17, 2003.

"Journal of Marches by the First United States Dragoons: 1834–1835." *Iowa Journal of History and Politics* 7, no. 3 (1909): 331–78.

Kalishek, Bill. Interview by author. Decorah, Iowa, October 6, 2003.

Kambesis, Patricia. Interview by author. Decorah, Iowa, April 7, 2004.

Keyes, Charles Reuben. "Federal Project 1047." *Palimpsest* 15, no. 10 (1934): 332–38.

———. "In the Day's Work." *Palimpsest* 15, no. 10 (1934): 339–54.

Kittleson, Kenneth K., and Raymond I. Dideriksen. *Soil Survey, Winneshiek County, Iowa.* Washington, DC: Government Printing Office, 1968.

Kittelson, Richard. Interview by author. Decorah, Iowa, April 1, 2004.

Knudson, George. *A Guide to the Upper Iowa River.* Decorah, IA: Luther College, 1970.

Knudson, Karl. Interview by author. Decorah, Iowa, September 18, 2003, and on canoe trip, November 16, 2003.

———. *Multiple Use Preservation of Iowa's Rivers.* Des Moines: Sierra Club, Iowa Chapter, 1979.

Koren, Elisabeth. *The Diary of Elisabeth Koren, 1853–1855,* trans. David T. Nelson. Northfield, MN: Norwegian-American Historical Association, 1955.

Kurz, Rudolf Friedrich. *Journal of Rudolf Friedrich Kurz: An Account of His Experiences among Fur Traders and American Indians on the Mississippi and the Upper Missouri Rivers during the Years 1846 to 1852*, trans. Myrtis Jarrell. Lincoln: University of Nebraska Press, 1970.

La Potherie, Claude Charles Le Roy, Bacqueville de. "History of the Savage Peoples Who Are Allies of New France." In Blair, *Indian Tribes*. Vol. 1.

La Salle, René Robert Cavelier, Sieur de. Letter in *The French Regime in Wisconsin 1, 1634–1727*. Vol. 16 of *Collections of the State Historical Society of Wisconsin*, ed. Reuben Gold Thwaites. Madison: State Historical Society of Wisconsin, 1902.

Lace, Mike. Interview by author. Decorah, Iowa, April 17, 2004.

Land Survey. Vol. 69. West 5th Meridian, Iowa Townships 94–99, Range 8. Filed with the State Land Office. Office of the Iowa Secretary of States. Des Moines.

Leopold, Aldo. *A Sand County Almanac: With Essays on Conservation from Round River*. New York: Ballantine Books, 1986.

Long, Major Stephen. "Voyage in a Six-oared Skiff to the Falls of Saint Anthony, in 1817." *Collections of the Minnesota Historical Society* 2 (1860–1867): 9–88.

Lowry, Rev. David. "Moral Questions Relative to Practical Plans for Educating and Civilizing the Aborigines." In *History of the Indian Tribes of the United States*, ed. Henry R. Schoolcraft. Vol. 2. Philadelphia: Lippincott, Grambo, and Company, 1857.

Lubke, Alice and Fred. Interview by author. Ridgeway, Iowa, June 13 and 15, 1999.

Lubke, John. Interview by author. Ridgeway, Iowa, October 2003.

Lurie, Nancy Oestreich. "Winnebago." In *Handbook of North American Indians*, gen. ed. William C. Sturtevant. Vol. 15, *Northeast*, ed. B. G. Trigger. Washington, DC: Smithsonian Institution, 1978.

Lynch, E. A., S. Tomscha, and L. Schulte. "Historic Vegetation Composition and Structure at the Prairie-Forest Border in Northeastern Iowa." Poster presentation, US-International Association of Landscape Ecology Symposium, Madison, WI, April 6–10, 2008.

Mallam, R. Clark. *The Iowa Effigy Mound Manifestation: An Interpretive Model*. Report 9. Iowa City: Office of the State Archeologist, 1976.

Mancall, Peter. *Deadly Medicine: Indians and Alcohol in Early America*. Ithaca, NY: Cornell University Press, 1997.

Marquette, Fr. Jacques. "The Mississippi Voyage Made by Father Marquette." In *Early Narratives of the Northwest: 1634–1699*, ed. Louise Phelps Kellogg. New York: C. Scribner's Sons, 1917.

Marston, Morrell. "Letter to Reverend Dr. Jedidiah Morse." In Blair, *Indian Tribes*. Vol. 2.

Matteson, Sumner W. *Ramblings on the Upper Iowa River: An Interesting Description of One of Nature's Paradises.* Decorah, IA: Leonard and Son, 1890.

McGee, W. J. W. "Notes on the Passenger Pigeon." *Science* 32 (1910): 958–64.

———. *The Pleistocene History of Northeastern Iowa.* Eleventh Annual Report of the Director of the U.S. Geological Survey. Pt. 1, Geology. Washington, DC: Government Printing Office, 1891.

McHugh, Tom. *The Time of the Buffalo.* New York: Knopf, 1972.

McKusick, Marshall Bassford. "Art that Predates Columbus." *The Iowan* 19, no. 4 (1971): 8–13.

———. *The Grant Oneota Village.* Report 4. Office of the State Archaeologist. Iowa City: University of Iowa Press, 1973.

McMullen, Lee Dennis. "Water Quality Study of the Upper Iowa." MS thesis, University of Iowa, 1972.

Meggers, Betty J. *Prehistoric America.* Chicago: Aldine and Atherton, 1972.

Meyer, Roy W. *History of the Santee Sioux.* Lincoln: University of Nebraska Press, 1967.

National Archives (NA). Microcopies of papers related to the Winnebago. Referenced by microcopy, roll, and frame.

"Narrative of Spoon Decorah." *Wisconsin Historical Collections* 13 (1895): 448–62.

Neill, Edward D. *History of Fillmore County, Minnesota.* Minneapolis: Minnesota Historical Company, 1882.

Newhall, John. *A Glimpse of Iowa in 1846.* 1846. Reprint, Iowa City: State Historical Society of Iowa, 1957.

Nixon, Richard. "Reorganization Plan No. 3 of 1970." Delivered to Congress, July 9, 1970. http://www.epa.gov/history/org/origins/reorg.htm (accessed August 26, 2006).

Northwest Ordinance: July 13, 1787. *U.S. Historical Documents.* http://www.law.ou.edu/ushistory/ordinanc.shtml (acccessed August 1, 2006).

Orr, Ellison. "Iowa Archaeological Reports: 1934–1939." 10 vols. Manuscripts at Effigy Mounds National Monument. McGregor, Iowa.

Paquette, Moses. "The Wisconsin Winnebagos." *Wisconsin Historical Collections* 12 (1892): 399–433.

Park, Ed. *The World of the Bison.* New York: J. B. Lippincott, 1969.

Parker, Nathan. *Iowa As It Is: A Gazetteer for Citizens, and a Hand-book for Immigrants, Embracing a Full Description of the State of Iowa.* Chicago: Keen and Lee, 1855.

Perrot, Nicolas. "Memoir of the Manners, Customs, and Religion of the Savages of North America." In Blair, *Indian Tribes of the Upper Mississippi.* Vol. 1.

Peterson, Howard and Marie. Interview by author. Decorah, Iowa, January 1997.

"Petition for Flood Control on Dry Run," October 18, 1906. Vertical file, Decorah Geneological Library, Decorah, Iowa.

Pike, Zebulon. *The Journals of Zebulon Montgomery Pike: With Letters and Related Documents,* ed. Donald Jackson. 2 vols. Norman: University of Oklahoma Press, 1966.

Portman, R. F. B. *Decorah's English Colony of 1872: A Biographical Sketch.* N.p., 1931.

Pusateri, W. P., D. M. Roosa, and D. R. Farrar. "Habitat and Distribution of Plants Special to Iowa's Driftless Area." *Journal of the Iowa Academy of Science* (1993) 100: 29–53.

Radin, Paul. *The Winnebago Tribe.* 1923. Reprint, Lincoln: University of Nebraska Press, 1973.

Rayman, Ronald. "Confrontation at the Fever River Lead Mining District: Joseph Montfort Street vs. Henry Dodge, 1827–1828." *Annals of Iowa,* 44 no.4 (1978): 278–95.

Reed, William R. "Narrative of the March of Morgan's Mounted Volunteers (from Fort Atkinson, Iowa, to Long Prairie, Minnesota Guarding Removal of the Winnebago Indians)." Photocopy of typed manuscript. Iowa State Historical Society, Des Moines.

Reque Collection. Luther College Archives, Decorah, Iowa.

Robb, John S. "A Journalist at Old Fort Snelling." Ed. John Frances McDermott. *Minnesota History 31* (1950): 209–21.

Robinson, Gerry. Interview by author. Old Town, Iowa, August 22, 2004.

Roosa, Dean M. "Profile of an Endangered Species." *Iowa Conservationist* 42, nos. 4–5 (April–May 1983): 47.

Rosell, Vance. Interview by author. Decorah, Iowa, August 1996.

Ross, Earle D. *Iowa Agriculture: An Historical Survey.* Iowa City: State Historical Society of Iowa, 1951.

Roverud, Jeff. Interview by author. Decorah, Iowa, September 1996.

Sandoz, Mari. *The Beaver Men: Spearheads of Empire.* New York: Hastings House, 1964.

Scanlan, Peter Lawrence. *Prairie du Chien: French, British, American.* Menasha, WI: George Banta, 1937.

Schultz, Gwen. *Glaciers and the Ice Age: Earth and Its Inhabitants during the Pleistocene.* New York: Holt, Rinehart, and Winston, 1963.

Seastedt, Timothy. "Soil Systems and Nutrient Cycles of the North American Prairie." In *The Changing Prairie: North American Grasslands,* eds. Anthony Joern and Kathleen H. Keeler. New York: Oxford University Press, 1995.

Sibley, Henry H. "Reminiscences of the Early Days of Minnesota." In *Collections of the Minnesota Historical Society 3* (1880): 242–288.

Sires, Iris, and Patricia Fitzpatrick. *The First 100 Years of New Albin*. N.p., 1995.

Skinner, Alanson. "Societies of the Iowa, Kansa and Ponca Indians." *Journal of the Anthropological Papers of the American Museum of Natural History* 11, no. 9 (1915): 679–740.

Smith, David Lee. *Folklore of the Winnebago Tribe*. Norman: University of Oklahoma Press, 1997.

———. *Ho-Chunk Tribal History*. N.p., 1996.

———. Public appearance at Fort Atkinson, Iowa, September 1996.

Soils and Men. Washington, DC: U.S. Department of Agriculture, 1938.

Sparks, Charles H. *History of Winneshiek County with Biographical Sketches of its Eminent Men*. Decorah, IA: Jas. Alex Leonard, 1877.

Standard Historical Atlas of Winneshiek County Iowa. Davenport, IA: Anderson and Goodwin, 1905.

Street, Aaron. Letter to *Friends Review* 8 (1855): 455.

Sullivan, John O. "Annexation." *United States Democratic Review* 17, no. 85 (1845): 5–10.

Surveyor's section line field notes. Secretary of state. State Historical Society of Iowa, Des Moines.

Theler, James L., and Robert F. Boszhardt. *Twelve Millennia: Archaeology of the Upper Mississippi River Valley*. Iowa City: University of Iowa Press, 2003.

Thompson, Dean. Interview by author. Chester, Iowa, October 4, 2003.

United States Department of Agriculture. National Agricultural Statistics Service. *Agricultural Prices Summary*. 1976, 1986, 2004. http://usda.mannlib.cornell.edu/MannUsda/viewDocumentInfo.do?document ID=1003.

Unrau, William E. *White Man's Wicked Water: Alcohol Trade and Prohibition in Indian Country, 1802–1892*. Lawrence: University Press of Kansas, 1996.

Upper Iowa Wild and Scenic River Study. Washington, DC: Department of the Interior, U.S. Government Printing Office, 1971.

Van der Zee, Jacob. "The Neutral Ground." *Iowa Journal of History and Politics* 13, no. 3 (1915): 311–48.

Veysey, Steve. "French Creek Defense Project." *Iowa Sierran: The Sierra Club Iowa Chapter Newsletter* 29, no. 3. (1999). http://iowa.sierraclub.org/iasieran/autumn99/frenchck1.html.

Wedel, Mildred Mott. "Oneota Sites on the Upper Iowa River." *Missouri Archeologist* 21, nos. 2–4 (1959).

———. "Peering at the Ioway Indians through the Mist of Time: 1650–circa 1700." *Journal of the Iowa Archeological Society* 33 (1986): 1–74.

White, Bruce M. "The Power of Whiteness: Or, the Life and Times of Joseph Rolette, Jr." *Minnesota History* 56, no. 4 (1998–1999): 179–97.

Whitney, Josiah, D. *The Climatic Changes of Later Geological Times: A Discussion Based on Observations Made in the Cordilleras of North America*. Memoirs of the Museum of Comparative Zoölogy at Harvard College, 7, no. 2, Cambridge, MA: Museum of Comparative Zoölogy, Harvard College, 1882.

"Wisconsin Winnebagoes: An Interview with Moses Paquette, by the Editor." *Wisconsin Historical Collections* 12 (1892): 399–433.

Wise, David. Interview by author. Decorah, Iowa, October 28, 2004.

Wise, Samuel, Jr. Diary. In "Roots Grow Strong and Deep in Winneshiek County, Iowa: Wise Old Oak Tree Planted 1854. Vol. 1. Comp. Susan Jacobsen, with Madelyn Wise (2001). Decorah Geneology Library, Decorah, Iowa.

Young, Otis. "The United States Mounted Ranger Battalion, 1832–33." *Mississippi Valley Historical Review* 41, no. 3 (1954): 453–70.

Index

U.S. Geological Survey, 2

Voisin, André, 194

Wal-Mart, 16
War of 1812, 76
Washington Prairie, 30
Washington Prairie Lutheran Church, 121
waste water treatment, 16–17, 158, 171, 189
Waterloo Creek, 54, 87–88
Waukon, Iowa, 52, 111, 124, 127, 138–39, 143, 172
weather, 1, 3, 115, 116, 126, 140, 153, 161
weeds, 165, 167, 198, 199
wells, 11, 106, 108, 124, 178, 188–89, 193
Welsh, 104
wetlands, 38, 42–43, 114, 123, 141
whiskey, 59, 76, 80, 93, 96–98
Whitney, Josiah D., 13, 24, 32
Wild and Scenic Rivers Act, 179, 181, 183, 197
wild plants: potato, 57; raspberries, 111; strawberries, 44, 111; sumac, 109
wildflowers, 44, 178; coneflower, 44; gentian, 178; golden saxifrage, 29; harebells, 65; Maximilian sunflower, 44; northern monkshood, 29; ox eye, 44; shooting star, 178; wild aster, 178; wild rose, 44
wildlife: bats, 71, 145, 180; bear, 26, 56, 79, 85, 95, 117; beaver, 4, 20, 22, 26, 32, 60, 67, 69–70, 79, 85, 95; bison, 26, 39, 44–45, 60–61, 64, 66–69, 85; bobcat, 79, 117; cougar, 117; coyote, 117; deer, 20, 42, 60, 67, 79, 82, 85, 95–96, 114; elk, 60, 64, 95, 114; fox, 117; mink, 79; muskrat, 79, 85, 114, 139; otter, 79, 85; rabbit, 42; raccoon, 28, 79, 95; wolf, 64, 95, 117
Winnebago, 49, 61, 66, 77, 85, 87–102; alcohol, 96–98; Big Canoe (One-

Eyed Decorah), 88, 91, 98, 106; Black Hawk, 88; census, 98; clans, 93, 95; Coming Thunder (Wakon-chaw-kooga Winneshiek), 87–88, 91–92, 95, 98, 100, 111; David Smith, 99; deaths, 94, 97; dwellings, 94, 111; Elk, 88, 98; Le Petit Garçon, 96; Little Decorah (Reaches the Skies), 88, 98; Little Hill, 92; Little Priest, 93; Margaret Porter, 94; mission, 89, 93; Spoon Decorah, 98; subagency, 89, 91–93; Tribe of Nebraska, 90, 99; Waukon Haga Decorah (Snake Skin), 88, 91–93, 97, 100; Old Walking Turtle, 77, 91, 98; Young Walking Turtle, 88, 98; Whirling Thunder, 88, 90, 92, 98–99; Yellow Thunder, 98
Winneshiek County, 30, 35, 52, 107, 117, 119, 129, 131, 133, 143, 145, 147–48, 150–52, 154–55, 173, 178, 181, 186; board of supervisors, 189; Citizens for Clean Groundwater, 189; Conservation Commission, 183; Dairy and Stock Association, 132; Soil Conservation Board, 166; state bank, 149–50
Wisconsin, 25, 31, 41, 89–90, 92, 105, 116; Wisconsin River, 50
Wise, Catherine, 136–37, 144
Wise, Samuel, Jr., 122, 125, 128–29, 136–37, 142, 144–45
Wise, Samuel, Sr., 191
Woodland culture, 52–55, 57–58
woodlots, 142
wool, 118
Works Progress Administration, 53–54, 156–59
World War I, 122, 145, 151
World War II, 162, 165–66, 172

Yellow River, 52, 62, 89
Young, Raymond, 150